CRE▲TIVE
HOMEOWNER®

D0772060

# SMALL

- 1–3 BATHS
- 1–4 BEDROOMS
- UP TO 2,500 SQ. FT.

## HOME PLANS

CREATIVE HOMEOWNER®, Upper Saddle River, New Jersey

President: Brian H. Toolan
VP/Editorial Director: Timothy O. Bakke
Production Manager: Kimberly H. Vivas

Home Plans Editor: Kenneth D. Stuts
Home Plans Designer Liaison: Timothy Mulligan

Design and Layout: Arrowhead Direct (David Kroha, Cindy DiPierdomenico, Judith Kroha)

Cover Design: David Geer

Printed In China

Current Printing (last digit)
10 9 8 7 6 5 4 3 2 1

Small Home Plans
Library of Congress Control Number: 2006902939
ISBN-10: 1-58011-324-9
ISBN-13: 978-1-58011-324-3

CREATIVE HOMEOWNER®
A Division of Federal Marketing Corp.
24 Park Way
Upper Saddle River, NJ 07458
**www.creativehomeowner.com**

*Note: The homes as shown in the photographs and renderings in this book may differ from the actual blueprints. When studying the house of your choice, please check the floor plans carefully.*

# Contents

# Getting Started

**M**aybe you can't wait to bang the first nail. Or you may be just as happy leaving town until the windows are cleaned. The extent of your involvement with the construction phase is up to you. Your time, interests, and abilities can help you decide how to get the project from lines on paper to reality. But building a house requires more than putting pieces together. Whoever is in charge of the process must competently manage people as well as supplies, materials, and construction. He or she will have to

- Make a project schedule to plan the orderly progress of the work. This can be a bar chart that shows the time period of activity by each trade.
- Establish a budget for each category of work, such as foundation, framing, and finish carpentry.
- Arrange for a source of construction financing.
- Get a building permit and post it conspicuously at the construction site.
- Line up supply sources and order materials.
- Find subcontractors and negotiate their contracts.
- Coordinate the work so that it progresses smoothly with the fewest conflicts.
- Notify inspectors at the appropriate milestones.
- Make payments to suppliers and subcontractors.

## You as the Builder

You'll have to take care of every logistical detail yourself if you decide to act as your own builder or general contractor. But along with the responsibilities of managing the project, you gain the flexibility to do as much of your own work as you want and subcontract out the rest. Before taking this path, however, be sure you have the time and capabilities. Do you also have the

time and ability to schedule the work, hire and coordinate subs, order materials, and keep ahead of the accounting required to manage the project successfully? If you do, you stand to save the amount that a general contractor would charge to take on these responsibilities, normally 15 to 30 percent of the construction cost. If you take this responsibility on but mismanage the project, the potential savings will erode and may even cost you more than if you had hired a builder in the first place. A subcontractor might charge extra for hav-

**Acting as the builder,** above, requires the ability to hire and manage subcontractors.

**Building a home,** opposite, includes the need to schedule building inspections at the appropriate milestones.

ing to return to the site to complete work that was originally scheduled for an earlier date. Or perhaps because you didn't order the windows at the beginning, you now have to pay for a recent cost increase. (If you had hired a builder in the first place he or she would absorb the increase.)

order direct: 1-800-523-6789

## Hiring a Builder to Handle Construction

A builder or general contractor will manage every aspect of the construction process. Your role after signing the construction contract will be to make regular progress payments and ensure that the work for which you are paying has been completed. You will also consult with the builder and agree to any changes that may have to be made along the way.

Leads for finding builders might come from friends or neighbors who have had contractors build, remodel, or add to their homes. Real-estate agents and bankers may have some names handy but are more likely familiar with the builder's ability to complete projects on time and budget than the quality of the work itself.

The next step is to narrow your list of candidates to three or four who you think can do a quality job and work harmoniously with you. Phone each builder to see whether he or she is interested in being considered for your project. If so, invite the builder to an interview at your home. The meeting will serve two purposes. You'll be able to ask the candidate about his or her experience, and you'll be able to see whether or not your personalities are compatible. Go over the plans with the builder to make certain that he or she understands the scope of the project. Ask if they have constructed similar houses. Get references, and check the builder's standing with the Better Business Bureau. Develop a short list of builders, say three, and ask them to submit bids for the project.

## Contracts

### Lump-Sum Contracts

A lump-sum, or fixed-fee, contract lets you know from the beginning just what the project will cost, barring any changes made because of your requests or unforeseen conditions. This form works well for projects that promise few surprises and are well defined from the outset by a complete set of contract documents. You can enter into a fixed-price contract by negotiating with a single builder on your short list or by obtaining bids from three or four builders. If you go the latter route, give each bidder a set of documents and allow at least two weeks for them to submit their bids. When you get the bids, decide who you want and call the others to thank them for their efforts. You don't have to accept the lowest bid, but it probably makes sense to do so since you have already honed the list to builders you trust. Inform this builder of your intentions to finalize a contract.

### Cost-Plus-Fee Contracts

Under a cost-plus-fee contract, you agree to pay the builder for the costs of labor and materials, as verified by receipts, plus a fee that represents the builder's overhead and profit. This arrangement is sometimes referred to as "time and materials." The fee can range between 15 and 30 percent of the incurred costs. Because you ultimately pick up the tab—whatever the costs—the contractor is never at risk, as he is with a lump-sum contract. You won't know the final total cost of a cost-plus-fee contract until the project is built and paid for. If you can live with that uncertainty, there are offsetting advantages. First, this form allows you to accommodate unknown conditions much more easily than does a lump-sum contract. And rather than being tied down by the project documents, you will be free to make changes at any point along the way. This can be a trap, though. Watching the project take shape will spark the desire to add something or do something differently. Each change costs more, and the accumulation can easily exceed your budget. Because of the uncertainty of the final tab and the built-in advantage to the contractor, you should think twice before entering into this form of contract.

### Contract Content

The conditions of your agreement should be spelled out thoroughly in writing and signed by both parties, whatever contractual arrangement you make with your builder. Your contract should include provisions for the following:

- The names and addresses of the owner and builder.
- A description of the work to be included ("As described in the plans and specifications dated . . .").
- The date that the work will be completed if time is of the essence.
- The contract price for lump-sum contracts and the builder's allowed profit and overhead costs for changes.
- The builder's fee for cost-plus-fee contracts and the method of accounting and requesting payment.
- The criteria for progress payments (monthly, by project milestones) and the conditions of final payment.
- A list of each drawing and specification section that is to be included as part of the contract.
- Requirements for guarantees. (One year is the standard period for which contractors guarantee the entire project, but you may require specific guarantees on

**When submitting bids,** all of the builders should base their estimates on the same specifications. Once the work begins, communicate with your builder to keep the work proceeding smoothly.

**Inspect your newly built home,** if possible, before the builder closes it up and finishes it.

certain parts of the project, such as a 20-year guarantee on the roofing.)
- Provisions for insurance.
- A description of how changes in the work orders will be handled.

The builder may have a standard contract that you can tailor to the specifics of your project. These contain complete specific conditions with blanks that you can fill in to fit your project and a set of "general conditions" that cover a host of issues from insurance to termination provisions. It's always a good idea to have an attorney review the draft of your completed contract before signing it.

## Working with Your Builder

The construction phase officially begins when you have a signed copy of the contract and copies of any insurance required from the builder. It's not unheard of for a builder to request an initial payment of 10 to 20 percent of the total cost to cover mobilization costs, those costs associated with obtaining permits and getting set up to begin the actual construction. If you agree to this, keep a careful eye on the progress of the work to ensure that the total paid out at any one time doesn't get too far out of sync with the actual work completed.

What about changes? From here on, it's up to you and your builder to proceed in good faith and to keep the channels of communication open. Even so, changes of one sort or another beset every project, and they usually add to its cost.

### Light at the End of the Tunnel.

The builder's request for a final inspection marks the end of the construction phase—almost. At the final inspection meeting, you and the builder will inspect the work, noting any defects or incomplete items on a "punch list." When the builder tidies up the punch list items, you should reinspect. Sometimes, builders go on to another job and take forever to clean up the last few details, so only after all items on the list have been completed satisfactorily should you release the final payment, which often accounts for the builder's profit.

## Some Final Words

Having a positive attitude is important when undertaking a project as large as building a home. A positive attitude can help you ride out the rigors and stress of the construction process.

**Stay Flexible.** Expect problems, because they certainly will occur. Weather can upset the schedule you have established for subcontractors. A supplier may get behind on deliveries, which also affects the schedule. An unexpected pipe may surprise you during excavation. Just as certain, every problem that comes along has a solution if you are open to it.

**Be Patient.** The extra days it may take to resolve a construction problem will be forgotten once the project is completed.

**Express Yourself.** If what you see isn't exactly what you thought you were getting, don't be afraid to look into changing it. Or you may spot an unforeseen opportunity for an improvement. Changes usually cost more money, though, so don't make frivolous decisions.

Finally, watching your home go up is exciting, so stay upbeat. Get away from your project from time to time. Dine out. Take time to relax. A positive attitude will make for smoother relations with your builder. An optimistic outlook will yield better-quality work if you are doing your own construction. And though the project might seem endless while it is under way, keep in mind that all the planning and construction will fade to a faint memory at some time in the future, and you will be getting a lifetime of pleasure from a home that is just right for you.

## Plan #161002

**Dimensions:** 64'2" W x 44'2" D

**Levels:** 1

**Square Footage:** 1,860

**Bedrooms:** 3

**Bathrooms:** 2

**Foundation:** Basement

**Materials List Available:** Yes

**Price Category:** D

The brick, stone, and cedar shake facade provides color and texture to the exterior, while the unique nooks and angles inside this delightful one-level home give it character.

### Features:

- **Great Room/Dining Room:** This spacious great room is furnished with a wood-burning fireplace, a high ceiling, and French doors. Wide entrances to the breakfast room and dining room expand its space to comfortably hold large gatherings.

- **Kitchen:** The breakfast bar offers additional seating. The covered porch lets you enjoy a view of the landscape and is conveniently located for outdoor meals off this kitchen and breakfast area.

- **Master Bedroom:** The master bedroom is a private retreat. An alcove creates a comfortable sitting area, and an angled entry leads to the bath with whirlpool and a double-bowl vanity.

*Images provided by designer/architect.*

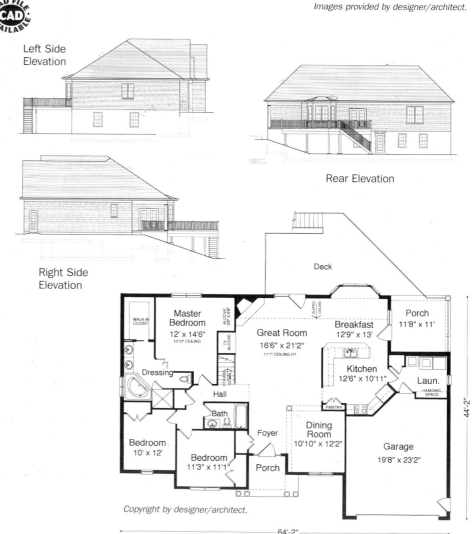

*Copyright by designer/architect.*

Dining Room

Living Room / Dining Room

Great Room/Breakfast Area

Great Room

SMARTtip

## Installing Rods and Poles

The way to install a rod or pole depends on the type it is, the brackets that will hold it, the weight of the window treatment, and the surface to which it is being fastened. Given below are some general guidelines, but for specific installation procedures, refer to the instructions that accompany the rod or pole.

· Use a stepladder to reach high places.

· Use the proper tools.

· Take accurate measurements.

· Work with a helper.

· If attaching a bracket to wood, first drill small pilot holes to avoid splitting the wood.

· Consider using wall anchors, particularly for the heavier window treatments.

· Use a level as needed to help you position the brackets for the pole or rod.

· Take care not to drill or hammer into any pipes or electrical wiring.

Because they're designed to stand out, decorative poles and their finials require more room for installation than conventional drapery rods. Finials add inches to the ends of a window treatment, so make sure you have enough wall room to display your hardware to its full advantage. And because decorative rods are often heavy, be certain your window frames and walls can support the weight.

## Plan #121001

**Dimensions:** 56' W x 58' D

**Levels:** 1

**Square Footage:** 1,911

**Bedrooms:** 3

**Bathrooms:** 2

**Foundation:** Basement

**Materials List Available:** Yes

**Price Category:** D

Detailed, soaring ceilings and top-notch amenities set this distinctive home apart.

**Features:**

- Ceiling Height: 8 ft. except as noted.

- Great Room: A soaring ceiling and six tall transom-topped windows make this a light and airy spot for entertaining.

- Formal Dining Room: The entry enjoys a pleasing view of this dining room's detailed 12-ft. ceiling and picture window.

- Great Room: At the back of the home, a see-through fireplace in this great room is joined by a built-in entertainment center.

- Hearth Room: This bayed room shares the see-through fireplace with the great room.

- Master Suite: Enjoy the stars and the sun in the private bath's whirlpool and separate shower. The bath features the same decorative ceiling as the dining room.

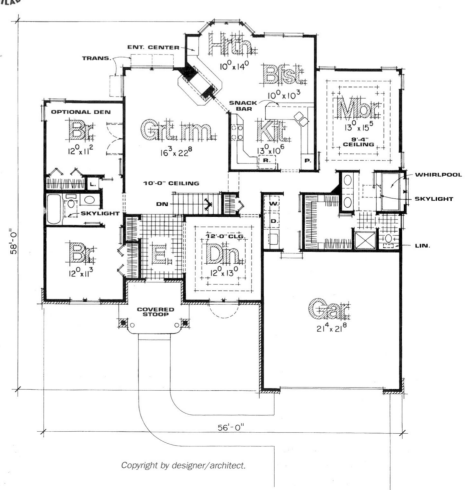

## Plan #151034

**Dimensions:** 58'6" W x 64'6" D

**Levels:** 1

**Square Footage:** 2,133

**Bedrooms:** 3

**Bathrooms:** 2

**Foundation:** Crawl space, slab, or basement

**CompleteCost List Available:** Yes

**Price Category:** D

*This home, as shown in the photograph, may differ from the actual blueprints. For more detailed information, please check the floor plans carefully.*

*Images provided by designer/architect.*

You'll love the high ceilings, open floor plan, and contemporary design features in this home.

**Features:**

- Great Room: A pass-through tiled fireplace between this lovely large room and the adjacent hearth room allows you to notice the mirror effect created by the 10-ft. boxed ceilings in both rooms.

- Dining Room: An 11-ft. ceiling and 8-in. boxed column give formality to this lovely room, where you're certain to entertain.

- Kitchen: If you're a cook, this room may become your favorite spot in the house, thanks to its great design, which includes plenty of work and storage space, and a very practical layout.

- Master Suite: A 10-ft. boxed ceiling gives elegance to this room. A pocket door opens to the private bath, with its huge walk-in closet, glass-blocked whirlpool tub, separate glass shower, and private toilet room.

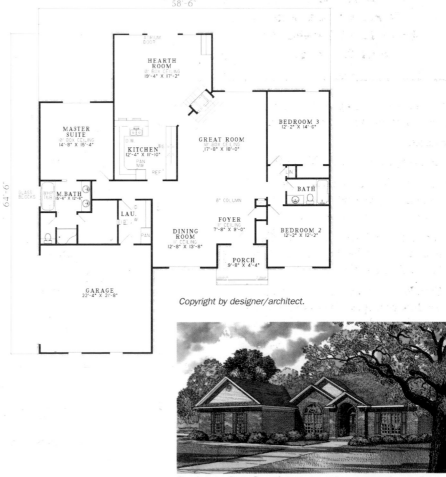

*Copyright by designer/architect.*

*Rendering reflects floor plan*

## Plan #131022

**Dimensions:** 54'8" W x 43' D

**Levels:** 2

**Square Footage:** 2,092

**Main Level Sq. Ft.:** 1,152

**Upper Level Sq. Ft.:** 940

**Bedrooms:** 4

**Bathrooms:** 2½

**Foundation:** Crawl space, slab, or basement

**Materials List Available:** Yes

**Price Category:** E

*This home, as shown in the photograph, may differ from the actual blueprints. For more detailed information, please check the floor plans carefully.*

*Images provided by designer/architect.*

You'll love the way this charming home reminds you of an old-fashioned farmhouse.

**Features:**

- Ceiling Height: 8 ft.
- Living Room: This large living room can be used as guest quarters when the need arises.
- Dining Room: This bayed, informal room is large enough for all your dining and entertaining needs. It could also double as an office or den.

- Garage: An expandable loft over the garage offers an ideal playroom or fourth bedroom.

Rear Elevation

## Main Level Floor Plan

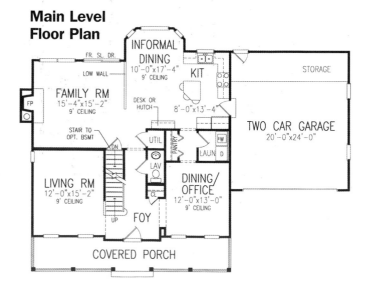

## Upper Level Floor Plan

*Copyright by designer/architect.*

12    order direct: 1-800-523-6789

Images provided by designer/architect.

## Plan #121064

**Dimensions:** 44' W x 40' D
**Levels:** 2
**Square Footage:** 1,846
**Main Level Sq. Ft.:** 919
**Upper Level Sq. Ft.:** 927
**Bedrooms:** 4
**Bathrooms:** 2½
**Foundation:** Basement
**Materials List Available:** Yes
**Price Category:** D

You'll love the features and design in this compact but amenity-filled home.

### Features:

- **Entry:** A balcony overlooks this two-story entry, where a plant shelf tops the coat closet.
- **Great Room:** A trio of tall windows points up the large dimensions of this room, which is sure to be the hub of your home. Arrange the furniture to create a cozy space around the fireplace, or leave it open to the room.
- **Kitchen:** You'll love to work in this well designed kitchen area.
- **Master Suite:** On the second floor, this master suite features a tiered ceiling and two walk-in closets. In the bath, you'll find a double vanity, whirlpool tub, and separate shower.

## Main Level Floor Plan

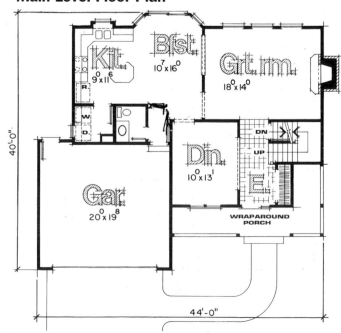

## Upper Level Floor Plan

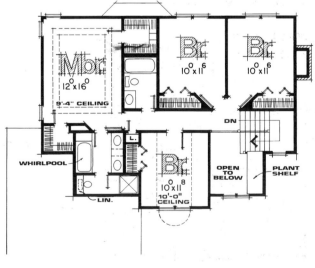

*Copyright by designer/architect.*

# Plan #101005

**Dimensions:** 63' W x 57'2" D

**Levels:** 1

**Square Footage:** 1,992

**Bedrooms:** 3

**Bathrooms:** 2½

**Foundation:** Crawl space, slab, or basement

**Materials List Available:** Yes

**Price Category:** D

*Images provided by designer/architect.*

Rear View

This midsized ranch is accented with Palladian windows and inviting front porch.

**Features:**

- Ceiling Height: 9 ft. unless otherwise noted.

- Special Ceilings: Tray or vaulted ceilings adorn the living room, family room, dining room, and master suite.

- Kitchen: This bright and airy kitchen is designed to be a pleasure in which to work. It shares a big bay window with the contiguous breakfast room.

- Breakfast Room: The light streaming in from the bay window makes this the perfect place to linger with coffee and the Sunday paper.

- Master Suite: This lovely suite is exceptional, with its sitting area and direct access to the deck, as well as a full-featured bath, and spacious walk-in closet.

- Secondary Bedrooms: The other bedrooms each measure about 13 ft. x 11 ft. They have walk-in closets and share a "Jack-and-Jill" bath.

*Copyright by designer/architect.*

Kitchen

Living Room

Dining Room

Family Room

Master Bedroom

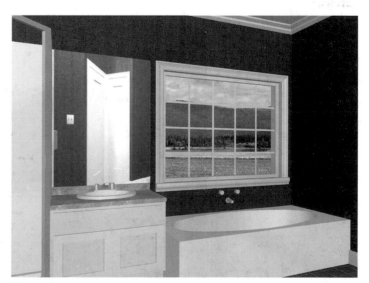

Master Bath

## Plan #111045

**Dimensions:** 41' W x 50' D
**Levels:** 2
**Square Footage:** 1,880
**Main Level Sq. Ft.:** 1,244
**Upper Level Sq. Ft.:** 636
**Bedrooms:** 3
**Bathrooms:** 2½
**Foundation:** Slab
**Materials List Available:** No
**Price Category:** D

*Images provided by designer/architect.*

This charming farmhouse has a unique design that's sure to fit the needs of a growing family.

**Features:**

- Porch: This traditional covered porch welcomes guests warmly into the home and invites neighbors to stop by on pleasant days.

- Living Room: The fireplace and a view of the back deck make this room a lovely place for the gathering of friends and family alike.

- Kitchen: This elongated kitchen is flanked by workspace and storage, surrounding the family chef with everything he or she needs.

An eating bar separates the kitchen and the breakfast nook, providing space for meals-on-the-run overlooking the sunlit area reserved for family breakfasts.

- Master Suite: This space, separated from the busy areas of the home for peace and quiet, features a walk-in closet and full master bath.

- Second Floor: The secondary bedrooms share the second full bathroom through individual vanities and walk-in closets.

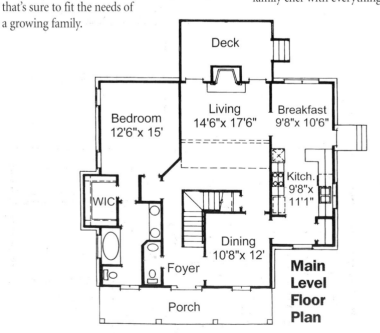

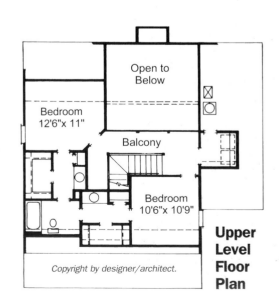

*Images provided by designer/architect.*

## Plan #211003

**Dimensions:** 62' W x 64' D
**Levels:** 1
**Square Footage:** 1,865
**Bedrooms:** 3
**Bathrooms:** 2
**Foundation:** Crawl space or slab
**Materials List Available:** Yes
**Price Category:** D

### SMARTtip

### Fire Extinguishers

The word PASS is an easy way to remember the proper way to use a fire extinguisher.

**P**ull the pin at the top of the extinguisher that keeps the handle from being accidentally pressed.

**A**im the nozzle of the extinguisher toward the base of the fire.

**S**queeze the handle to discharge the extinguisher. Stand approximately 8 feet away from the fire.

**S**weep the nozzle back and forth at the base of the fire. After the fire appears to be out, watch it carefully because it may reignite!

The traditional style of this home is blended with all the amenities required for today's lifestyle.

**Features:**

- Ceiling Height: 8 ft. unless otherwise noted.

- Front Porch: Guests will feel welcome arriving at the front door under this sheltering front porch.

- Dining Room: This large room will accommodate dinner parties of all sizes, from large formal gatherings to more intimate family get-togethers.

- Living Room: Guests and family alike will feel right at home in this inviting room. Sunlight streaming through the skylights in the 12-ft. ceiling, combined with the handsome fireplace, makes the space both airy and warm.

- Back Patio: When warm weather comes around, step out the sliding glass doors in the living room to enjoy entertaining or just relaxing on this patio.

- Kitchen: A cathedral ceiling soars over this efficient modern kitchen. It includes an eating area that is perfect for informal family meals.

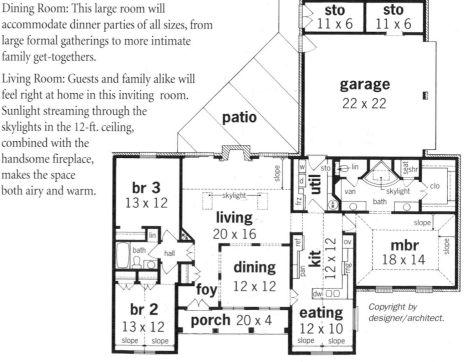

*Copyright by designer/architect.*

## Plan #121088

**Dimensions:** 56'8" W x 48' D

**Levels:** 2

**Square Footage:** 2,340

**Main Level Sq. Ft.:** 1,701

**Upper Level Sq. Ft.:** 639

**Bedrooms:** 4

**Bathrooms:** 2½

**Foundation:** Basement

**Materials List Available:** Yes

**Price Category:** E

*Images provided by designer/architect.*

You'll love this cheerful home, with its many large windows that let in natural light and cozy spaces that encourage family gatherings.

**Features:**

- Entry: Use the built-in curio cabinet here to display your best collector's pieces.

- Den: French doors from the entry lead to this room, with its built-in bookcase and triple-wide, transom-topped window.

- Great Room: The 14-ft. ceiling in this room accentuates the floor-to-ceiling windows that frame the raised-hearth fireplace.

- Kitchen: Both the layout and the work space make this room a delight for any cook.

- Master Suite: The bedroom has a tray ceiling for built-in elegance. A skylight helps to light the master bath, and an oval whirlpool tub, separate shower, and double vanity provide a luxurious touch.

### Main Level Floor Plan

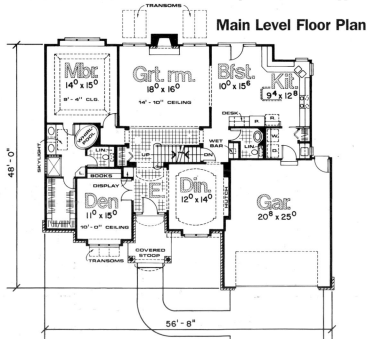

### Upper Level Floor Plan

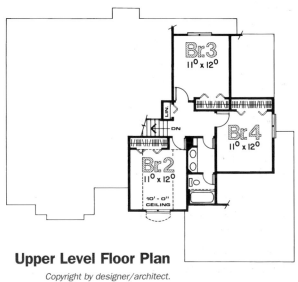

*Copyright by designer/architect.*

## Plan #131005

**Dimensions:** 70' W x 37'4" D
**Levels:** 1
**Square Footage:** 1,595
**Bedrooms:** 3
**Bathrooms:** 2
**Foundation:** Crawl space, slab, or basement
**Materials List Available:** Yes
**Price Category:** C

### SMARTtip

### Create a Courtyard

Create a private walled-garden retreat with fences covered by climbing vines. Add height with trellises, and divide spaces with clipped boxwood hedges. Include an (almost) instant patio by digging away an area of sod and then covering it with a layer of sand and landscaping mesh to discourage weeds. Then cover it with pea gravel, and add a garden bench, statuary, and perhaps an antique or two. The result? European ambiance for even the most nondescript suburban yard.

*Images provided by designer/architect.*

With the finest features of an open design in the main living areas, this home gives privacy where you need it. Best of all, it's wheelchair accessible.

**Features:**

- Foyer: A high ceiling gives this area real presence and serves to blend it seamlessly with the great room and the dining room.

- Great Room: The open design allows you to use this room as an extension of the dining room or, if you wish, furnish it to create a private reading nook or visually separate media center.

- Breakfast Room: Both this room and the adjacent well-appointed kitchen flow into the rest of the living area. However, access to the rear porch, where you can sit out and enjoy the weather while you eat, distinguishes this room.

- Master Suite: Located in the same wing as the other bedrooms, this suite has a separate entrance and features a vaulted ceiling, three closets, and a compartmented bath.

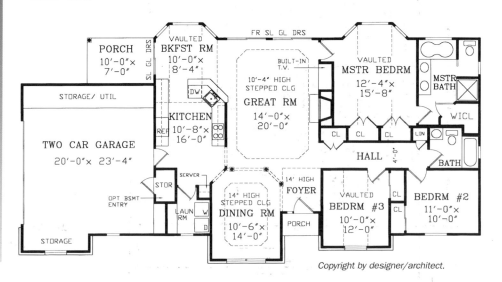

*Copyright by designer/architect.*

## Plan #131057

**Dimensions:** 79'2" W x 37'8" D
**Levels:** 1
**Square Footage:** 1,843
**Bedrooms:** 3
**Bathrooms:** 2
**Foundation:** Crawl space, slab, or basement
**Material List Available:** Yes
**Price Category:** D

*Images provided by designer/architect.*

The size of this traditionally styled brick ranch is deceiving; it more than accommodates all of the modern family's needs. Vaulted ceilings and an abundance of windows open the home up from the inside out.

**Features:**

- Covered Porch: Sit in peaceful privacy, looking out on your backyard while enjoying coffee on cool summer mornings.
- Great Room: Family and friends alike will be drawn to this expansive, window-lined room to sit by the fireplace on frosty winter days.
- Kitchen: Featuring lots of workspace and a raised bar, this kitchen is great for the family gourmet. The hub of the home, it links together the breakfast room, dining room, and

great room, giving you plenty of convenient choices for formal or informal dining.
- Master Bedroom: A large area, bay windows, his and her walk-in closets, and a fully equipped master bath combine to make a relaxing, romantic escape from everyday life. The compartmentalized master bath features a vaulted ceiling, his and her sinks, a standing shower, and a bathtub.

### Optional Laundry Room Floor Plan

*Copyright by designer/architect.*

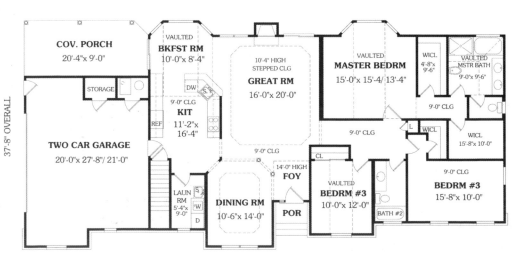

## Plan #161024

**Dimensions:** 54'4" W x 26'8" D
**Levels:** 2
**Square Footage:** 1,698
**Main Level Sq. Ft.:** 868
**Upper Level Sq. Ft.:** 830
**Bonus Space Sq. Ft.:** 269
**Bedrooms:** 3
**Bathrooms:** 2½
**Foundation:** Basement
**Materials List Available:** No
**Price Category:** C

The covered porch, dormers, and center gable that grace the exterior let you know how comfortable your family will be in this home.

**Features:**

- **Great Room:** Walk from windows overlooking the front porch to a door into the rear yard in this spacious room, which runs the width of the house.

- **Dining Room:** Adjacent to the great room, the dining area gives your family space to spread out and makes it easy to entertain a large group.

- **Kitchen:** Designed for efficiency, the kitchen area includes a large pantry.

- **Master Suite:** Tucked away on the second floor, the master suite features a walk-in closet in the bedroom and a luxurious attached bathroom.

- **Bonus Room:** Finish the 269-sq.-ft. area over the 2-bay garage as a guest room, study, or getaway for the kids.

*This home, as shown in the photograph, may differ from the actual blueprints.* *Images provided by designer/architect.*
*For more detailed information, please check the floor plans carefully.*

**CAD FILE AVAILABLE**

**Main Level Floor Plan**

*Copyright by designer/architect.*

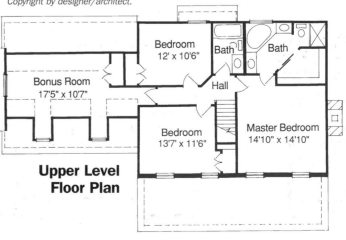

**Upper Level Floor Plan**

## Plan #151050

**Dimensions:** 69'2" W x 74'10" D

**Levels:** 1

**Square Footage:** 2,096

**Bedrooms:** 3

**Bathrooms:** 2½

**Foundation:** Crawl space, slab, or basement

**CompleteCost List Available:** Yes

**Price Category:** D

*Images provided by designer/architect.*

You'll love this spacious home for both its elegance and its convenient design.

### Features:

- Ceiling Height: 8 ft.

- Great Room: A 9-ft. boxed ceiling complements this large room, which sits just beyond the front gallery. A fireplace and door to the rear porch make it a natural gathering spot.

- Kitchen: This well-designed kitchen includes a central work island and shares an angled eating bar with the adjacent breakfast room.

- Breakfast Room: This room's bay window is gorgeous, and the door to the garage is practical.

- Master Suite: You'll love the 9-ft. boxed ceiling in the bedroom and the vaulted ceiling in the bath, which also includes two walk-in closets, a corner whirlpool tub, split vanities, a shower, and a compartmentalized toilet.

- Workshop: A huge workshop with half-bath is ideal for anyone who loves to build or repair.

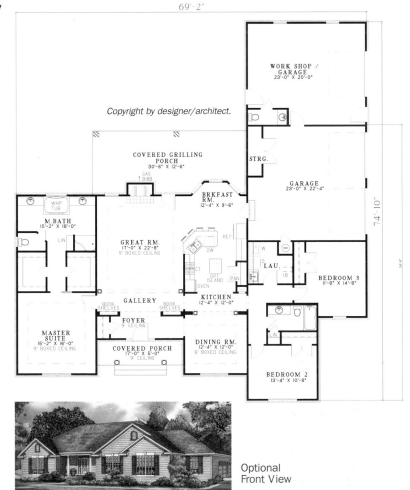

*Copyright by designer/architect.*

Optional
Front View

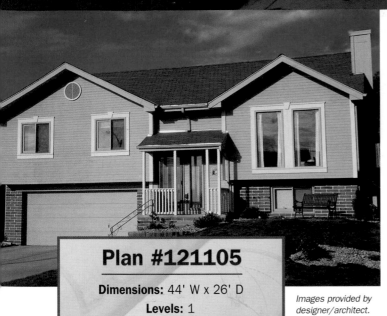

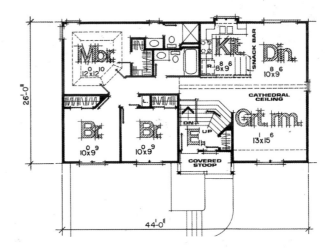

## Plan #121105

**Dimensions:** 44' W x 26' D

**Levels:** 1

**Square Footage:** 1,125

**Bedrooms:** 3

**Bathrooms:** 2

**Foundation:** Basement; crawl space for fee

**Material List Available:** Yes

**Price Category:** B

*Images provided by designer/architect.*

## Basement Level Floor Plan

*Copyright by designer/architect.*

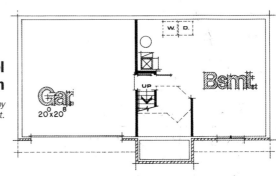

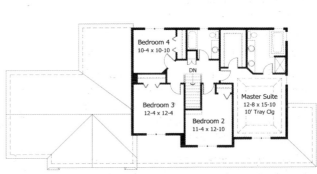

## Plan #481002

**Dimensions:** 67'8" W x 34' D

**Levels:** 2

**Square Footage:** 2,301

**Main Level Sq. Ft.:** 1,223

**Upper Level Sq. Ft.:** 1,078

**Bedrooms:** 4

**Bathrooms:** 2½

**Foundation:** Walkout

**Material List Available:** No

**Price Category:** E

*Images provided by designer/architect.*

## Main Level Floor Plan

## Upper Level Floor Plan

*Copyright by designer/architect.*

## Plan #101011

**Dimensions:** 71'2" W x 58'1" D

**Levels:** 1

**Square Footage:** 2,184

**Bedrooms:** 3

**Bathrooms:** 3

**Foundation:** Crawl space, slab, basement, or walkout

**Materials List Available:** Yes

**Price Category:** D

*Images provided by designer/architect.*

A classic design and spacious interior add up to a flexible design suitable to any modern lifestyle.

**Features:**

- Ceiling Height: 9 ft. unless otherwise noted.

- Formal Dining Room: A decorative square column and a tray ceiling adorn this elegant dining room.

- Screened Porch: Enjoy summer breezes in style by stepping out of the French doors into this vaulted screened porch.

- Kitchen: Does everyone want to hang out in the kitchen while you are cooking? No problem. True to the home's country style, this huge 14-ft.-3-in. x 22-ft.-6-in. has plenty of room for helpers.

- The kitchen is open to the vaulted family room.

- Patio or Deck: This pleasant outdoor area is accessible from both the screened porch and the master bedroom.

- Master Suite: This luxurious suite includes a double tray ceiling, a sitting area, two walk-in closets, and an exquisite bath.

Kitchen

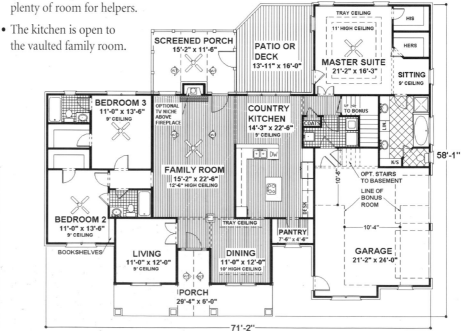

*Copyright by designer/architect.*

## Plan #101008

**Dimensions:** 68' W x 53' D
**Levels:** 1
**Square Footage:** 2,088
**Bedrooms:** 3
**Bathrooms:** 2½
**Foundation:** Crawl space, slab, or basement
**Materials List Available:** Yes
**Price Category:** D

*Images provided by designer/architect.*

This ranch sports an attractive brick-and-stucco exterior accented with quoins and layered trim.

**Features:**

- Ceiling Height: 11 ft. unless otherwise noted.

- Kitchen: You'll love cooking in this bright, airy kitchen, which is lit by an abundance of windows.

- Breakfast room: Off the kitchen is this breakfast room, the perfect spot for informal family meals.

- Master Suite: You'll look forward to retiring at the end of the day to this truly exceptional master suite, with its grand bath, spacious walk-in closet, and direct access to the porch.

- Morning Porch: Greet the day with your first cup of coffee on this porch, which is accessible from the master suite.

- Secondary Bedrooms: These bedrooms measure a generous 11 ft. x 14 ft. They share a compartmented bath.

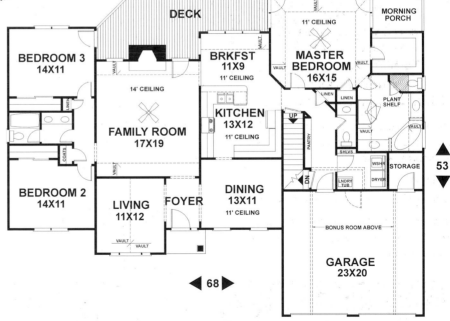

*Copyright by designer/architect.*

## SMARTtip

### Accentuating Your Bathroom with Details

No matter how big or small the room, details will pull the style together. Some of the best details that you can include are the smallest—drawer pulls from an antique store or shells in a glass jar or just left on the countertop. Add period flavor with crown molding, or dress up contemporary fixtures with polished stone fittings.

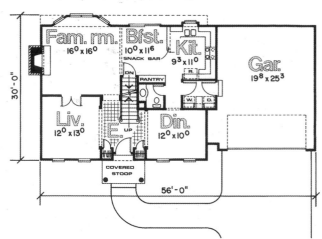

## Main Level Floor Plan

# Plan #121115

**Dimensions:** 56' W x 30' D

**Levels:** 2

**Square Footage:** 1,993

**Main Level Sq. Ft.:** 1,000

**Upper Level Sq. Ft.:** 993

**Bedrooms:** 4

**Bathrooms:** 2½

**Foundation:** Basement; crawl space for fee

**Material List Available:** Yes

**Price Category:** D

*Images provided by designer/architect.*

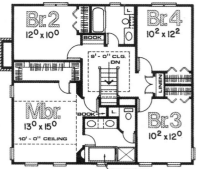

### Upper Level Floor Plan

*Copyright by designer/architect.*

---

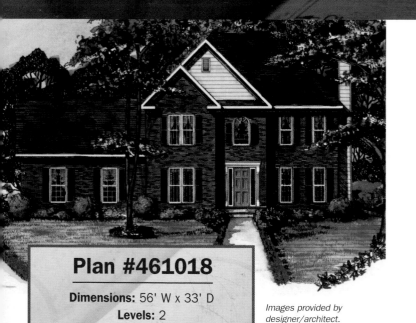

# Plan #461018

**Dimensions:** 56' W x 33' D

**Levels:** 2

**Square Footage:** 1,887

**Main Level Sq. Ft.:** 997

**Upper Level Sq. Ft.:** 910

**Bedrooms:** 3

**Bathrooms:** 2½

**Foundation:** Slab or basement

**Material List Available:** No

**Price Category:** D

*Images provided by designer/architect.*

## Main Level Floor Plan

### Upper Level Floor Plan

*Copyright by designer/architect.*

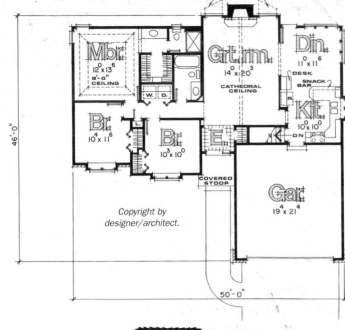

Images provided by designer/architect.

**CAD FILE AVAILABLE** CAD

# Plan #121215

**Dimensions:** 50' W x 46' D

**Levels:** 1

**Square Footage:** 1,271

**Bedrooms:** 3

**Bathrooms:** 2

**Foundation:** Basement; crawl space or slab for fee

**Material List Available:** Yes

**Price Category:** B

*Copyright by designer/architect.*

Rear Elevation

# Plan #151009

**Dimensions:** 44' W x 86'2" D

**Levels:** 1

**Square Footage:** 1,601

**Bedrooms:** 3

**Bathrooms:** 2

**Foundation:** Crawl space or slab

**CompleteCost List Available:** Yes

**Price Category:** C

Images provided by designer/architect.

**CAD FILE AVAILABLE** CAD

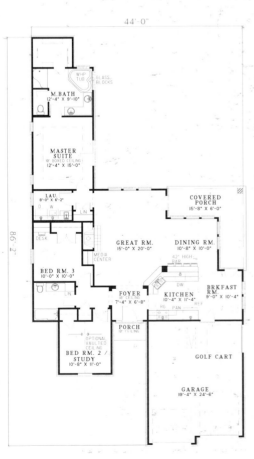

*Copyright by designer/architect.*

## Plan #341304

**Dimensions:** 40' W x 35'4" D

**Levels:** 1

**Square Footage:** 1,248

**Bedrooms:** 3

**Bathrooms:** 2

**Foundation:** Crawl space, slab, basement, or walkout

**Material List Available:** Yes

**Price Category:** B

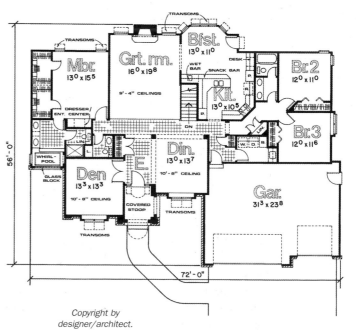

## Plan #121116

**Dimensions:** 72' W x 56' D

**Levels:** 1

**Square Footage:** 2,276

**Bedrooms:** 3

**Bathrooms:** 2½

**Foundation:** Basement; crawl space for fee

**Material List Available:** Yes

**Price Category:** E

## Plan #521055

**Dimensions:** 49' W x 44'4" D

**Levels:** 1

**Square Footage:** 1,401

**Bedrooms:** 3

**Bathrooms:** 2

**Foundation:** Crawl space

**Material List Available:** No

**Price Category:** B

*Images provided by designer/architect.*

**CAD FILE AVAILABLE**

*Copyright by designer/architect.*

MASTER BEDROOM (12'0"x14'4")

LIVING ROOM (14'0"x21'0")

DINING AREA (9'2"x14'2")

KITCHEN (10'6"x11'4")

MSTR BATH

LAUNDRY (6'0"x6'0")

BATH

BEDROOM #3 (10'8"x10'0")

2-CAR GARAGE (19'4"x23'4")

BEDROOM #2 (11'0"x10'0")

FRONT PORCH (15'0"x5'0")

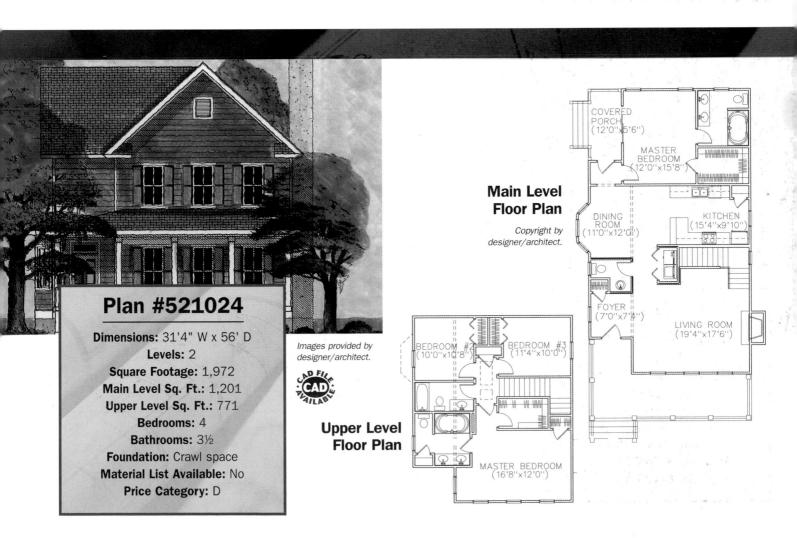

## Plan #521024

**Dimensions:** 31'4" W x 56' D

**Levels:** 2

**Square Footage:** 1,972

**Main Level Sq. Ft.:** 1,201

**Upper Level Sq. Ft.:** 771

**Bedrooms:** 4

**Bathrooms:** 3½

**Foundation:** Crawl space

**Material List Available:** No

**Price Category:** D

*Images provided by designer/architect.*

**CAD FILE AVAILABLE**

**Main Level Floor Plan**

*Copyright by designer/architect.*

COVERED PORCH (12'0"x5'6")

MASTER BEDROOM (12'0"x15'8")

DINING ROOM (11'0"x12'0")

KITCHEN (15'4"x9'10")

FOYER (7'0"x7'4")

LIVING ROOM (19'4"x17'6")

**Upper Level Floor Plan**

BEDROOM #2 (10'0"x10'8")

BEDROOM #3 (11'4"x10'0")

MASTER BEDROOM (16'8"x12'0")

## Plan #141025

**Dimensions:** 52' W x 36' D

**Levels:** 2

**Square Footage:** 1,721

**Main Level Sq. Ft.:** 902

**Upper Level Sq. Ft.:** 819

**Bedrooms:** 4

**Bathrooms:** 2½

**Foundation:** Basement

**Materials List Available:** Yes

**Price Category:** C

This traditional two-story home, with its typical roof and multi-directional ridge lines, presents a grand appearance. While modest in size, this lovely home incorporates many amenities found in much larger offerings.

**Features:**

• Living Room: This formal living room, certain to become a gathering place for friends and family, is accessible through an open foyer, with U-shaped stairs leading to the second floor.

• Dining Room: This formal dining room is particularly well-suited for those special entertainment occasions.

• Kitchen: This kitchen, which is designed for convenience and easy work patterns, makes food preparation a pleasure.

• Bedrooms: In addition to the master bedroom, this delightful home offers two secondary bedrooms. Also, you can convert the bonus room above the garage into a fourth bedroom.

Family Room

**Main Level Floor Plan**

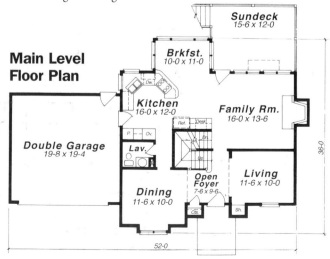

**Upper Level Floor Plan**

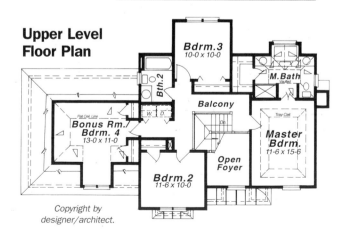

*Copyright by designer/architect.*

## Plan #131032

**Dimensions:** 69'2" W x 46' D
**Levels:** 2
**Square Footage:** 2,455
**Main Level Sq. Ft.:** 1,499
**Upper Level Sq. Ft.:** 956
**Bedrooms:** 4
**Bathrooms:** 3
**Foundation:** Crawl space, slab, or basement
**Materials List Available:** Yes
**Price Category:** F

If you love Victorian styling, you'll be charmed by the ornate, rounded front porch and the two-story bay that distinguish this home.

*Images provided by designer/architect.*

**Features:**

- **Living Room:** You'll love the 13-ft. ceiling in this room, as well as the panoramic view it gives of the front porch and yard.

- **Kitchen:** Sunlight streams into this room, where an angled island with a cooktop eases both prepping and cooking.

- **Breakfast Room:** This room shares an eating bar with the kitchen, making it easy for the family to congregate while the family chef is cooking.

- **Guest Room:** Use this lovely room on the first level as a home office or study if you wish.

- **Master Suite:** The dramatic bayed sitting area with a high ceiling has an octagonal shape that you'll adore, and the amenities in the private bath will soothe you at the end of a busy day.

*Rear View*

**Main Level Floor Plan**

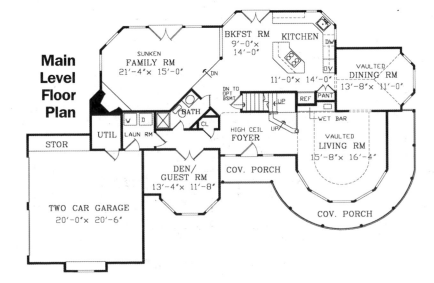

**Upper Level Floor Plan**

*Copyright by designer/architect.*

## Plan #351018

**Dimensions:** 40'8" W x 38'6" D

**Levels:** 1

**Square Footage:** 1,251

**Bedrooms:** 3

**Bathrooms:** 2

**Foundation:** Crawl space or slab

**Materials List Available:** Yes

**Price Category:** C

This traditional home has great curb appeal and a great floor plan.

**Features:**

- Ceilings: All ceilings are a minimum of 9-ft. high.

- Great Room: This entertainment area, with a 12-ft.-high ceiling, features a gas fireplace and has views of the front yard through round-top windows and doors.

- Kitchen: This kitchen fulfills all the needs of the active family, plus it has a raised bar.

- Dining Room: Being adjacent to the kitchen allows this room to be practical as well as beautiful by means of the numerous windows overlooking the porch and backyard.

- Bedrooms: Vaulted ceilings in two of the three bedrooms provide a feeling of spaciousness. One bedroom has its own bathroom.

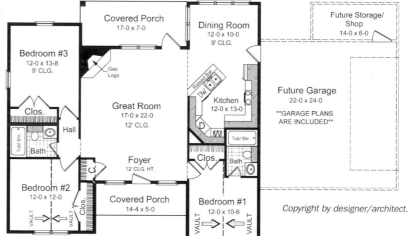

Front View

## Plan #121217

**Dimensions:** 40' W x 47'8" D

**Levels:** 1

**Square Footage:** 1,212

**Bedrooms:** 2

**Bathrooms:** 2

**Foundation:** Basement; crawl space or slab for fee

**Material List Available:** Yes

**Price Category:** B

*Images provided by designer/architect.*

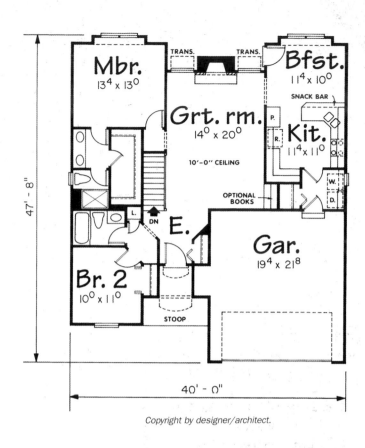

*Copyright by designer/architect.*

## Plan #461053

**Dimensions:** 37'6" W x 71' D

**Levels:** 2

**Square Footage:** 2,379

**Main Level Sq. Ft.:** 1,395

**Upper Level Sq. Ft.:** 984

**Bedrooms:** 3

**Bathrooms:** 2½

**Foundation:** Slab; crawl space, or basement for fee

**Material List Available:** No

**Price Category:** E

*Images provided by designer/architect.*

**Main Level Floor Plan**

**Upper Level Floor Plan**

*Copyright by designer/architect.*

## Plan #141028

**Dimensions:** 48' W x 36'4" D

**Levels:** 2

**Square Footage:** 2,215

**Main Level Sq. Ft.:** 1,075

**Upper Level Sq. Ft.:** 1,140

**Bedrooms:** 4

**Bathrooms:** 3

**Foundation:** Basement

**Materials List Available:** Yes

**Price Category:** E

*Images provided by designer/architect.*

*This home, as shown in the photograph, may differ from the actual blueprints. For more detailed information, please check the floor plans carefully.*

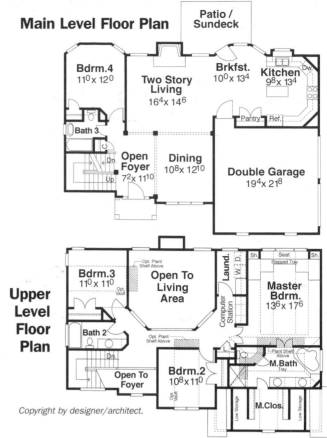

**Main Level Floor Plan**

Patio / Sundeck

Bdrm.4 11⁰ x 12⁰

Two Story Living 16⁴ x 14⁶

Brkfst. 10⁰ x 13⁴

Kitchen 9⁸ x 13⁴

Bath 3

Pantry  Ref.

Open Foyer 7² x 11¹⁰

Dining 10⁸ x 12¹⁰

Double Garage 19⁴ x 21⁸

**Upper Level Floor Plan**

Bdrm.3 11⁰ x 11⁰

Open To Living Area

Laund. W.D.

Master Bdrm. 13⁶ x 17⁶

Bath 2

Bdrm.2 10⁸ x 11⁰

Open To Foyer

M.Bath

M.Clos.

*Copyright by designer/architect.*

---

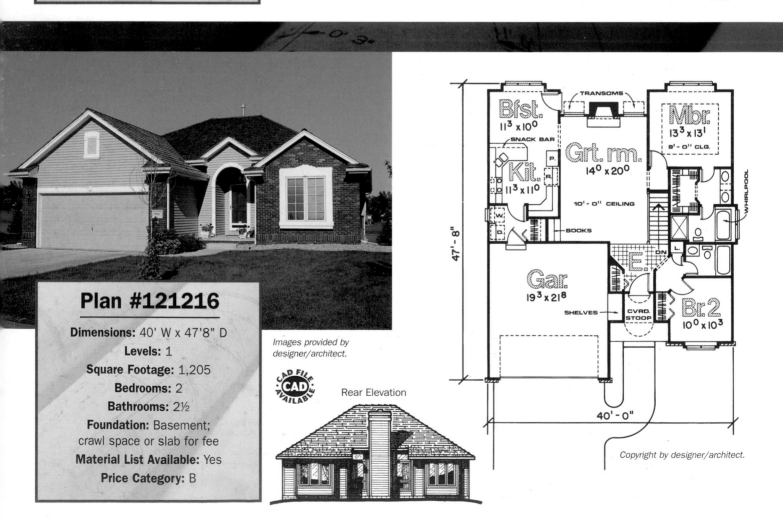

## Plan #121216

**Dimensions:** 40' W x 47'8" D

**Levels:** 1

**Square Footage:** 1,205

**Bedrooms:** 2

**Bathrooms:** 2½

**Foundation:** Basement; crawl space or slab for fee

**Material List Available:** Yes

**Price Category:** B

*Images provided by designer/architect.*

CAD FILE AVAILABLE

**Rear Elevation**

Bfst. 11³ x10⁰

Mbr. 13³ x 13¹ 9'-0" CLG.

Kit. 11³ x11⁰

Grt. rm. 14⁰ x 20⁰ 10'-0" CEILING

WHIRLPOOL

Gar. 19³ x 21⁸

Br. 2 10⁰ x 10³

CVRD. STOOP

47'-8"

40'-0"

*Copyright by designer/architect.*

## Plan #101012

**Dimensions:** 69'4" W x 62'9" D

**Levels:** 1

**Square Footage:** 2,288

**Bedrooms:** 3

**Bathrooms:** 2½

**Foundation:** Crawl space, slab, basement, or walkout

**Materials List Available:** No

**Price Category:** E

*Images provided by designer/architect.*

This classic brick ranch boasts traditional styling and an exciting up-to-date floor plan.

### Features:

• Ceiling Height: 9 ft. unless otherwise noted.

• Front Porch: Guests will be welcome by this inviting front porch, which features a 12-ft. ceiling.

• Family Room: This warm and inviting room measures 16 ft. x 19 ft. It features a 14-ft. ceiling and a rear wall of windows. French doors lead to an enormous deck.

• Kitchen: This unique angled kitchen is open to the hearth room and eating areas, all of which enjoy vaulted ceilings and are surrounded by windows. The hearth room has a TV niche.

• Master Suite: This 16-ft. x 15-ft. master suite is truly sumptuous, with its

12-ft. ceiling, sitting area, two walk-in closets, and full-featured bath.

• Bonus Room: Here is plenty of storage or room for future expansion. Just beyond the entry are stairs leading to a bonus room measuring approximately 12 ft. x 21 ft.

*Copyright by designer/architect.*

Living Room

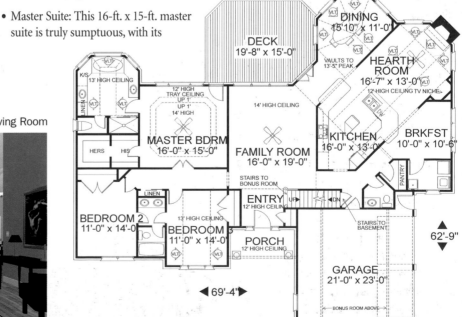

# Plan #131051

**Dimensions:** 64'4" W x 53'4" D

**Levels:** 2

**Square Footage:** 2,431

**Main Level Sq. Ft.:** 1,293

**Upper Level Sq. Ft.:** 1,138

**Bedrooms:** 4

**Bathrooms:** 2½

**Foundation:** Crawl space, slab, or basement

**Materials List Available:** Yes

**Price Category:** F

Gracious and charming with a wraparound front porch and a backyard terrace, this home also has a ready-to-finish third floor all-purpose room and a full bath.

**Features:**

• Main Level Ceiling Height: 8 ft.

• Family Room: A comfortable space for the entire family to gather, this delightful room can be warmed by a heat-circulating fireplace.

• Dining Room: A cozy dinette boasts a sliding glass door with access to a gorgeous backyard terrace with an optional calm reflecting pool.

• Kitchen: Adjoining the dining area, the kitchen offers plenty of storage and counter space. The laundry room and half-bath are nearby for convenience.

• Garage: The garage is tucked way back to keep it from intruding into the traditional facade.

## Main Level Floor Plan

*Images provided by designer/architect.*

*This home, as shown in the photograph, may differ from the actual blueprints. For more detailed information, please check the floor plans carefully.*

Rear Elevation

## Upper Level Floor Plan

## Optional 3rd Level Floor Plan

*Copyright by designer/architect.*

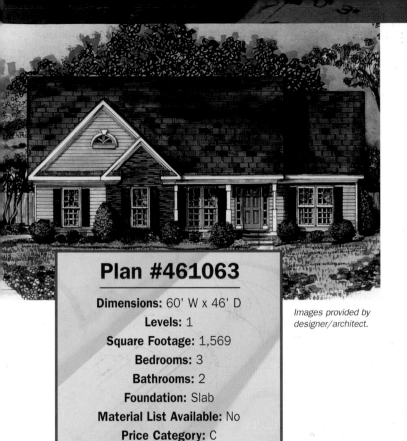

## Plan #461063

**Dimensions:** 60' W x 46' D

**Levels:** 1

**Square Footage:** 1,569

**Bedrooms:** 3

**Bathrooms:** 2

**Foundation:** Slab

**Material List Available:** No

**Price Category:** C

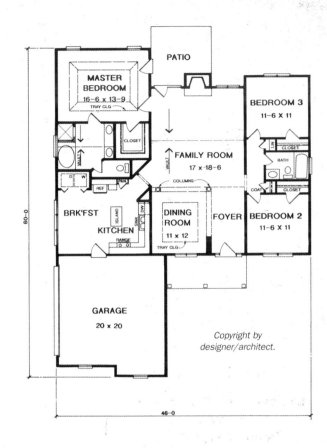

*Images provided by designer/architect.*

*Copyright by designer/architect.*

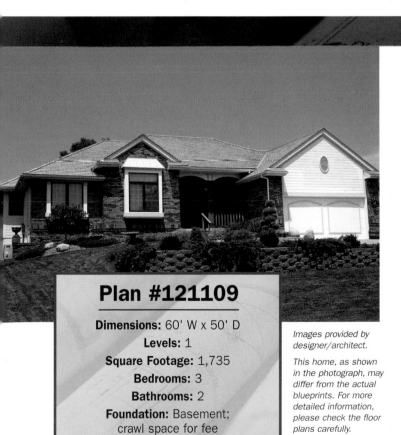

## Plan #121109

**Dimensions:** 60' W x 50' D

**Levels:** 1

**Square Footage:** 1,735

**Bedrooms:** 3

**Bathrooms:** 2

**Foundation:** Basement; crawl space for fee

**Material List Available:** Yes

**Price Category:** C

*Images provided by designer/architect.*

*This home, as shown in the photograph, may differ from the actual blueprints. For more detailed information, please check the floor plans carefully.*

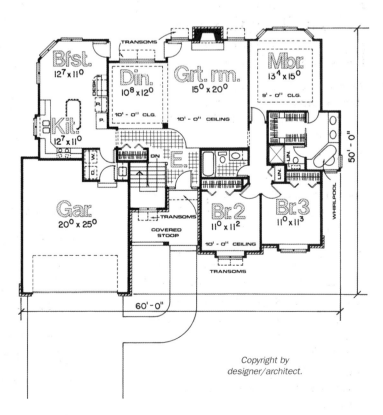

*Copyright by designer/architect.*

## Plan #151089

**Dimensions:** 84' W x 55'6" D
**Levels:** 1
**Square Footage:** 1,921
**Bedrooms:** 3
**Bathrooms:** 3
**Foundation:** Crawl space, slab, or basement
**CompleteCost List Available:** Yes
**Price Category:** D

If your family loves to combine indoor and outdoor living, this home's fabulous porches and deck space make it perfect.

**Features:**

- Porches: A huge wraparound front porch, sizable rear porch, and deck that joins them give you space for entertaining or simply lounging.

- Living Room: A fireplace and built-in media center could be the focal points in this large room.

- Hearth Room: Open to both the living room and kitchen, this hearth room also features a fireplace.

- Kitchen: This step-saving kitchen includes ample storage and work space, as well as an angled bar it shares with the hearth room. Atrium doors lead to the rear porch.

- Bonus Upper Level: A large game room and a full bath make this area a favorite with the children.

**Bonus Area Floor Plan**

## Plan #141031

**Dimensions:** 58'4" W x 30' D

**Levels:** 2

**Square Footage:** 2,367

**Main Level Sq. Ft.:** 1,025

**Upper Level Sq. Ft.:** 1,342

**Bedrooms:** 4

**Bathrooms:** 2½

**Foundation:** Basement

**Materials List Available:** No

**Price Category:** E

Images provided by designer/architect.

This inviting home combines traditional exterior lines, luxurious interior amenities, and innovative design to present a package that will appeal to all members of your family.

**Features:**

- Foyer: Formal living and dining rooms flank this impressive two-story foyer, which welcomes you to this delightful home with a staircase leading to a balcony.

- Command Center: You will enjoy the open flow of the main floor from the family room to this command center, beyond the kitchen, where you can plan your family activities.

- Master Suite: This master bedroom with optional window seat features a stepped tray ceiling. The master bath with cathedral ceiling offers an optional radius window.

- Additional Bedrooms: The secondary bedroom, next to the master, offers an over look to the foyer, well suited for a sitting room or study.

**Main Level Floor Plan**

**Upper Level Floor Plan**

Copyright by designer/architect.

# Decorative Paint Technique: Sponging

**S**ponging creates a dappled finish, a subtle play of color that ranges from delicate to bold. It all depends on the colors you choose, the transparency and glossiness of your glaze, and how heavily you apply it. Sponging is the easiest and most versatile decorative paint finish. Realistically, it's also one of the most tedious, especially if you're decorating all of the walls in a room. Remember, your hand will touch every inch of those walls many times over before the job is done.

## Sponging: The Basics

Starting with simple sponging helps you learn a number of important skills, including mixing paint and glaze, applying a glaze properly, getting a feeling for the decorative paint process, and developing coordination of your eye and hand.

Because it produces a textured surface with great visual depth, sponging disguises imperfect walls and hides dirt in hard-use areas such as children's rooms. It's also a way to enhance furniture made of inexpensive wood.

Appropriately, the technique takes its name from the only tool usually used to apply the finish, a sponge. Not just any sponge, however. It must be a natural sea sponge, the only sponge that has the irregular shape and uneven surface necessary to create a mottled texture. Sea sponges come in round and flat shapes and are sold in paint and craft stores. The flat shape works best for sponging. (Always use the flat side, which was attached to the rock.) If you can't find a flat sponge, cut a round sea sponge in half to create a similar effect. If you use the sponge correctly, you won't be able to see the individual strokes of paint on the wall.

Apply the glaze quickly; you could use a fast-drying latex or acrylic glaze in most cases. If you use a water-based glaze, immediately correct any mistakes you make with a clean sponge and water. Slower-drying oil glazes also work well with

This article was reprinted from *Decorative Painting and Faux Finishes* (Creative Homeowner 2004).

**Sponge painting,** above, is one way to create texture. On the wall, here, it leaves the illusion of a slightly uneven or aged surface, which intensifies the room's rustic country feeling.

**The finished effect,** below, of sponging a wall can be subtle and yet highly decorative.

**Subtle tonal variations,** opposite, create a sophisticated effect on walls with sponged-on color.

**A natural sea sponge,** above, has the uneven, irregular texture required for creating a mottled finish.

this technique. Whatever type of glaze you use, you'll need a damp sponge. Prepare it by dipping it into clean water and wringing it out until the sponge is damp but not wet.

## Sure Strokes

As with most decorative finishes, individual strokes shouldn't be visible when they're done. To achieve this subtle effect, apply the glaze over a color-coordinated base coat that is thoroughly dry.

To make the proper stroke, hold the sponge flat and, working from your wrist, quickly and lightly pounce it straight up and down over the surface of the wall.

Don't let the sponge slip or slide on the glaze. Apply each stroke of the sponge so that it just barely touches the last one, and work consistently across the surface—don't hop around the room sponging at random or the effect will be uneven. Give the sponge a one-quarter turn before you make each stroke, and turn your hand from side to side to avoid any tendency to create an identifiable pattern. To sponge into corners, cut off a small piece of the sponge to make a flat edge.

About 40 percent of the base-coat color will show through after you finish the first sponged coat. The second sponged coat will overlap some of the base color and some of the first sponged strokes, covering about 40 percent of the wall. When you're finished, about 25 percent of the base-coat color will be visible.

Effective sponging keeps color contrasts to a minimum and puts the emphasis on subtle tonal variations that are applied over a pale or light base. As you become more secure with the technique, try for more dramatic color combinations.

## Sponging On Two Colors

This is the basic sponging technique. It is a positive (additive) method, which means you dab glaze over the base coat to create the desired effect. First, the surface receives a light base coat. When it's thoroughly dry, sponge on two slightly contrasting coats of glaze using the application method described on the previous page. Let the first coat dry before applying the second coat. In the examples, the base coat is a warm white paint applied with a roller. The first sponged coat is a medium taupe; the second sponged coat, a deep golden beige. Custom-mixed latex paints were used as the colorants and then blended with an acrylic glazing medium and water to make a slightly opaque, fast-drying finish. Use artist's acrylics for the colorant if you want a more translucent finish. You might want to add a gel retarder to the glaze beforehand to slow down drying and allow yourself more time to work.

**A Variation.** Apply two coats of light glaze over a dark base coat to add dramatic flair to a room. Be sure to constantly vary your strokes because a repetitive pattern is more noticeable when you put light glazes over a dark base coat.

**Step One: Mix The First Glaze.** Pour a small amount into the tray. Hold a dampened sponge flat side down, and dip it into the glaze. Gently slide the sponge over the ridges so that it becomes evenly coated. Always off-load any excess glaze onto old newspapers.

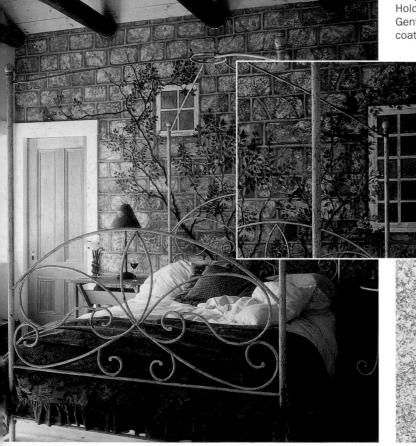

**Sponge on "weathered stone,"** above, provides a distinctive addition to this bedroom.

**Step Three: Add a Second Color.** Repeat Step 2 with the second color, sponging it on so that it covers about 40 percent of the wall. Let the glaze dry.

**Step Two: Sponge on the Glaze.** Sponge the surface as described in the introduction. Avoid creating an identifiable pattern. Reload and off-load the sponge as necessary. This step covers about 40 percent of the base coat. Let the glaze dry.

**Step Four: The Final Finish.** The final finish reveals about 25 percent of the base-coat color. The overlapping areas create the illusion of depth and texture, and the strokes are indistinguishable from one another.

## Sponging On Two Colors

### (Positive Method 1)

**Skill Level:** Beginner

**Recommended For:** Any flat or smooth surface, including floors and ceilings. Especially good for walls with flaws that need hiding and in hard-use areas such as children's rooms. Also good for furniture that doesn't have intricate carving or elaborate trim

**Not Recommended For:** Uneven surfaces with intricate carving or elaborate trim

**Pairs Of Hands Needed:** 1

**Tools:** Paint buckets; mixing sticks; paint tray; sea sponges; bucket of clear water; old newspaper; clean rags; gloves

**Base Coat:** Latex paint

**Glaze Colorants:** Custom-mixed eggshell latex paints or artist's acrylics, or custom-mixed eggshell alkyd paints or universal tints

**Glaze Formula:**
**Latex glaze:** 1 part colorant, 1 part latex or acrylic glazing medium, and 1 part water.
**Oil glaze:** 1 part colorant, 1 part alkyd glazing medium, and 1 part mineral spirits

**Typical Workable Section:** A 2-foot-wide wall or surface

**Clear Top Coat:** Optional

### Color Palette

Warm White

Medium Taupe

Golden Beige

## Sponging On Three Colors

This version of the technique results in a denser surface than the first sponging-on method, so less of the base coat will show through. Use three glazes over a light base coat to create the finish. In this example, the glaze colors are the taupe and golden beige used in the first method, with a dark terra-cotta color accent. They are slightly opaque and fast-drying glazes made with equal parts of custom-mixed latex paint, acrylic glazing medium, and water. For a more translucent look, use artist's acrylic paints instead of latex paint.

**Covering Percentages:** When you cover 40 percent of the base coat, 60 percent of it still shows. A second coat that covers 40 percent of the wall, covers 40 percent of the base and first coats. Of the 60 percent of the base coat that was showing after the first coat, just 60 percent of *that* is now visible (leaving 25 percent), therefore, a third coat will allow about 10 percent of it to be visible.

**Applying consecutive layers,** above, of sponged on color looks rich.

**Step One: Use a Light Touch.** Make your first strokes subtle. After mixing your glaze, gently dip the dampened sponge into the paint, flat side down. Then off-load the excess onto newspaper before applying the glaze to the surface.

**Step Three: Add a More Color.** Repeat Step 2 with the second color, sponging it on so that it covers about 40 percent of the wall. Let it dry. Apply the third color the same way. It should cover about 40 percent of the wall. Let the glaze dry.

**Step Two: Sponge on the Entire Surface.** Go over the surface with the glaze, avoiding an identifiable pattern. Reload and off-load the sponge often to create a consistent look. This step covers about 40 percent of the base coat. Let the glaze dry.

**Step Four: The Final Finish.** The final finish reveals about 10 percent of the base-coat color. The overlapping light and dark areas create the illusion of depth and texture. The strokes are indistinguishable from one another.

## Sponging On Three Colors
### (Positive Method 2)

**Skill Level:** Beginner to Intermediate

**Recommended For:** Any flat or smooth surface, including floors and ceilings. Especially good for walls with flaws that need hiding and in hard-use areas such as children's rooms. Also good for furniture that doesn't have intricate carving or elaborate trim

**Not Recommended For:** Uneven surfaces with intricate carving or elaborate trim

**Pairs Of Hands Needed:** 1

**Tools:** Paint buckets; mixing sticks; paint tray; sea sponges; bucket of water for cleaning sponge; newspapers; rags; gloves

**Base Coat:** Latex paint

**Glaze Colorants:** Custom-mixed eggshell latex paints or artist's acrylics or alkyd paints or universal tints

**Glaze Formula:**
**Latex glaze:** 1 part colorant, 1 part latex or acrylic glazing medium, and 1 part water.
**Oil glaze:** 1 part colorant, 1 part alkyd glazing medium, and 1 part mineral spirits

**Typical Workable Section:**
A 2-foot-wide wall or surface

**Clear Top Coat:** Optional

### Color Palette

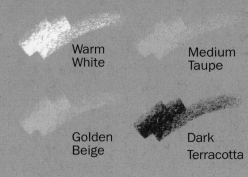

Warm White

Medium Taupe

Golden Beige

Dark Terracotta

# Random Sponging: Four Colors

This method involves a slightly different sponging technique. It's called random because of the loose arrangement of the strokes. The effect is a texture that is more ephemeral or diffused and very close to color washing in some respects. It gets away from the tight texture of the first two sponging-on techniques by letting you drag the sponge lightly to roughen the surface and blend the colors as you make your strokes. Random sponging creates a colorful, painterly look that's particularly appropriate for doors, small walls such as accent or transition walls, and unornamented furniture.

**Intermingled hues,** above, give a painterly look to this wall.

## SMARTtip

If you want an even denser appearance, use different paint finishes for the consecutive coats. For example, start with a flat base coat followed by paint in an eggshell finish, then a satin coat, then semigloss paint.

**Step One: Pounce the Sponge.** Mix the first glaze. To apply the technique, randomly pounce on the color in a straight up and down motion, shifting the sponge slightly to get the blending effect. Cover only 30 percent of the base coat. Let the glaze dry.

**Step Three: Blend More Color.** Mix the third color and apply it to the surface, filling in areas left untouched by the second glaze. Let the glaze dry.

**Step Two: Use Random Strokes.** Mix the second color, and apply it the same way. Use a random pattern that allows areas of the first glaze to remain untouched. Let the glaze dry.

**Step Four: The Final Finish.** The fourth color is thinned out and almost transparent. Pat it over the entire surface using a light touch, overlapping and filling in areas as needed.

## Random Sponging: Four Colors

### (Positive Method 3)

**Skill Level:** Advanced Beginner to Intermediate

**Recommended For:** Small walls, doors, and other flat surfaces free of intricate carving or elaborate trim, as well as furniture with little or no ornamentation.

**Not Recommended For:** Ceilings or areas with intricate carving or elaborate trim or ornate furniture.

**Pairs Of Hands Needed:** 1

**Tools:** Paint buckets; mixing sticks; paint tray; four sea sponges; bucket of clear water; mineral spirits; old newspapers; clean rags; gloves

**Base Coat:** Latex paint

**Glaze Colorants:** Custom-mixed eggshell latex paints or artist's acrylics or alkyd paints or universal tints

**Glaze Formula:**
**Latex glaze:** 1 part colorant, 1 part latex or acrylic glazing medium, and 1 part water.
**Oil glaze:** 1 part colorant, 1 part alkyd glazing medium, and 1 part mineral spirits

**Typical Workable Section:** A 2-foot-wide wall or surface

**Clear Top Coat:** Optional

## Color Palette

Warm White

Golden Beige

Taupe

Moss Green

## Plan #161034

**Dimensions:** 56' W x 53' D
**Levels:** 2
**Square Footage:** 2,156
**Main Level Sq. Ft.:** 1,605
**Upper Level Sq. Ft.:** 551
**Bedrooms:** 3
**Bathrooms:** 2½
**Foundation:** Basement
**Materials List Available:** No
**Price Category:** D

*Images provided by designer/architect.*

Multiple gables, a covered porch, and circle-topped windows combine to enhance the attractiveness of this exciting home.

**Features:**

• **Great Room:** A raised foyer introduces this open combined great room and dining room. Enjoy the efficiency of a dual-sided fireplace that warms both the great room and kitchen.

• **Kitchen:** The kitchen, designed for easy traffic patterns, offers an abundance of counter space and features a cooktop island.

• **Master Suite:** This first-floor master suite, separated for privacy, includes twin vanities and a walk-in closet. A deluxe corner bath and walk-in shower complete its luxurious detail.

• **Additional Rooms:** Two additional bedrooms lead to the second-floor balcony, which overlooks the great room. You can use the optional bonus room as a den or office.

**Main Level Floor Plan**

**Upper Level Floor Plan**

# Plan #321006

**Dimensions:** 76' W x 45' D

**Levels:** 1, optional lower

**Square Footage:** 1,977

**Optional Basement Level Sq. Ft.:** 1,416

**Bedrooms:** 4

**Bathrooms:** 2½

**Foundation:** Basement

**Materials List Available:** Yes

**Price Category:** D

*Images provided by designer/architect.*

This design is ideal if you're looking for a home with space to finish as your family and your budget grow.

**Features:**

- Great Room: A vaulted ceiling in this room sets an elegant tone that the gorgeous atrium windows pick up and amplify.

- Atrium: Elegance marks the staircase here that leads to the optional lower level.

- Kitchen: Both experienced cooks and beginners will appreciate the care that went into the design of this step-saving kitchen, with its ample counter space and generous cabinets.

- Master Suite: Enjoy the luxuries you'll find in this suite, and revel in the quiet that the bedroom can provide.

- Lower Level: Finish the 1,416 sq. ft. here to create a family room, two bedrooms, two bathrooms, and a study.

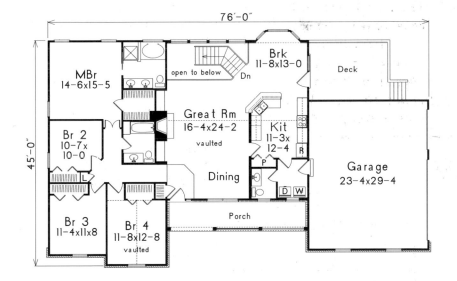

**Optional Basement Level Floor Plan**

*Copyright by designer/architect.*

## Plan #121117

**Dimensions:** 76' W x 46' D

**Levels:** 1

**Square Footage:** 2,172

**Bedrooms:** 4

**Bathrooms:** 3

**Foundation:** Basement; crawl space for fee

**Material List Available:** Yes

**Price Category:** D

*Images provided by designer/architect.*

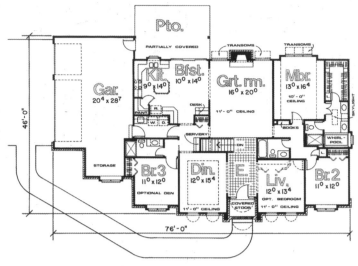

*Copyright by designer/architect.*

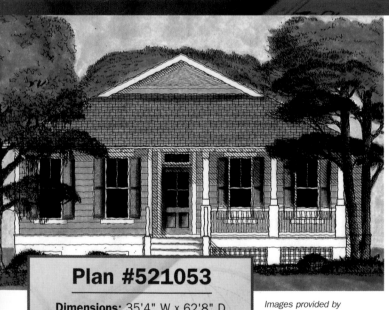

## Plan #521053

**Dimensions:** 35'4" W x 62'8" D

**Levels:** 1

**Square Footage:** 1,453

**Bedrooms:** 2

**Bathrooms:** 2

**Foundation:** Crawl space

**Material List Available:** No

**Price Category:** B

*Images provided by designer/architect.*

*Copyright by designer/architect.*

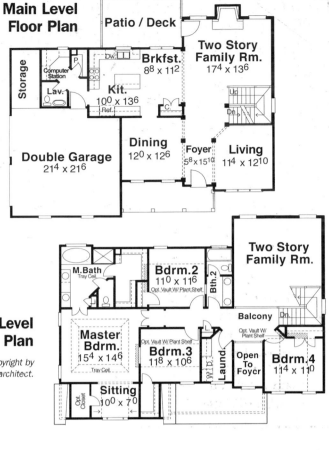

## Main Level Floor Plan

Patio / Deck

Storage

Computer Station

Lav.

P.

Dw.

Brkfst.
8⁸ x 11²

Kit.
10⁰ x 13⁶

Ref.

C.

Up

Dn

Two Story Family Rm.
17⁴ x 13⁶

Double Garage
21⁴ x 21⁶

Dining
12⁰ x 12⁶

Foyer
5⁸ x 15¹⁰

Living
11⁴ x 12¹⁰

## Upper Level Floor Plan

M.Bath
Tray Ceil.

Bdrm.2
11⁰ x 11⁶
Opt. Vault W/ Plant Shelf

Bth.2

Two Story Family Rm.

Master Bdrm.
15⁴ x 14⁶
Tray Ceil.

Opt. Vault W/ Plant Shelf

Bdrm.3
11⁸ x 10⁶

W.I.C.

Laund.

Balcony

Open To Foyer

Opt. Vault W/ Plant Shelf

Bdrm.4
11⁴ x 11⁰

Dn

Opt. Closet

Sitting
10⁰ x 7⁰

# Plan #141032

**Dimensions:** 52' W x 44' D

**Levels:** 2

**Square Footage:** 2,476

**Main Level Sq. Ft.:** 1,160

**Upper Level Sq. Ft.:** 1,316

**Bedrooms:** 4

**Bathrooms:** 2½

**Foundation:** Basement

**Materials List Available:** Yes

**Price Category:** E

---

# Plan #521029

**Dimensions:** 32' W x 42' D

**Levels:** 2

**Square Footage:** 1,688

**Main Level Sq. Ft.:** 844

**Upper Level Sq. Ft.:** 844

**Bedrooms:** 3

**Bathrooms:** 3

**Foundation:** Pier/pole

**Material List Available:** No

**Price Category:** C

**CAD FILE AVAILABLE**

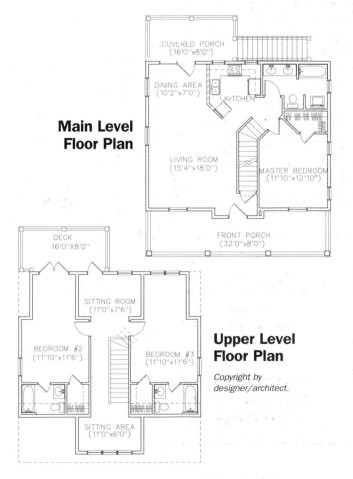

## Main Level Floor Plan

COVERED PORCH
(16'0"x8'0")

DINING AREA
(10'2"x7'0")

KITCHEN

LIVING ROOM
(15'4"x18'0")

MASTER BEDROOM
(11'10"x12'10")

FRONT PORCH
(32'0"x8'0")

## Upper Level Floor Plan

DECK
16'0"X8'0"

SITTING ROOM
(11'0"x7'6")

BEDROOM #2
(11'10"x11'6")

BEDROOM #3
(11'10"x11'6")

SITTING AREA
(11'0"x6'0")

*Images provided by designer/architect.*

## Plan #121085

**Dimensions:** 42' W x 54' D

**Levels:** 2

**Square Footage:** 1,948

**Main Level Sq. Ft.:** 1,517

**Upper Level Sq. Ft.:** 431

**Bedrooms:** 4

**Bathrooms:** 3

**Foundation:** Basement

**Materials List Available:** Yes

**Price Category:** D

You'll love the spacious feeling in this home, with its generous rooms and excellent design.

**Features:**

- Great Room: This room is lofty and open, thanks in part to the transom-topped windows that flank the fireplace. However, you can furnish to create a cozy nook for reading or a private spot to watch TV or enjoy some quiet music.

- Kitchen: Wrapping counters add an unusual touch to this kitchen, and a pantry gives extra storage area. A snack bar links the kitchen with a separate breakfast area.

- Master Suite: A tiered ceiling adds elegance to this area, and a walk-in closet adds practicality. The private bath features a sunlit whirlpool tub, separate shower, and double vanity.

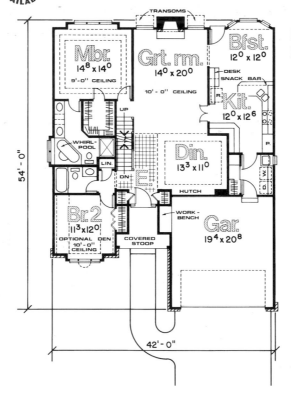

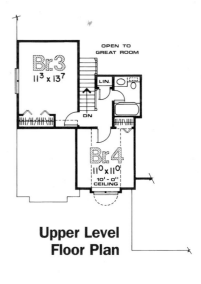

**Main Level Floor Plan**

**Upper Level Floor Plan**

*Copyright by designer/architect.*

- Upper-Level Bedrooms: The upper-level placement is just right for these bedrooms, which share an amenity-filled full bathroom.

## Plan #521051

**Dimensions:** 49'8" W x 61' D

**Levels:** 1

**Square Footage:** 1,492

**Bedrooms:** 3

**Bathrooms:** 2

**Foundation:** Slab

**Material List Available:** No

**Price Category:** B

*Images provided by designer/architect.*

*This home, as shown in the photograph, may differ from the actual blueprints. For more detailed information, please check the floor plans carefully.*

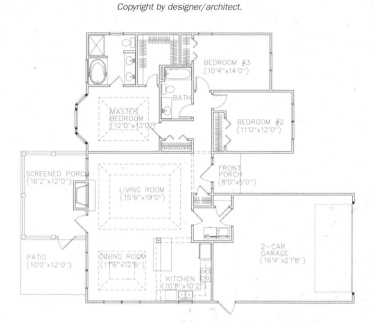

## Plan #121107

**Dimensions:** 48'8" W x 48' D

**Levels:** 1

**Square Footage:** 1,604

**Bedrooms:** 3

**Bathrooms:** 2

**Foundation:** Basement; crawl space for fee

**Material List Available:** Yes

**Price Category:** C

*Images provided by designer/architect.*

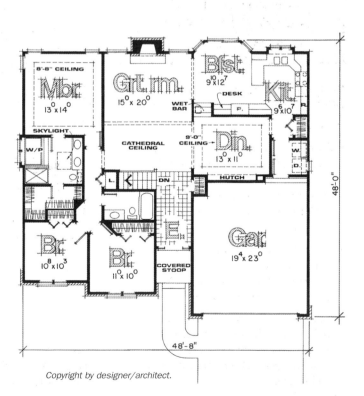

# Plan #521021

**Dimensions:** 60' W x 74'4" D

**Levels:** 1

**Square Footage:** 2,132

**Bedrooms:** 3

**Bathrooms:** 3

**Foundation:** Crawl space or slab

**Material List Available:** No

**Price Category:** D

*Images provided by designer/architect.*

CAD FILE AVAILABLE

BREAKFAST (15'0"x12'0")

SCREENED PORCH (31'10"x10'0")

BEDROOM #3 (13'10"x10'0")

LIVING ROOM (18'0"x18'10")

KITCHEN (13'0"x13'10")

MASTER BEDROOM (13'2"x18'10")

BEDROOM #2 (10'0"x13'6")

STUDY (13'2"x12'2")

FOYER

FRONT PORCH

2-CAR GARAGE (25'8"x20'2")

BONUS ROOM (14'0"x16'4")

**Bonus Area Floor Plan**

*Copyright by designer/architect.*

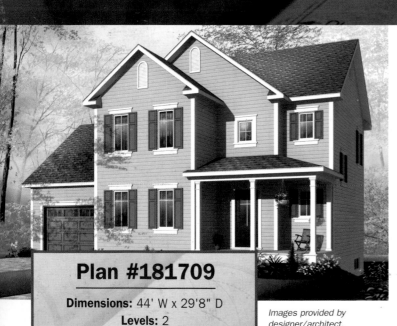

# Plan #181709

**Dimensions:** 44' W x 29'8" D

**Levels:** 2

**Square Footage:** 1,485

**Main Level Sq. Ft.:** 735

**Upper Level Sq. Ft.:** 750

**Bedrooms:** 3

**Bathrooms:** 1½

**Foundation:** Basement

**Material List Available:** Yes

**Price Category:** B

*Images provided by designer/architect.*

CAD FILE AVAILABLE

29'-8"
8,9 m

15'-4" X 22'-4"
4,60 X 6,70

9'-8" X 10'-0"
2,90 X 3,00

10'-4" X 13'-4"
3,10 X 4,00

12'-8" X 14'-8"
3,80 X 4,40

**Main Level Floor Plan**

44'-0"
13,2 m

9'-9" X 10'-0"
2,93 X 3,00

9'-9" X 10'-0"
2,93 X 3,00

12'-8" X 14'-8"
3,80 X 4,40

**Upper Level Floor Plan**

*Copyright by designer/architect.*

## Plan #121080

**Dimensions:** 56' W x 49' D
**Levels:** 2
**Square Footage:** 2,384
**Main Level Sq. Ft.:** 1,616
**Upper Level Sq. Ft.:** 768
**Bedrooms:** 4
**Bathrooms:** 2½
**Foundation:** Slab
**Materials List Available:** Yes
**Price Category:** E

*This home, as shown in the photograph, may differ from the actual blueprints. Images provided by designer/architect. For more detailed information, please check the floor plans carefully.*

This design is ideal if you want a generously sized home now and room to expand later.

**Features:**

• Living Room: Your eyes will be drawn towards the ceiling as soon as you enter this lovely room. The ceiling is vaulted, giving a sense of grandeur, and a graceful balcony from the second floor adds extra interest to this room.

• Kitchen: Designed with lots of counter space to make your work convenient, this kitchen also shares an eating bar with the breakfast nook.

• Breakfast Nook: Eat here or go out to the adjoining private porch where you can enjoy your meal in the morning sunshine.

• Master Suite: The bayed area in the bedroom makes a picturesque sitting area. French doors in the bedroom open to a private bath that's fitted with a whirlpool tub, separate shower, two vanities, and a walk-in closet.

**Main Level Floor Plan**

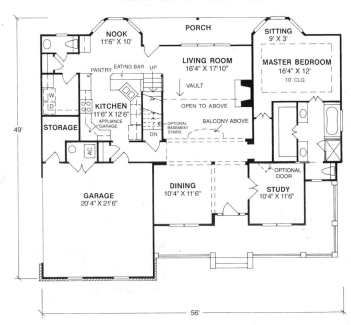

**Upper Level Floor Plan**

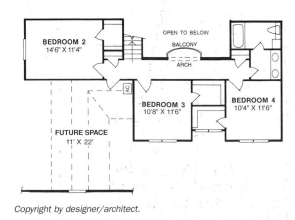

*Copyright by designer/architect.*

## Plan #321008

**Dimensions:** 57' W x 52'2" D

**Levels:** 1

**Square Footage:** 1,761

**Bedrooms:** 4

**Bathrooms:** 2

**Foundation:** Basement

**Materials List Available:** Yes

**Price Category:** C

*Images provided by designer/architect.*

One look at the roof dormers and planter boxes that grace the outside of this ranch, and you'll know that the interior is planned for comfortable family living.

**Features:**

- **Great Room:** A vaulted ceiling in this room points up its generous dimensions. Put a grouping of chairs near the fireplace to take advantage of the cozy spot it creates in chilly weather.

- **Kitchen:** Open to the great room, this kitchen has been planned for convenience. It features a pass-through to the dining area for easy serving when you've got a crowd to feed.

- **Master Bedroom:** A vaulted ceiling here makes you feel especially pampered, and the walk-in closet and amenity-filled bath add to that feeling.

- **Additional Bedrooms:** Great closet space characterizes all the rooms in this home, making it easy for children of any age to keep it organized and tidy.

*Copyright by designer/architect.*

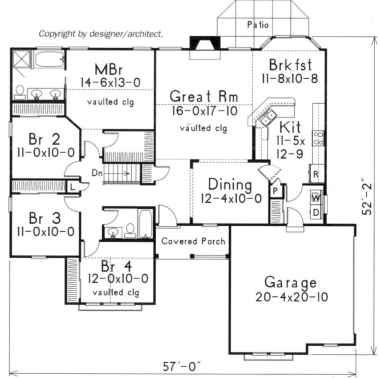

## SMARTtip

### Hanging Wallpaper

Use liner paper to smooth out a damaged wall and to provide uniform support for expensive paper.

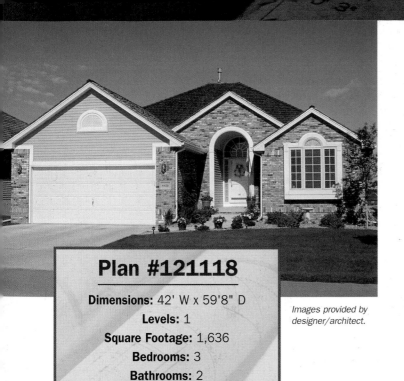

## Plan #121118

**Dimensions:** 42' W x 59'8" D

**Levels:** 1

**Square Footage:** 1,636

**Bedrooms:** 3

**Bathrooms:** 2

**Foundation:** Basement; crawl space for fee

**Material List Available:** Yes

**Price Category:** C

*Images provided by designer/architect.*

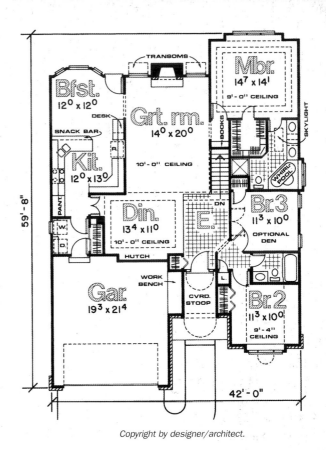

*Copyright by designer/architect.*

## Plan #341252

**Dimensions:** 62' W x 29'5" D

**Levels:** 2

**Square Footage:** 2,140

**Main Level Sq. Ft.:** 1,069

**Upper Level Sq. Ft.:** 1,071

**Bedrooms:** 3

**Bathrooms:** 2½

**Foundation:** Crawl space, slab, basement, or walkout

**Material List Available:** Yes

**Price Category:** D

*Images provided by designer/architect.*

CAD FILE AVAILABLE

**Upper Level Floor Plan**

**Main Level Floor Plan**

*Copyright by designer/architect.*

## Plan #131007

**Dimensions:** 59'10" W x 47'8" D

**Levels:** 1

**Square Footage:** 1,595

**Bedrooms:** 3

**Bathrooms:** 2

**Foundation:** Crawl space, slab, basement, or walkout

**Materials List Available:** Yes

**Price Category:** D

*Images provided by designer/architect.*

Imagine living in this home, with its traditional country comfort and individual brand of charm.

### Features:

- Exterior elements: The mixture of a front porch with a cameo front door, decorative posts, bay windows, and dormers will delight you.

- Great Room: A tray ceiling gives distinction to this large room, and a wet bar eases entertaining.

- Screened Porch: At dusk and dawn, this porch is sure to be your favorite outdoor spot.

- Kitchen: Eat any meal in this large kitchen for a touch of homey charm.

- Dining Room: Perfect for hosting a formal dinner, this bayed dining room can increase your enjoyment of simple family meals.

- Master Bedroom: For the sake of privacy, this room is somewhat secluded. Decorate to emphasize the elegant tray ceiling.

**SCREENED PORCH** 13'-4" x 12'-8"

**BEDRM #3** 13'-4" x 11'-0"

**GREAT RM** 14'-0" x 22'-8"

TRAY CEIL

WET BAR

**MSTR BEDRM** 12'-0" x 18'-0"

TRAY CEIL

**MSTR BATH**

WICL

DRSG

W D

**STOR**

**UTIL**

LOCATION OF OPT BSMT STAIR

**BEDRM #2** 11'-0" x 14'-0"

**BATH**

CL

CL

**FOY**

**DINING RM** 10'-0" x 13'-0"

**KITCHEN** 10'-0" x 11'-0"

REF

DW

**TWO CAR GARAGE** 20'-0" x 21'-4"

**COV. PORCH**

*Copyright by designer/architect.*

Rear Elevation

Alternate Front View

Foyer / Dining Room

Great Room

## Add the Extras

Simple or plain, it's the little conveniences and miscellaneous touches that push the dining experience to perfection. Here are some extra things to think about.

- You can never have too many serving trays when you entertain outside. For carrying food or drinks from the kitchen or the grill, trays are indispensable.

- A serving cart on wheels makes a perfect movable outdoor bar and provides an additional serving surface. Look for one at yard sales or buy one new.

- Chances are you won't have a sideboard, but a few small tables to hold excess items are great substitutes for one. They're also easier to position in the different places where you need them.

- For cooler weather or even a summer's evening with a bit of nip in the air, nothing beats an outdoor fireplace for comfort. You could build one into the house, but various types of stand-alone units are sold in home centers. To add a Southwest ambiance, consider a chiminea, a clay fireplace. Try burning some piñon pine, and you'll feel as if you're in Santa Fe. Be sure to follow manufacturers' instructions when using these fireplaces. You might also have to store them during the winter.

- Pots of fragrant plants—lavender, scented geraniums, flowering tobacco, or jasmine—provide a sensual aroma. Flowers such as roses climbing up an arbor or trellis are beautiful, evoke a romantic feeling, and lend a delicate scent to the atmosphere as well.

Nothing adds romance and intrigue to an evening soiree as candlelight does. Include just a few candles for an intimate dinner. Use more for a larger gathering, placing one or more on each table. Scatter luminaries around the yard. As the beautiful evening dusk begins, light candles, a few at a time, so your eyes can adjust to the dimming light. Not only do the candles illuminate the night in a magical way but they can also keep bugs at bay.

## Plan #321003

**Dimensions:** 67'4" W x 48' D
**Levels:** 1
**Square Footage:** 1,791
**Bedrooms:** 4
**Bathrooms:** 2
**Foundation:** Basement
**Materials List Available:** Yes
**Price Category:** C

*Images provided by designer/architect.*

The traditional good looks of the exterior of this home are complemented by the stunning contemporary design of the interior.

**Features:**

- Great Room: With a vaulted ceiling to highlight its spacious dimensions, this room is certain to be the central gathering spot for friends and family.

- Dining Room: Also with a vaulted ceiling, this room has an octagonal shape for added interest. Windows here and in the great room look out to the covered patio.

- Kitchen: A center island gives a convenient work space in this well-designed kitchen, which features a pass-through to the dining room for easy serving, and large, walk-in pantry for storage.

- Breakfast Room: A bay window lets sunshine pour in to start your morning with a smile.

- Master Bedroom: A vaulted ceiling and a sitting area make you feel truly pampered in this room.

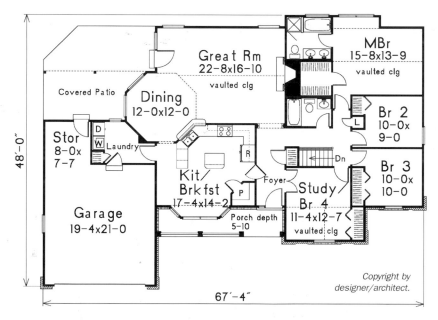

*Copyright by designer/architect.*

## SMARTtip

### Bay & Bow Windows

Occasionally too little room exists between the window frame (if there is one) and the ceiling. In this situation you might be able to use ceiling-mounted hardware. Alternatively, a cornice across the top and a rod mounted inside the cornice will give you the dual benefit of visually lowering the top of the window and concealing the hardware.

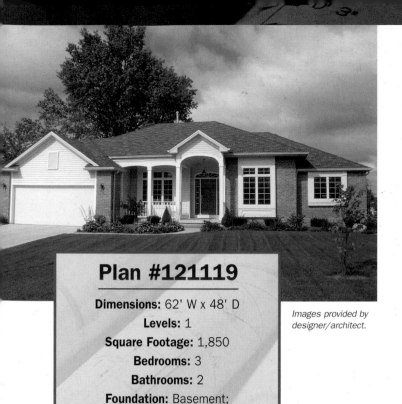

## Plan #121119

**Dimensions:** 62' W x 48' D

**Levels:** 1

**Square Footage:** 1,850

**Bedrooms:** 3

**Bathrooms:** 2

**Foundation:** Basement; crawl space for fee

**Material List Available:** Yes

**Price Category:** D

*Images provided by designer/architect.*

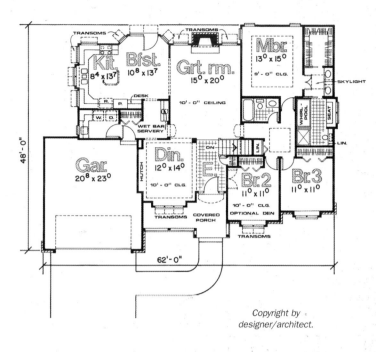

*Copyright by designer/architect.*

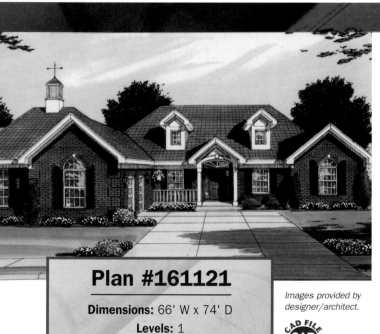

## Plan #161121

**Dimensions:** 66' W x 74' D

**Levels:** 1

**Square Footage:** 1,824

**Bedrooms:** 3

**Bathrooms:** 2

**Foundation:** Basement

**Material List Available:** Yes

**Price Category:** D

*Images provided by designer/architect.*

*Copyright by designer/architect.*

Rear Elevation

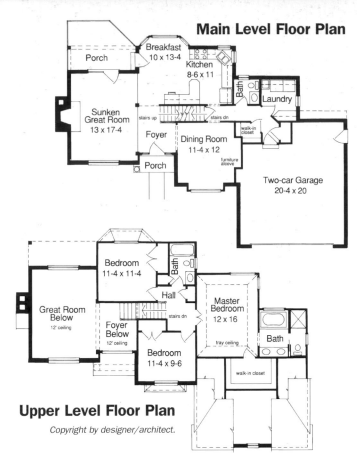

## Main Level Floor Plan

Porch

Breakfast
10 x 13-4

Kitchen
8-6 x 11

Bath

Laundry

Sunken
Great Room
13 x 17-4

stairs up

stairs dn

walk-in
closet

Foyer

Dining Room
11-4 x 12

Two-car Garage
20-4 x 20

Porch

furniture
alcove

Bedroom
11-4 x 11-4

Bath

Great Room
Below
12' ceiling

Hall

Master
Bedroom
12 x 16

Foyer
Below
12' ceiling

stairs dn

tray ceiling

Bath

Bedroom
11-4 x 9-6

walk-in
closet

## Upper Level Floor Plan

*Copyright by designer/architect.*

*Images provided by designer/architect.*

# Plan #161015

**Dimensions:** 55'4" W x 40'4" D

**Levels:** 2

**Square Footage:** 1,768

**Main Level Sq. Ft.:** 960

**Upper Level Sq. Ft.:** 808

**Bedrooms:** 3

**Bathrooms:** 2½

**Foundation:** Basement

**Materials List Available:** Yes

**Price Category:** C

---

*Copyright by designer/architect.*

9'-0" X 11'-0"
2,70 X 3,30

17'-8" X 12'-4"
5,30 X 3,70

12'-8" X 23'-4"
3,80 X 7,00

35'-0"
10,5 m

13'-8" X 14'-4"
4,10 X 4,30

13'-0" X 13'-4"
3,90 X 4,00

50'-0"
15,0 m

*Images provided by designer/architect.*

**CAD FILE AVAILABLE**

# Plan #181729

**Dimensions:** 50' W x 35' D

**Levels:** 1

**Square Footage:** 1,155

**Bedrooms:** 2

**Bathrooms:** 1

**Foundation:** Basement

**Material List Available:** Yes

**Price Category:** B

# Plan #121106

**Dimensions:** 74'4" W x 58' D

**Levels:** 1

**Square Footage:** 2,133

**Bedrooms:** 3

**Bathrooms:** 2½

**Foundation:** Basement; crawl space for fee

**Material List Available:** Yes

**Price Category:** D

*Images provided by designer/architect.*

**CAD FILE AVAILABLE**

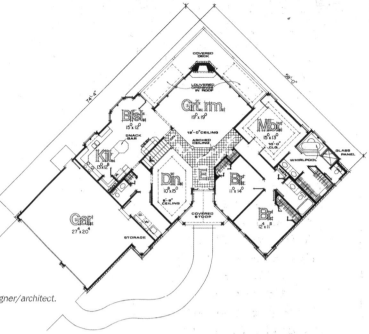

*Copyright by designer/architect.*

# Plan #181721

**Dimensions:** 47' W x 53'4" D

**Levels:** 1

**Square Footage:** 1,828

**Bedrooms:** 3

**Bathrooms:** 2

**Foundation:** Basement

**Material List Available:** Yes

**Price Category:** D

*Images provided by designer/architect.*

**CAD FILE AVAILABLE**

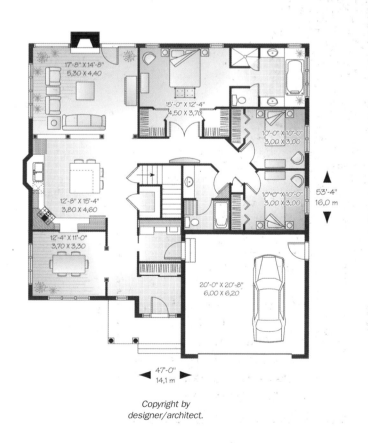

*Copyright by designer/architect.*

## Main Level Floor Plan

## Plan #181645

**Dimensions:** 50' W x 42' D

**Levels:** 2

**Square Footage:** 2,300

**Main Level Sq. Ft.:** 1,212

**Upper Level Sq. Ft.:** 1,088

**Bedrooms:** 3

**Bathrooms:** 2½

**Foundation:** Basement

**Material List Available:** Yes

**Price Category:** E

*Images provided by designer/architect.*

CAD FILE AVAILABLE

## Upper Level Floor Plan

*Copyright by designer/architect.*

---

## Main Level Floor Plan

38'-0"
11,4 m

## Plan #181653

**Dimensions:** 36' W x 38' D

**Levels:** 2

**Square Footage:** 1,722

**Main Level Sq. Ft.:** 804

**Upper Level Sq. Ft.:** 918

**Bedrooms:** 3

**Bathrooms:** 2½

**Foundation:** Basement

**Material List Available:** Yes

**Price Category:** C

*Images provided by designer/architect.*

CAD FILE AVAILABLE

Rear Elevation

## Upper Level Floor Plan

*Copyright by designer/architect.*

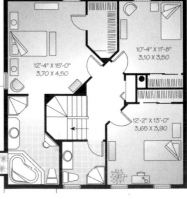

## Plan #121086

**Dimensions:** 55'4" W x 37'8" D

**Levels:** 2

**Square Footage:** 1,998

**Main Level Sq. Ft.:** 1,093

**Upper Level Sq. Ft.:** 905

**Bedrooms:** 3

**Bathrooms:** 2½

**Foundation:** Basement

**Materials List Available:** Yes

**Price Category:** D

You'll love the open design of this comfortable home if sunny, bright rooms make you happy.

**Features:**

- Entry: Walk into this two-story entry, and you're sure to admire the open staircase and balcony from the upper level.
- Dining Room: To the left of the entry, you'll see this dining room, with its special ceiling detail and built-in display cabinet.
- Living Room: Located immediately to the right, this living room features a charming bay window.
- Family Room: French doors from the living room open into this sunny space, where a handsome fireplace takes center stage.
- Kitchen: Combined with the breakfast area, this kitch-- features an island cooktop, a large pantry, and a built-in d--k.

**Main Level Floor Plan**

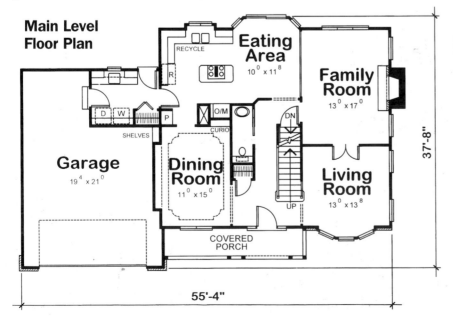

**Upper Level Floor Plan**

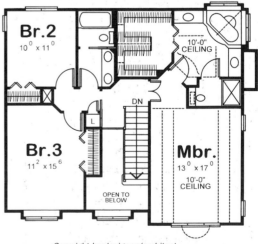

## Upper Level Floor Plan

BEDROOM 3
10'-10" X 11'-5"

LINEN
BA.2
CLOS
CLOS
BA.1
1/2" WALL
SHWR

UNFINISHED BONUS ROOM
23'-2" X 11'-10"

RAILING

BEDROOM 2
14'-6" X 11'-6"

OPEN

BEDROOM 1
15'-8" X 15'-0"

## Main Level Floor Plan

*Copyright by designer/architect.*

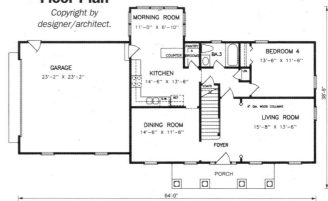

MORNING ROOM
11'-0" X 6'-10"

PANTRY &
BROOMS

COUNTER

BA.3

BEDROOM 4
13'-6" X 11'-6"

GARAGE
23'-2" X 23'-2"

KITCHEN
14'-6" X 13'-6"

COATS

LIN.

D.W. REF

8" DIA. WOOD COLUMNS

DINING ROOM
14'-6" X 11'-6"

LIVING ROOM
15'-8" X 13'-6"

FOYER

PORCH

64'-0"

38'-8"

# Plan #341251

**Dimensions:** 64' W x 38'8" D

**Levels:** 2

**Square Footage:** 2,254

**Main Level Sq. Ft.:** 1,127

**Upper Level Sq. Ft.:** 1,127

**Bedrooms:** 4

**Bathrooms:** 3

**Foundation:** Crawl space, slab, basement, or walkout

**Material List Available:** Yes

**Price Category:** E

*Images provided by designer/architect.*

CAD FILE AVAILABLE

---

# Plan #121148

**Dimensions:** 36' W x 50' D

**Levels:** 2

**Square Footage:** 2,076

**Main Level Sq. Ft.:** 1,117

**Upper Level Sq. Ft.:** 959

**Bedrooms:** 3

**Bathrooms:** 2½

**Foundation:** Basement; crawl space for fee

**Material List Available:** Yes

**Price Category:** D

*Images provided by designer/architect.*

CAD FILE AVAILABLE

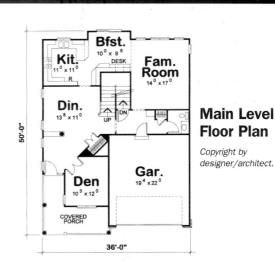

Bfst.
10'0 x 9'8
DESK

Kit.
11'0 x 11'0
R

Fam. Room
14'0 x 17'0

Din.
13'8 x 11'0

UP
DN

Den
10'3 x 12'0

Gar.
19'4 x 22'0

COVERED PORCH

50'-0"

36'-0"

## Main Level Floor Plan

*Copyright by designer/architect.*

## Upper Level Floor Plan

Mbr.
13'8 x 19'0

Br.4
10'4 x 11'0

DN
COMP. DESK
W D

LOFT

OPEN TO BELOW

L

Br.3
10'0 x 11'0

PLANTS

Br.2
10'3 x 14'0

## Optional Upper Level Floor Plan

Mbr.
13'8 x 11'0

OPEN TO BELOW

DN
COMP. DESK
W D

OPEN TO BELOW

L

Br.3
10'0 x 11'0

PLANTS

Br.2
10'3 x 14'0

## Plan #121066

**Dimensions:** 46' W x 41'5" D
**Levels:** 2
**Square Footage:** 2,078
**Main Level Sq. Ft.:** 1,113
**Upper Level Sq. Ft.:** 965
**Bedrooms:** 4
**Bathrooms:** 2½
**Foundation:** Basement
**Materials List Available:** Yes
**Price Category:** D

*Images provided by designer/architect.*

This lovely home has an unusual dignity, perhaps because its rooms are so well-proportioned and thoughtfully laid out.

**Features:**

• **Family Room:** This room is sunken, giving it an unusually cozy, comfortable feeling. Its abundance of windows let natural light stream in during the day, and the fireplace warms it when the weather's chilly.

• **Dining Room:** This dining room links to the parlor beyond through a cased opening.

• **Parlor:** A tall, angled ceiling highlights a large, arched window that's the focal point of this room.

• **Breakfast Area:** A wooden rail visually links this bayed breakfast area to the family room.

• **Master Suite:** A roomy walk-in closet adds a practical touch to this luxurious suite. The bath features a skylight, whirlpool tub, and separate shower.

### Main Level Floor Plan

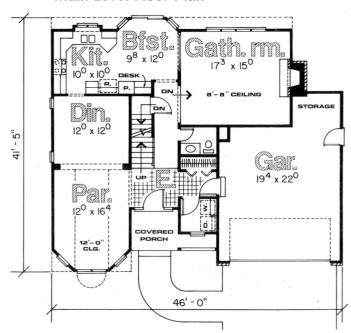

### Upper Level Floor Plan

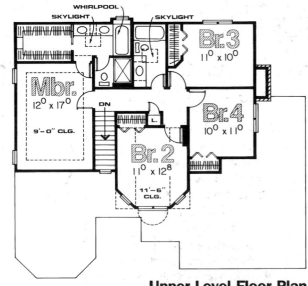

*Copyright by designer/architect.*

# Plan #151037

**Dimensions:** 50' W x 56' D

**Levels:** 1

**Square Footage:** 1,538

**Bedrooms:** 3

**Bathrooms:** 2

**Foundation:** Crawl space, slab, or basement

**CompleteCost List Available:** Yes

**Price Category:** C

You'll love this traditional-looking home, with its covered porch and interesting front windows.

**Features:**

- Ceiling Height: 8 ft.

- Great Room: This large room has a boxed window that emphasizes its dimensions and a fireplace where everyone will gather on chilly evenings. A door opens to the backyard.

- Dining Room: A bay window overlooking the front porch makes this room easy to decorate.

- Kitchen: This well-planned kitchen features ample counter space, a full pantry, and an eating bar that it shares with the dining room.

- Master Suite: A pan ceiling in this lovely room gives an elegant touch. The huge private bath includes two walk-in closets, a whirlpool tub, a dual-sink vanity, and a skylight in the ceiling.

- Additional Bedrooms: On the opposite side of the house, these bedrooms share a large bath, and both feature excellent closet space.

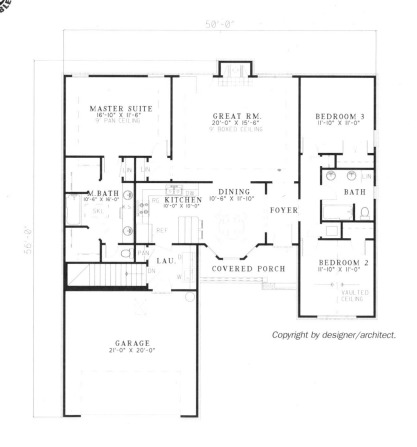

*Copyright by designer/architect.*

# Plan #161007

**Dimensions:** 66'4" W x 43'10" D

**Levels:** 1

**Square Footage:** 1,611

**Bedrooms:** 3

**Bathrooms:** 2

**Foundation:** Basement; crawl space option for fee

**Materials List Available:** Yes

**Price Category:** C

A lovely front porch and an entry with side-lights invite you to experience the impressive amenities offered in this exceptional ranch home.

**Features:**

- Great Room: Grand openings, featuring columns from the foyer to this great room and continuing to the bayed dining area, convey an open, spacious feel. The fireplace and matching windows on the rear wall of the great room enhance this effect.

- Kitchen: This well-designed kitchen offers convenient access to the laundry and garage. It also features an angled counter with ample space and an abundance of cabinets.

- Master Suite: This deluxe master suite contains many exciting amenities, including a lavishly appointed dressing room and a large walk-in closet.

- Porch: Sliding doors lead to this delightful screened porch for relaxing summer interludes.

CAD FILE AVAILABLE

*Images provided by designer/architect.*

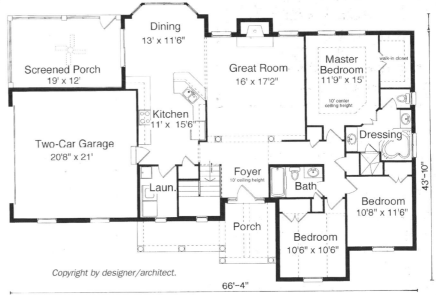

Screened Porch 19' x 12'

Two-Car Garage 20'8" x 21'

Dining 13' x 11'6"

Kitchen 11' x 15'6"

Great Room 16' x 17'2"

Master Bedroom 11'9" x 15'

walk-in closet

10' center ceiling height

Dressing

Laun.

Foyer 10' ceiling height

Bath

Bedroom 10'8" x 11'6"

Porch

Bedroom 10'6" x 10'6"

43'-10"

66'-4"

*Copyright by designer/architect.*

Rear Elevation

## Plan #341176

**Dimensions:** 76'6" W x 34' D

**Levels:** 2

**Square Footage:** 2,170

**Main Level Sq. Ft.:** 1,550

**Lower Level Sq. Ft:** 620

**Bedrooms:** 3

**Bathrooms:** 2½

**Foundation:** Crawl space, slab, basement, or walkout

**Materials List Available:** Yes

**Price Category:** D

*Images provided by designer/architect.*

A columned portico and brick facade combine to create this classically beautiful home, which has an ideal design for the modern family.

**Features:**

- **Foyer:** Double doors swing into this welcoming space, with closets ready to take your guests' coats and an attached formal living room that introduces them comfortably to your home.

- **Family Room:** With built-in entertainment and storage space and an unfettered connection with the dining room and kitchen, this is a space where the whole family can gather and enjoy each other's company.

- **Kitchen:** The sweeping design of this space is both efficient and attractive. It features a working island with a range and stands open to the dining room. And whether it's a cool, sunny day or a warm, rainy one, you'll enjoy relaxing meals on the screened porch that is just a few steps away.

- **Master Suite:** In this space, a walk-in closet and full master bath adorn the bedroom, all waiting to be transformed into your personal retreat.

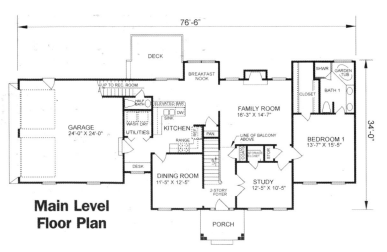

**Main Level Floor Plan**

*Copyright by designer/architect.*

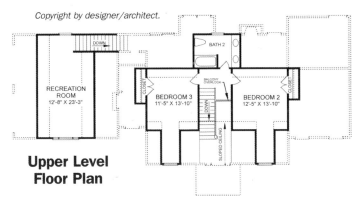

**Upper Level Floor Plan**

## Plan #141046

**Dimensions:** 54'4" W x 35' D
**Levels:** 2
**Square Footage:** 2,375
**Main Level Sq. Ft.:** 977
**Lower Level Sq. Ft:** 1,398
**Bedrooms:** 4
**Bathrooms:** 2½
**Foundation:** Basement
**Materials List Available:** No
**Price Category:** E

*Images provided by designer/architect.*

Dormers and two-story bay windows add architectural beauty and expansive light to this innovative home, which is an ideal space for the growing family.

**Features:**

- **Living Room:** Go from relaxing on the front porch in summer to lounging in this spacious living room in front of the fireplace during winter.

- **Kitchen:** Budding gourmet and experienced chef alike will appreciate being surrounded by workspace and storage in this efficient kitchen. The space is flanked by the formal dining room, which faces the bay windows, and the sweet breakfast room, which will fill with the morning sun.

- **Master Suite:** This space is so luxurious that it has its own wing. The large bedroom area is full of interior design possibilities and features his and her walk-in closets. The master bath has dual sinks and an oversized tub, over which moonlight will pour from the adjacent window.

- **Secondary Bedrooms:** With three additional bedrooms, there is room to grow. One features bay windows, another a walk-in closet, while all three are close to the shared second full bathroom.

*Copyright by designer/architect.*

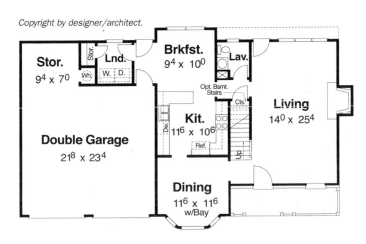

**Main Level Floor Plan**

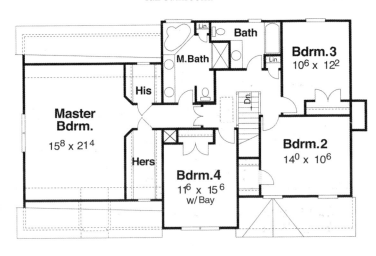

**Upper Level Floor Plan**

## Plan #121006

**Dimensions:** 46' W x 58' D

**Levels:** 1

**Square Footage:** 1,762

**Bedrooms:** 3

**Bathrooms:** 2

**Foundation:** Slab

**Materials List Available:** Yes

**Price Category:** C

*Images provided by designer/architect.*

The entry has a trio of arched openings that leads you to other areas of this amenity-packed home.

**Features:**

- Ceiling Height: 8 ft. except as noted.

- Eating Bar: Conveniently located between the kitchen and family room, this is sure to be a favorite spot for informal entertaining and family gatherings.

- Family room: A wall of windows, a fireplace, and a vaulted ceiling stretching to 11 ft. work together to make this a bright and warm room.

- Kitchen: There's no shortage of counter space in this well-planned kitchen that features a center island in addition to the eating bar.

- Master Suite: Luxuriate at the end of the day in this large bedroom with its decorative tray ceiling and walk-in closet. Enjoy the pampering bath with its sunlit corner whirlpool flanked by vanities.

- Garage: Two bays provide room for cars and plenty of storage as well.

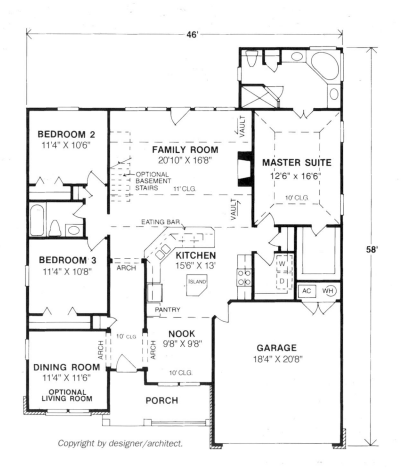

*Copyright by designer/architect.*

## Main Level Floor Plan

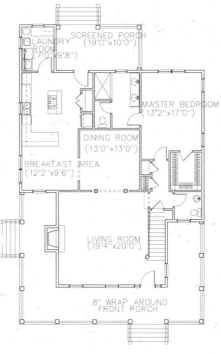

LAUNDRY ROOM (7'0"x9'8")

SCREENED PORCH (19'0"x10'0")

MASTER BEDROOM (13'2"x17'0")

DINING ROOM (13'0"x13'0")

BREAKFAST AREA (12'2"x9'6")

LIVING ROOM (19'4"x20'0")

8' WRAP AROUND FRONT PORCH

## Upper Level Floor Plan

*Copyright by designer/architect.*

BEDROOM #2 (12'0"x13'0")

STORAGE

BEDROOM #3 (12'0"x12'8")

*Images provided by designer/architect.*

**CAD FILE AVAILABLE**

## Plan #521018

**Dimensions:** 40' W x 64'10" D

**Levels:** 2

**Square Footage:** 2,306

**Main Level Sq. Ft.:** 1,678

**Upper Level Sq. Ft.:** 628

**Bedrooms:** 3

**Bathrooms:** 2½

**Foundation:** Crawl space

**Material List Available:** No

**Price Category:** E

---

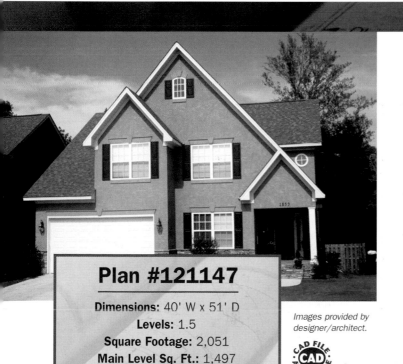

## Plan #121147

**Dimensions:** 40' W x 51' D

**Levels:** 1.5

**Square Footage:** 2,051

**Main Level Sq. Ft.:** 1,497

**Upper Level Sq. Ft.:** 554

**Bedrooms:** 3

**Bathrooms:** 2½

**Foundation:** Basement; crawl space for fee

**Material List Available:** Yes

**Price Category:** D

*Images provided by designer/architect.*

**CAD FILE AVAILABLE**

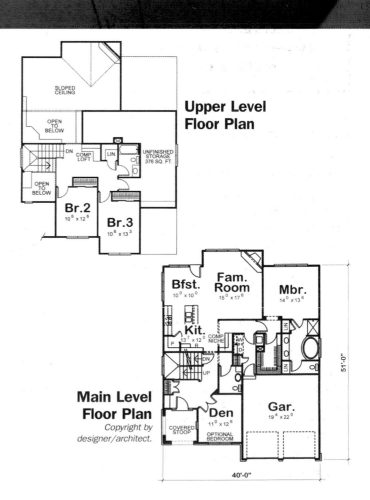

## Upper Level Floor Plan

SLOPED CEILING

OPEN TO BELOW

COMP LOFT

LIN.

UNFINISHED STORAGE 376 SQ. FT.

OPEN TO BELOW

DN

Br.2 10'6 x 12'6

Br.3 10'6 x 13'3

Bfst. 10'0 x 10'0

Fam. Room 15'0 x 17'6

Mbr. 14'0 x 13'6

Kit. 13'7 x 12'0

COMP NICHE

Den 11'0 x 12'6

Gar. 19'4 x 22'0

COVERED STOOP

OPTIONAL BEDROOM

## Main Level Floor Plan

*Copyright by designer/architect.*

40'-0"

51'-0"

**Main Level Floor Plan**

Porch 22'1"x 8'

Breakfast 10'x 10'

Utility

Living 20'5"x 15'6"

Kitchen 12'x 13'6"

Ma. Ba.

Two Car Garage 22'8"x 21'4"

Master Bedroom 13'x 17'8"

Dining 12'x 12'8"

Foyer

Porch 34'10"x 6'

*Copyright by designer/architect.*

## Plan #111022

**Dimensions:** 62' W x 36'4" D

**Levels:** 2

**Square Footage:** 3,105

**Main Level Sq. Ft.:** 1,470

**Upper Level Sq. Ft.:** 1,635

**Bedrooms:** 4

**Bathrooms:** 2½

**Foundation:** Finished basement

**Materials List Available:** Yes

**Price Category:** G

*Images provided by designer/architect.*

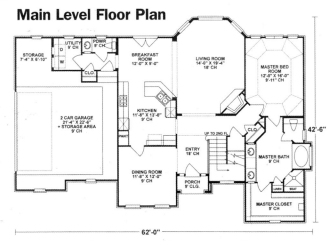

Computer Area

Future Gameroom 18'9"x 12'6"

Bedroom 12'3"x 14'

Bedroom 12'5"x 14'

**Upper Level Floor Plan**

---

**Main Level Floor Plan**

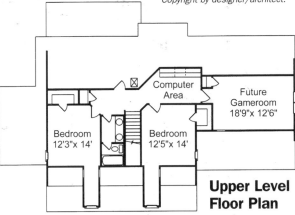

STORAGE 7'-4" X 6'-10"

UTILITY 9' CH

PDWR 9' CH

CLO

BREAKFAST ROOM 12'-0" X 9'-0"

LIVING ROOM 14'-0" X 19'-4" 18' CH

MASTER BED ROOM 12'-0" X 16'-0" 9'-11" CH

2 CAR GARAGE 21'-4" X 22'-8" + STORAGE AREA 9' CH

KITCHEN 11'-8" X 13'-0" 9' CH

PANT

UP TO 2ND FL

CLO

MASTER BATH 9' CH

ENTRY 18' CH

DINING ROOM 11'-8" X 12'-0" 9' CH

PORCH 9' CLG.

LINEN SEAT

MASTER CLOSET 9' CH

42'-6"

62'-0"

## Plan #121153

**Dimensions:** 62' W x 42'6" D

**Levels:** 1.5

**Square Footage:** 1,984

**Main Level Sq. Ft.:** 1,487

**Upper Level Sq. Ft.:** 497

**Bedrooms:** 3

**Bathrooms:** 2½

**Foundation:** Slab; basement for fee

**Material List Available:** Yes

**Price Category:** D

*Images provided by designer/architect.*

CAD FILE AVAILABLE

**Upper Level Floor Plan**

*Copyright by designer/architect.*

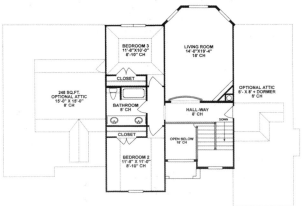

BEDROOM 3 11'-8"X10'-0" 8'-10" CH

LIVING ROOM 14'-0"X19'-4" 18' CH

CLOSET

248 SQ.FT. OPTIONAL ATTIC 15'-0" X 15'-0" 8' CH

BATHROOM 8' CH

OPTIONAL ATTIC 8'- X 8' + DORMER 5' CH

CLOSET

HALL-WAY 8' CH

DOWN

BEDROOM 2 11'-8" X 11'-0" 8'-10" CH

OPEN BELOW 18' CH

# Plan #431005

**Dimensions:** 55' W x 52'6" D

**Levels:** 2

**Square Footage:** 1,693

**Main Level Sq. Ft.:** 1,263

**Upper Level Sq. Ft.:** 430

**Bedrooms:** 3

**Bathrooms:** 2½

**Foundation:** Crawl space or basement

**Material List Available:** Yes

**Price Category:** C

*Images provided by designer/architect.*

**Main Level Floor Plan**

**Upper Level Floor Plan**

*Copyright by designer/architect.*

Great Room

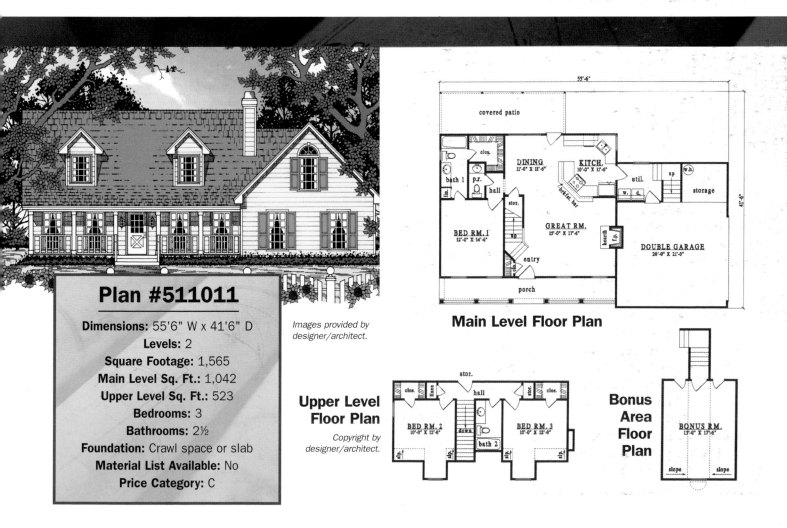

# Plan #511011

**Dimensions:** 55'6" W x 41'6" D

**Levels:** 2

**Square Footage:** 1,565

**Main Level Sq. Ft.:** 1,042

**Upper Level Sq. Ft.:** 523

**Bedrooms:** 3

**Bathrooms:** 2½

**Foundation:** Crawl space or slab

**Material List Available:** No

**Price Category:** C

*Images provided by designer/architect.*

**Main Level Floor Plan**

**Upper Level Floor Plan**

*Copyright by designer/architect.*

**Bonus Area Floor Plan**

## Plan #351087

**Dimensions:** 66'8" W x 70'8" D
**Levels:** 1.5
**Square Footage:** 2,250
**Bedrooms:** 4
**Bathrooms:** 3
**Foundation:** Crawl space or slab
**Materials List Available:** Yes
**Price Category:** E

The dashing contemporary-country style of brick and wood siding with attractive architectural details, like a string of dormers, makes this home's exterior as lovely as its interior.

**Features:**

- **Great Room:** Vaulted ceilings give this great room an enormous sense of freedom. The space also opens onto the rear covered porch for the overflow of relaxing warm-weather gatherings and features a fireplace and built-in storage for staying comfortable inside during the cold months.

- **Kitchen:** This efficiently designed kitchen features an L-shaped work area, a pantry,

and an island with a raised eating bar. Because the space is open to the formal dining room, bay-windowed breakfast room, and large great room, you'll have plenty of mealtime possibilities.

- **Master Suite:** In a space of its own, the bedroom in this space speaks volumes of relaxation and privacy. One door leads onto the covered porch while the other leads to the expansive master bath, with its dual sinks, oversize jetted tub, stall shower, and his and her walk-in closets.

- **Secondary Bedrooms:** The other bedrooms have hallways of their own and are all just steps away from the other full bathrooms.

- **Flex Space:** A small room adjacent to the master bedroom is in perfect proximity for use as a home office, a nursery, or extra storage space. Above the garage is unfinished bonus space, which can be used however you like.

*Images provided by designer/architect.*

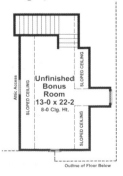

*Rear Elevation*

9' WIDE COVERED PORCH

CANTILEVERED 2nd FLOOR

OPTIONAL TWO CAR GARAGE

SHOP/ STORAGE
7'-7"x11'-9"

LNDRY 1/2 BATH

DINING
10'-3"x10'-5"
(9' CLG)

KITCHEN
10'-6"x10'-5"
(9' CLG)

FRIG

COATS PNTRY

ARCH OVER COLUMNS

LIVING ROOM
20'-9"x15'-6"
(9' CLG)

8' WIDE COVERED PORCH

GARAGE
14'-0"x22'-2"

VENTLESS GAS FIREPLACE

8' WIDE COVERED PORCH

10' OVERHEAD DOOR

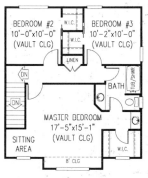

Images provided by designer/architect.

**CAD FILE AVAILABLE**

# Plan #421002

**Dimensions:** 46'9" W x 43'6" D

**Levels:** 2

**Square Footage:** 1,399

**Main Level Sq. Ft.:** 732

**Upper Level Sq. Ft:** 667

**Bedrooms:** 3

**Bathrooms:** 1½

**Foundation:** Crawl space, slab, or basement

**Material List Available:** Yes

**Price Category:** B

BEDROOM #2
10'-0"x10'-0"
(VAULT CLG)

BEDROOM #3
10'-2"x10'-0"
(VAULT CLG)

W.I.C.

W.I.C.

LINEN

BATH

TUB/SHWR

## Upper Level Floor Plan

Copyright by designer/architect.

MASTER BEDROOM
17'-5"x15'-1"
(VAULT CLG)

SITTING AREA

8' CLG

W.I.C.

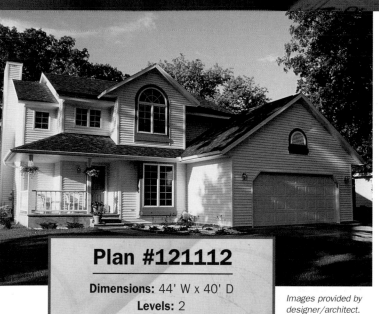

# Plan #121112

**Dimensions:** 44' W x 40' D

**Levels:** 2

**Square Footage:** 1,650

**Main Level Sq. Ft.:** 891

**Upper Level Sq. Ft.:** 759

**Bedrooms:** 3

**Bathrooms:** 2½

**Foundation:** Basement; crawl space for fee

**Material List Available:** Yes

**Price Category:** C

Images provided by designer/architect.

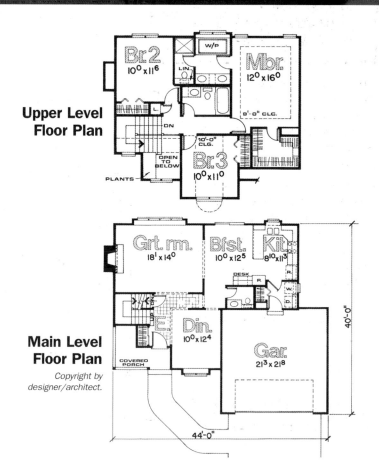

Br. 2
10⁰x11⁶

W/P

Mbr.
12⁰x16⁰

LIN

8'-0" CLG.

**Upper Level Floor Plan**

10'-0" CLG.

OPEN TO BELOW

Br. 3
10⁰x11⁰

DN

PLANTS

Grt. rm.
18'x14⁰

Bfst.
10⁰x12⁵

Kit.
8¹⁰x11³

DESK

Din.
10⁰x12⁴

Gar.
21³x21⁸

40'-0"

COVERED PORCH

**Main Level Floor Plan**

Copyright by designer/architect.

44'-0"

## Plan #521020

**Dimensions:** 98'11" W x 67'8" D

**Levels:** 1

**Square Footage:** 2,139

**Bedrooms:** 3

**Bathrooms:** 3

**Foundation:** Crawl space

**Material List Available:** No

**Price Category:** D

## Bonus Area Floor Plan

*Copyright by designer/architect.*

### Main Level Floor Plan

*Copyright by designer/architect.*

## Plan #181654

**Dimensions:** 40'8" W x 51' D

**Levels:** 2

**Square Footage:** 2,008

**Main Level Sq. Ft.:** 1,080

**Upper Level Sq. Ft.:** 928

**Bedrooms:** 3

**Bathrooms:** 2½

**Foundation:** Basement

**Material List Available:** Yes

**Price Category:** D

Rear Elevation

### Upper Level Floor Plan

## Plan #181085

**Dimensions:** 56'4" W x 44' D
**Levels:** 2
**Square Footage:** 2,183
**Main Level Sq. Ft.:** 1,232
**Second Level Sq. Ft.:** 951
**Bedrooms:** 3
**Bathrooms:** 2½
**Foundation:** Basement
**Materials List Available:** Yes
**Price Category:** D

*Images provided by designer/architect.*

This country home features an inviting front porch and a layout designed for modern living.

**Features:**

- Ceiling Height: 8 ft.

- Solarium: Sunlight streams through the windows of this solarium at the front of the house.

- Living Room: Walk through French doors, and you will enter this inviting living room. Family and friends will be drawn to the corner fireplace.

- Formal Dining Room: Usher your guests directly from the living room into this formal dining room. The kitchen is located on the other side of the dining room for convenient service.

- Kitchen: This generously sized kitchen is a delight, it offers a center island, separate eat-in area, and access to the back deck.

- Bonus Room: This room just off the entry hall can become a family room, a bedroom, or an office.

- Master Suite: Curl up by the corner fireplace in this master retreat, with its walk-in closet and lavish bath with separate shower and tub.

**Main Level Floor Plan**

**Upper Level Floor Plan**

*Copyright by designer/architect.*

# Plans and Ideas for Your Landscape

**L**andscapes change over the years. As plants grow, the overall look evolves from sparse to lush. Trees cast cool shade where the sun used to shine. Shrubs and hedges grow tall and dense enough to provide privacy. Perennials and ground covers spread to form colorful patches of foliage and flowers. Meanwhile, paths, arbors, fences, and other structures gain the patina of age.

Constant change over the years—sometimes rapid and dramatic, sometimes slow and subtle—is one of the joys of landscaping. It is also one of the challenges. Anticipating how fast plants will grow and how big they will eventually get is difficult, even for professional designers, and was a major concern in formulating the designs for this book.

To illustrate the kinds of changes to expect in a planting, these pages show a landscape design at three different "ages." Even though a new planting may look sparse at first, it will soon fill in. And because of careful spacing, the planting will look as good in 10 to 15 years as it does after 3 to 5. It will, of course, look different, but that's part of the fun.

**At Planting**

Crape myrtle

Carolina jasmine or clematis

Spirea

Bluebeard

Barberry

Annuals

Mondo grass

**Three to Five Years**

Carolina jasmine or clematis

Crape myrtle

Spirea

Barberry

Mondo grass

**At Planting**—Here's how a corner planting might appear in spring immediately after planting. The fence and mulch look conspicuously fresh, new, and unweathered. The crape myrtle is only 4 to 5 ft. tall, with trunks no thicker than broomsticks. It hasn't leafed out yet. The spirea and barberries are 12 to 18 in. tall and wide, and the Carolina jasmine (or clematis) just reaches the bottom rail of the fence. Evenly spaced tufts of mondo grass edge the sidewalk. The bluebeards are stubby now but will grow 2 to 3 ft. tall by late summer, when they bloom. Annuals such as vinca and ageratum start flowering right away and soon form solid patches of color. The first year after planting, be sure to water during dry spells and to pull or spray any weeds that pop through the mulch.

**Three to Five Years**—Shown in summer now, the planting has begun to mature. The mondo grass has spread to make a continuous, weed-proof patch. The Carolina jasmine (or clematis) reaches partway along the fence. The spirea and barberries have grown into bushy, rounded specimens. From now on, they'll get wider but not much taller. The crape myrtle will keep growing about 1 ft. taller every year, and its crown will broaden. As you continue replacing the annuals twice a year, keep adding compost or organic matter to the soil and spreading fresh mulch on top.

**Ten to Fifteen Years**—As shown here in late summer, the crape myrtle is now a fine specimen, about 15 ft. tall, with a handsome silhouette, beautiful flowers, and colorful bark on its trunks. The bluebeards recover from an annual spring pruning to form bushy mounds covered with blooms. The Carolina jasmine, (or clematis) spirea, and barberry have reached their mature size. Keep them neat and healthy by pruning out old, weak, or dead stems every spring. If you get tired of replanting annuals, substitute low-growing perennials or shrubs in those positions.

## Ten to Fifteen Years

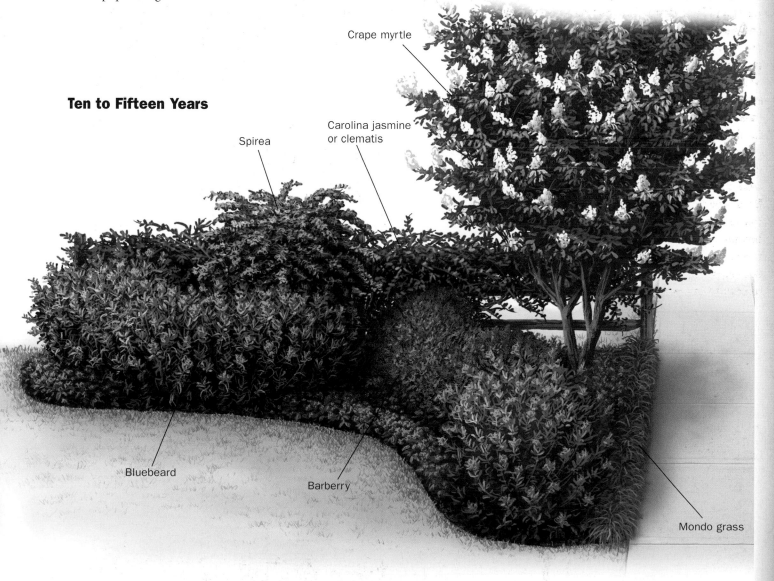

Crape myrtle

Carolina jasmine or clematis

Spirea

Bluebeard

Barberry

Mondo grass

# "Around Back"

## Dress Up the Area between the House and a Detached Garage

When people think of landscaping the entrance to their home, the public entry at the front of the house comes immediately to mind. It's easy to forget that the back door often gets more use. If you make the journey between back door and driveway or garage many times each day, why not make it as pleasant a trip as possible? For many properties, a simple planting can trans-

form the space bounded by the house, garage, and driveway, making it at once more inviting and more functional.

In a high-traffic area frequented by ball-bouncing, bicycle-riding children as well as busy adults, delicate, fussy plants have no place. The design shown here employs a few types of tough low-care plants, all of which look good year-round. The low yew hedge links

the house and the garage and separates the more private backyard from the busy driveway. The star magnolia is just the right size for its spot. Its early-spring flowers will be a delight whether viewed coming up the driveway or from a window overlooking the backyard. The wide walk makes passage to and from the car easy—even with your arms full of groceries.

*Note: All plants are appropriate for USDA Hardiness Zones 5, 6, and 7.*

A Star magnolia

See site plan for F

**Site:** Sunny
**Season:** Summer
**Concept:** A planting to raise spirits weighed down by shopping bags and to separate activities in the backyard from the driveway.

'Steeds' C
Japanese holly

B 'Hicksii' hybrid yew

D 'Hidcote' hypericum

E 'Big Blue' lilyturf

Walkway G

'Big Blue' lilyturf E

order direct: 1-800-523-6789

# Plants & Projects

The watchword in this planting is evergreen. Except for the magnolia, all the plants here are fully evergreen or are nearly so. Spring and summer see lovely flowers from the magnolia and hypericum, and the carpet of lilyturf turns a handsome blue in August. For a bigger splash in spring, underplant the lilyturf with daffodils. Choose a single variety for uniform color, or select several varieties for a mix of colors and bloom times. Other than shearing the hedge, the only maintenance required is cutting back the lilyturf and hypericum in late winter.

**A Star magnolia** *Magnolia stellata* (use 1 plant)
Lovely white flowers cover this small deciduous tree before the leaves appear. Starlike blooms, slightly fragrant and sometimes tinged with pink, appear in early spring and last up to two weeks. In summer, the dense leafy crown of dark green leaves helps provide privacy in the backyard. A multi-trunked specimen will fill the space better and display more of the interesting winter bark.

**B 'Hicksii' hybrid yew** *Taxus x media* (use 9)
A fast-growing evergreen shrub that is ideal for this 3-ft.-tall, neatly sheared hedge. Needles are glossy dark green and soft, not prickly. Eight plants form the L-shaped portion, while a single sheared plant extends the hedge on the other side of the walk connecting it to the house. (If the hedge needs to play a part in confining a family pet, you could easily set posts either side of the walk and add a gate.)

**C 'Steeds' Japanese holly** *Ilex crenata* (use 3 or more)
Several of these dense, upright evergreen shrubs can be grouped at the corner as specimen plants or to tie into an existing foundation planting. You could also extend them along the house to create a foundation planting, as shown here. The small dark green leaves are thick and leathery and have tiny spines. Plants attain a pleasing form when left to their own devices. Resist the urge to shear them; just prune to control size if necessary.

**D 'Hidcote' hypericum** *Hypericum* (use 1)
All summer long, clusters of large golden flowers cover the arching stems of this tidy semievergreen shrub, brightening the entrance to the backyard.

**E 'Big Blue' lilyturf** *Liriope muscari* (use 40 or more)
Grasslike evergreen clumps of this perennial ground cover grow together to carpet the ground flanking the driveway and walk. (Extend the planting as far down the drive as you like.) Slim spires of tiny blue flowers rise above the dark green leaves in June. Lilyturf doesn't stand up to repeated tromping. If the drive is also a basketball court, substitute periwinkle (*Vinca minor*) a tough ground cover with late-spring lilac flowers.

**F Stinking hellebor** *Helleborus foetidus* (use 5 or more) This clump-forming perennial is ideal for filling the space between the walk and house on the backyard side of the hedge. (You might also consider extending the planting along the L-shaped side of the hedge.) Its pale green flowers are among the first to bloom in the spring and continue for many weeks; dark green leaves are attractive year-round.

**G Walkway**
Precast concrete pavers, 2 ft. by 2 ft., replace an existing walk or form a new one.

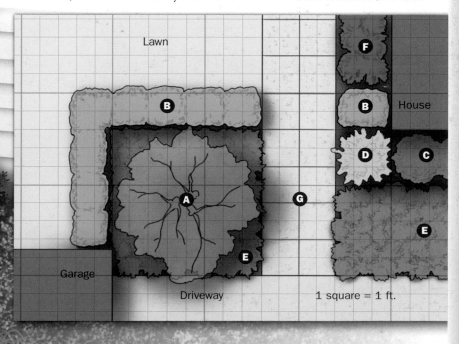

Lawn · House · Garage · Driveway · 1 square = 1 ft.

# Beautify Your Garden Shed

Just as you enhance your living room by hanging paintings on the walls, you can decorate blank walls in your outdoor "living rooms." The design shown here transforms a nondescript shed wall into a living fresco, showcasing lovely plants in a framework of roses and flowering vines. Instead of a view of peeling paint, imagine gazing at this scene from a nearby patio, deck, or kitchen window.

This symmetrical composition frames two crape myrtles between arched latticework trellises. Handsome multitrunked shrubs, the crape myrtles perform year-round, providing sumptuous pink flowers in summer, orange-red foliage in fall, and attractive bark in winter. On either side of the crape myrtles, roses and clematis scramble over the trellis in a profusion of yellow and purple flowers.

A tidy low boxwood hedge sets off a shallow border of shrubs and perennials at the bottom of the "frame." Cheerful long-blooming daylilies and asters, airy Russian sage, and elegant daphne make sure that the ground-level attractions hold their own with the aerial performers covering the wall above. The flowers hew to a color scheme of yellows, pinks, blues, and purples.

Wider or narrower walls can be accommodated by expanding the design to include additional "panels," or by reducing it to one central panel. To set off the plants, consider painting or staining the wall and trellises in an off-white, an earth tone, or a light gray color.

Jackman clematis

'Golden Showers' rose

'Carol Mackie' daphne **F**

'Happy Returns' daylily **H**

'Green Beauty' littleleaf boxwood **E**

## Plants and Projects

These plants will all do well in the hot, dry conditions often found near a wall with a sunny exposure. Other than training and pruning the vines, roses, and hedge, maintenance involves little more than fall and spring cleanup. The trellises, supported by 4x4 posts and attached to the garage, are well within the reach of average do-it-yourselfers.

**A** **'Hopi' crape myrtle** *Lagerstroemia indica* (use 2 plants)
Large multitrunked deciduous shrubs produce papery pink flowers for weeks in summer. They also contribute colorful fall foliage and attractive flaky bark for winter interest.

**B** **'Golden Showers' rose** *Rosa* (use 3)
Tied to each trellis, the long canes of these climbers dis-

play large, fragrant, double yellow flowers in abundance all summer long.

**C** **Golden clematis** *Clematis tangutica* (use 1)
Twining up through the rose canes, this deciduous vine adds masses of small yellow flowers to the larger, more elaborate roses all summer. Feathery silver seed heads in fall.

**D** **Jackman clematis** *Clematis x jackmanii* (use 2)
These deciduous vines clamber among the rose canes at the corners of the wall. The combination of their large but simple purple flowers and the double yellow roses is spectacular.

**E** **'Green Beauty' littleleaf boxwood** *Buxus microphylla* (use 15)
Small evergreen leaves make this an ideal shrub for this

neat hedge. The leaves stay bright green all winter. Trim it about 12 to 18 in. high so it won't obscure the plants behind.

**F** **'Carol Mackie' daphne** *Daphne x burkwoodii* (use 2)
This small rounded shrub marks the far end of the bed with year-round green-and-cream variegated foliage. In spring, pale pink flowers fill the yard with their perfume.

**G** **Russian sage** *Perovskia atriplicifolia* (use 7)
Silver-green foliage and tiers of tiny blue flowers create a light airy effect in the center of the design from midsummer until fall. Cut stems back partway in early summer to control the size and spread of this tall perennial.

**H** **'Happy Returns' daylily** *Hemerocallis* (use 6)
These compact grassy-leaved

perennials provide yellow trumpet-shaped flowers from early June to frost. A striking combination of color and texture with the Russian sage behind.

**I** **'Monch' aster** *Aster x frikartii* (use 4)
Pale purple daisylike flowers bloom gaily from June until frost on these knee-high perennials. Cut stems partway back in midsummer if they start to flop over the hedge.

**J** **Trellis**
Simple panels of wooden lattice frame the crape myrtles while supporting the roses and clematis.

**K** **Steppingstones**
Rectangular flagstone slabs provide a place to stand while pruning and tying nearby shrubs and vines.

**J** Trellis

**D** Jackman clematis

**B** 'Golden Showers' rose

**A** 'Hopi' crape myrtle

**C** Golden clematis

**B** 'Golden Showers' rose

**G** Russian sage

**F** 'Carol Mackie' daphne

**I** 'Monch' aster

**G** Russian sage

**H** 'Happy Returns' daylily

See site plan for **K**

**Site:** Sunny
**Season:** Late summer
**Concept:** Perennials, vines, and shrubs in a narrow bed make a focal point of an uninteresting wall.

Garage

**J** **B** **D** **G** **J** **B** **C** **G** **A** **G** **D** **B** **J**

**F** **H** **A** **F**

**K** **I** **K** **I** **K**

**E**

Lawn

1 square = 1 ft.

*Note: All plants are appropriate for USDA Hardiness Zones 5, 6, and 7.*

# Pleasing Passage to a Garden Landscape

Entrances are an important part of any landscape. They can welcome visitors onto your property; highlight a special feature, such as a rose garden; or mark passage between two areas with different character or function. The design shown here can serve in any of these situations. A picket fence and perennial plantings create a friendly, attractive barrier, just enough to signal the confines of the front

yard or contain the family dog. The vine-covered arbor provides welcoming access.

The design combines uncomplicated elements imaginatively, creating interesting details to catch the eye and a slightly formal but comfortable overall effect. Picketed enclosures and compact evergreen shrubs

broaden the arbor, giving it greater presence. The wide flagstone apron, flanked by neat deciduous shrubs, reinforces this effect and frames the entrance. Massed perennial plantings lend substance to the fence, which serves as a backdrop to their handsome foliage and colorful flowers.

Note: *All plants are appropriate for USDA Hardiness Zones 5, 6, and 7.*

order direct: 1-800-523-6789

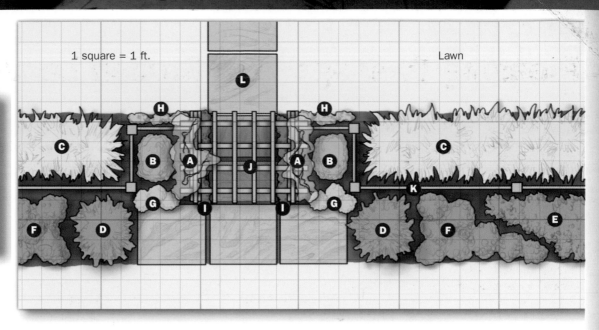

1 square = 1 ft.　　　　　　　　　　　Lawn

**Site:** Sunny
**Season:** Late summer
**Concept:** Perennials, and flowering vines accent traditional fence entry and arbor.

**K** Picket fence

**E** 'Wargrave Pink' geranium

**F** 'Autumn Joy' sedum

**D** 'Longwood Blue' bluebeard

# Plants and Projects

For many people, a picket fence and vine-covered arbor represent old-fashioned "Cottage" style. The plantings here further encourage this feeling.

Pretty white flowers cover the arbor for much of the summer. Massed plantings of daylilies, geraniums, and sedums along the fence produce wide swaths of flowers and attractive foliage from early summer to fall. Plant drifts of snowdrops in these beds; their late-winter flowers are a welcome sign that spring will soon come.

The structures and plantings are easy to build, install, and care for. You can extend the fence and plantings as needed. To use an existing concrete walk, just pour pads either side to create the wide apron in front of the arbor.

**A White clematis** *Clematis* (use 4 plants)
Four of these deciduous climbing vines, one at each post, will cover the arbor in a few years. For large white flowers, try the cultivar 'Henryi', which blooms in early and late summer.

**B 'Green Beauty' littleleaf boxwood** *Buxus microphylla* (use 2)
This evergreen shrub forms a neat ball of small bright green leaves without shearing. It is colorful in winter when the rest of the plants are dormant.

**C Pale yellow daylily** *Hemerocallis* (use 24)
A durable perennial whose cheerful trumpet-shaped flowers nod above clumps of arching foliage. Choose from the many yellow-flowered cultivars (some fragrant); mix several to extend the season of bloom.

**D 'Longwood Blue' bluebeard** *Caryopteris x clandonensis* (use 2)
A pair of these small deciduous shrubs with soft gray foliage frame the entry. Sky blue late-summer flowers cover the plants for weeks.

**E 'Wargrave Pink' geranium** *Geranium endressii* (use 9)
This perennial produces a mass of bright green leaves and a profusion of pink flowers in early summer. Cut it back in July and it will bloom intermittently until frost.

**F 'Autumn Joy' sedum** *Sedum* (use 13)
This perennial forms a clump of upright stems with distinctive fleshy foliage. Pale flower buds that appear during summer are followed by pink flowers during fall and rusty seed heads that stand up in winter.

**G Evergreen candytuft** *Iberis sempervirens* (use 12)
A perennial ground cover that spreads to form a small welcome mat at the foot of the boxwoods. White flowers stand out against glossy evergreen leaves in spring.

**H Lamb's ears** *Stachys byzantina* (use 6)
Favorites of children, the long woolly gray leaves of this perennial form a soft carpet. In early summer, thick stalks carry scattered purple flowers.

**I White bugleweed** *Ajuga reptans 'Alba'* (use 20)
Edging the walk under the arbor, this perennial ground cover has pretty green leaves and, in late spring, short spikes of white flowers.

**J Arbor** Thick posts give this simple structure a sturdy visual presence. Paint or stain it, or make it of cedar and let it weather as shown here.

**K Picket fence** Low picket fence adds character to the planting; materials and finish should match the arbor.

**L Walkway** Flagstone walk can be large pavers, as shown here, or made up of smaller rectangular flags.

*Images provided by designer/architect.*

## Plan #141012

**Dimensions:** 44'4" W x 38' D

**Levels:** 2

**Square Footage:** 1,870

**Main Level Sq. Ft.:** 1,159

**Upper Level Sq. Ft.:** 711

**Bedrooms:** 3

**Bathrooms:** 2½

**Foundation:** Basement

**Materials List Available:** Yes

**Price Category:** D

Country charm comes to mind with this classic two story design.

**Features:**

- Ceiling Height: 8 ft.
- Porch: This full shed porch with dormers creates a look few can resist.
- Living/Dining: This open living/dining area invites you to come in and sit a spell.
- Kitchen: This kitchen allows the host to see their guests from the sink through the opening in the angled walls.

- Breakfast Area: The cathedral ceiling in this breakfast area creates a sunroom effect at the rear of the house.
- Master Suite: This spacious master suite has all the amenities, including a double bowl vanity, corner tub, walk in closet, and 5-ft. shower.
- Bedrooms: Two large bedrooms upstairs share a hall bath.
- Balcony: This upstairs balcony is lit by the center dormer, creating a cozy study alcove.

*Copyright by designer/architect.*

### Main Level Floor Plan

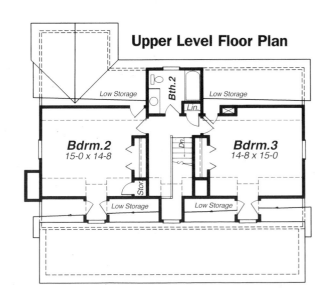

### Upper Level Floor Plan

## Plan #121035

**Dimensions:** 45'4" W x 38' D

**Levels:** 2

**Square Footage:** 1,471

**Main Level Sq. Ft.:** 716

**Upper Level Sq. Ft.:** 755

**Bedrooms:** 3

**Bathrooms:** 2½

**Foundation:** Basement

**Materials List Available:** Yes

**Price Category:** B

*Images provided by designer/architect.*

This convenient and elegant home is designed to expand as the family does.

**Features:**

- Ceiling Height: 8 ft. unless otherwise noted.

- Family Room: An open staircase to the second level visually expands this room where a built-in entertainment center maximizes the floor space. The whole family will be drawn to the warmth from the handsome fireplace.

- Kitchen: Cooking will be a pleasure in this

bright and efficient kitchen that features an island and a corner pantry. A snack bar offers a convenient spot for informal family meals.

- Dining Area: This lovely bayed area adjoins the kitchen.

- Room to Expand: Upstairs is 258 sq. ft. of unfinished area offering plenty of space for expansion as the family grows.

- Garage: This two-bay garage offers plenty of storage space in addition to parking for cars.

**CAD FILE AVAILABLE**

### Main Level Floor Plan

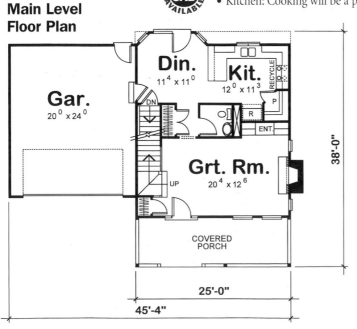

### Upper Level Floor Plan

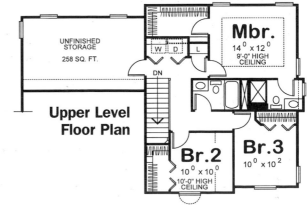

*Copyright by designer/architect.*

## Plan #121045

**Dimensions:** 40' W x 48' D

**Levels:** 2

**Square Footage:** 1,575

**Main Level Sq. Ft.:** 787

**Upper Level Sq. Ft.:** 788

**Bedrooms:** 3

**Bathrooms:** 2½

**Foundation:** Basement

**Materials List Available:** Yes

**Price Category:** C

*This home, as shown in the photograph, may differ from the actual blueprints.* *Images provided by designer/architect.* *For more detailed information, please check the floor plans carefully.*

This home is carefully laid out to provide the convenience demanded by busy family life.

**Features:**

• Ceiling Height: 8 ft.

• Family Room: This charming family room, with its fireplace and built-in cabinetry, will become the central gathering place for family and friends.

• Kitchen: This kitchen offers a central island that makes food preparation more convenient and doubles

as a snack bar for a quick bite on the run. The breakfast area features a pantry and planning desk.

• Computer Loft: The second-floor landing includes this loft designed to accommodate the family computer.

• Room to Grow: Also on the second-floor landing you will find a large unfinished area waiting to accommodate the growing family.

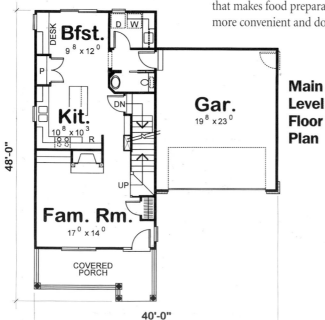

**Main Level Floor Plan**

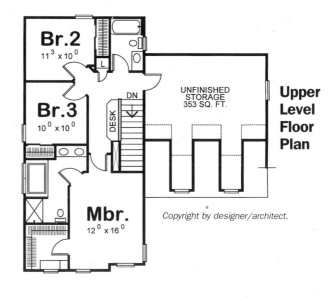

**Upper Level Floor Plan**

*Copyright by designer/architect.*

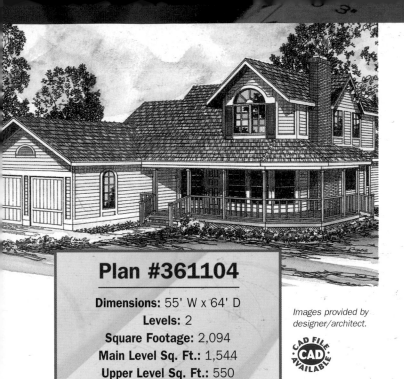

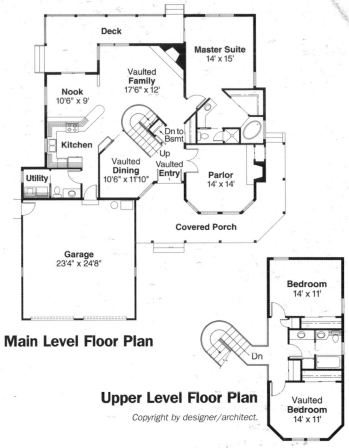

**Main Level Floor Plan**

Deck

Master Suite
14' x 15'

Vaulted Family
17'6" x 12'

Nook
10'6" x 9'

Kitchen

Dn to Bsmt

Up

Vaulted Entry

Parlor
14' x 14'

Vaulted Dining
10'6" x 11'10"

Utility

Covered Porch

Garage
23'4" x 24'8"

Bedroom
14' x 11'

Dn

**Upper Level Floor Plan**

*Copyright by designer/architect.*

Vaulted Bedroom
14' x 11'

*Images provided by designer/architect.*

# Plan #361104

**Dimensions:** 55' W x 64' D

**Levels:** 2

**Square Footage:** 2,094

**Main Level Sq. Ft.:** 1,544

**Upper Level Sq. Ft.:** 550

**Bedrooms:** 3

**Bathrooms:** 2½

**Foundation:** Crawl space

**Materials List Available:** No

**Price Category:** D

CAD FILE AVAILABLE

---

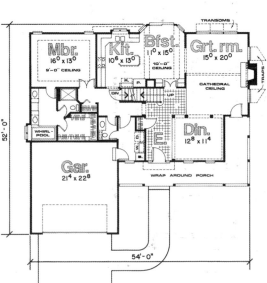

**Upper Level Floor Plan**

Br. 2
12⁰ x 12⁰

Br. 4
12⁰ x 11⁰

Open to Below

Br. 3
12⁰ x 11⁰

Plant Shelf

**Main Level Floor Plan**

Mbr.
16⁰ x 13⁰
9'-0" Ceiling

Kit.
10⁶ x 13⁰

Bfst.
11⁰ x 15⁰
10'-0" Ceiling

Grt. rm.
15⁰ x 20⁰

Cathedral Ceiling

Whirl-Pool

Din.
12⁸ x 11⁴

Gar.
21⁴ x 22⁸

Wrap Around Porch

52'-0"

54'-0"

Transoms

*Copyright by designer/architect.*

*Images provided by designer/architect.*

# Plan #121123

**Dimensions:** 54' W x 52' D

**Levels:** 1.5

**Square Footage:** 2,277

**Main Level Sq. Ft.:** 1,570

**Upper Level Sq. Ft.:** 707

**Bedrooms:** 4

**Bathrooms:** 2½

**Foundation:** Basement; crawl space for fee

**Material List Available:** Yes

**Price Category:** E

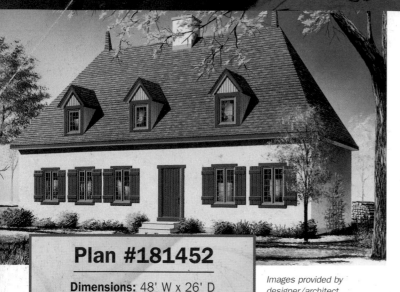

# Plan #181452

**Dimensions:** 48' W x 26' D
**Levels:** 2
**Square Footage:** 2,496
**Main Level Sq. Ft.:** 1,248
**Upper Level Sq. Ft.:** 1,248
**Bedrooms:** 4
**Bathrooms:** 1½
**Foundation:** Basement
**Material List Available:** Yes
**Price Category:** E

*Images provided by designer/architect.*

## Main Level Floor Plan

12'-8" X 24'-8"
3,80 X 7,40

10'-10" X 11'-2"
3,25 X 3,35

22'-10" X 24'-8"
6,86 X 7,40

26'-0"
7,8 m

48'-0"
14,4 m

9'-6" X 10'-0"
2,86 X 3,00

3'-10" X 9'-0"
4,15 X 2,70

14'-2" X 15'-4"
4,25 X 4,80

11'-0" X 10'-8"
3,30 X 3,20

13'-10" X 13'-0"
4,15 X 3,90

## Upper Level Floor Plan

*Copyright by designer/architect.*

Rear Elevation

---

# Plan #521043

**Dimensions:** 36' W x 43'8" D
**Levels:** 2
**Square Footage:** 1,536
**Main Level Sq. Ft.:** 1,038
**Upper Level Sq. Ft.:** 498
**Bedrooms:** 3
**Bathrooms:** 2½
**Foundation:** Crawl space
**Material List Available:** No
**Price Category:** C

*Images provided by designer/architect.*

## Main Level Floor Plan

*Copyright by designer/architect.*

MASTER BEDROOM
(16'4"x11'10")

SCREENED PORCH
(10'2"x10'4")

LAUNDRY
8'2"x6'0"

KITCHEN
(12'8"x8'0")

DINING AREA
(9'10"x9'8")

ENTRY
8'6"x4'10"

LIVING ROOM
(17'8"x14'2")

8' FRONT WRAP AROUND PORCH

Side View

BEDROOM #2
(11'4"x9'10")

BATH

BEDROOM #3
(11'4"x9'10")

## Upper Level Floor Plan

## Plan #461013

**Dimensions:** 80' W x 50' D
**Levels:** 2
**Square Footage:** 2,368
**Main Level Sq. Ft.:** 1,765
**Lower Level Sq. Ft:** 603
**Bedrooms:** 3
**Bathrooms:** 2½
**Foundation:** Slab or basement; crawl space for fee
**Materials List Available:** No
**Price Category:** E

*Images provided by designer/architect.*

The kind of house in which you make memories, this traditional country home is charming and practical for the modern family.

**Features:**

- Family Room: Also designed as part of a free-flowing space, the family room will always be full of inviting sunlight and warmth. Imagine the family gathering together in front of the fireplace, looking through the windows onto a bright, snowy scene.

- Kitchen: This L-shaped kitchen features an island with an eating bar and flows freely into the breakfast room, family room, and formal dining room for plenty of mealtime possibilities. It's also only a few steps from

the rear deck, perfect for barbecues or morning coffee out in the sun.

- Master Suite: Designed with privacy in mind, this area is separated from the others. It features his and her walk-in closets, and the master bath has dual vanities and a tub and shower stall, both oversized.

- Second Floor: Two additional bedrooms feature privacy, walk-in closets, and proximity to the second full bathroom with a dressing area. There is also a bonus space above the garage for whatever you might imagine.

## Main Level Floor Plan

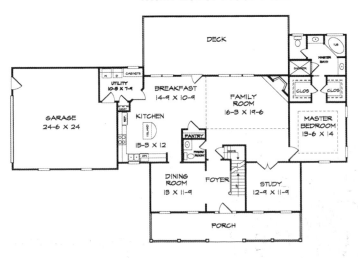

## Upper Level Floor Plan

*Copyright by designer/architect.*

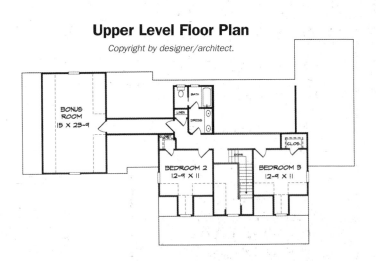

## Plan #131002

**Dimensions:** 70'1" W x 60'7" D
**Levels:** 1
**Square Footage:** 1,709
**Bedrooms:** 3
**Bathrooms:** 2½
**Foundation:** Crawl space, slab, or basement
**Materials List Available:** Yes
**Price Category:** D

*Images provided by designer/architect.*

Rear View

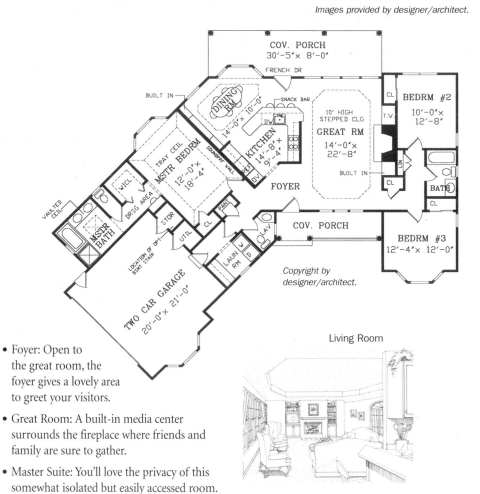

COV. PORCH
30'-5" x 8'-0"

FRENCH DR

BUILT IN

DINING RM
14'-0" x 10'-0"

SNACK BAR

KITCHEN
14'-8" x 9'-4"

TRAY CEIL
MSTR BEDRM
12'-0" x 18'-4"

VAULTED CEIL.

MSTR BATH

WICL

DR-SG AREA

STOR

LOCATION OF OPT. BSMT STAIR

UTIL

CL

PANT

LAV

LAUN RM

W D

TWO CAR GARAGE
20'-0" x 21'-0"

10' HIGH STEPPED CLG
GREAT RM
14'-0" x 22'-8"

BUILT IN

FOYER

COV. PORCH

CL

T.V

BEDRM #2
10'-0" x 12'-8"

CL

BATH

CL

BEDRM #3
12'-4" x 12'-0"

*Copyright by designer/architect.*

Living Room

You'll love the way this angled ranch brings out the best in a corner lot or on a slope.

**Features:**

- Ceiling Height: 8 ft.

- Front Porch: Hang baskets of plants from the roof of this porch, which is just the right size for a couple of rockers and a side table.

- Dining Room: Well-placed windows flood this room with sunlight during the day and a built-in cabinet gives ample storage space for all your china, linens, and collectables.

- Foyer: Open to the great room, the foyer gives a lovely area to greet your visitors.

- Great Room: A built-in media center surrounds the fireplace where friends and family are sure to gather.

- Master Suite: You'll love the privacy of this somewhat isolated but easily accessed room. Decorate to show off the large bay window and tray ceiling, and enjoy the luxury of a compartmented bathroom.

# Plan #341064

**Dimensions:** 58'6" W x 36'9" D

**Levels:** 1

**Square Footage:** 1,418

**Bedrooms:** 3

**Bathrooms:** 2

**Foundation:** Crawl space, slab, basement, or walkout

**Materials List Available:** Yes

**Price Category:** B

*Images provided by designer/architect.*

This sweet starter home has many of the amenities of a larger home.

## Features:

- **Family Room:** Already equipped with gas fireplace, all this room needs is some entertainment options and comfy furniture to welcome guests into the warmth of your home and out of the cold.

- **Dining Room:** This versatile space can be used for formal dinners or for barbecues that have been cooked on the deck.

- **Kitchen:** This efficiently designed space features a large pantry and an elevated bar for informal meals on the run. Or use the bar as a serving or buffet area for hosting dinner parties.

- **Master Suite:** A cozy retreat, this main bedroom features two walk-in closets and a full master bath with a garden tub.

*Copyright by designer/architect.*

## Main Level Floor Plan

80'

3 CAR GARAGE
21'4" X 28'4"

COVERED PORCH

SCREEN PORCH
17' X 16'
14' CLG.

COVERED PORCH

LAUND

D W

NOOK
12' X 12'6"
9' CLG.

MASTER BEDROOM
16' X 13'
9' CLG.

PANTRY

LIVING ROOM
17' X 20'
18' CLG.

EATING BAR

59'

DW

KITCHEN
12' X 14'

OPTIONAL BASEMENT STAIRS

UP

DN

REF

CAB

CAB

DINING
12' X 12'8"
9' CLG.

FOYER

STUDY/ BEDROOM 4
12' X 12'8"
9' CLG.

COVERED PORCH

### Upper Level Floor Plan

*Copyright by designer/architect.*

OPEN TO BELOW

OPT. GAMEROOM
16' X 25'-8
8' CLG.

JULIET BALCONY

ATTIC

LIN

DN

BEDROOM 2
12' X 12'8"
8' CLG.

BEDROOM 3
12' X 12'8"
8' CLG.

*Images provided by designer/architect.*

Front View

# Plan #121190

**Dimensions:** 80' W x 59' D

**Levels:** 1.5

**Square Footage:** 2,252

**Main Level Sq. Ft.:** 1,736

**Upper Level Sq. Ft.:** 516

**Bedrooms:** 4

**Bathrooms:** 3

**Foundation:** Slab; crawl space for fee

**Materials List Available:** Yes

**Price Category:** E

### Upper Level Floor Plan

BEDROOM #2
(10'0"x11'8")

BEDROOM #4
(11'2"x10'0")

BEDROOM #3
(10'0"x11'6")

### Main Level Floor Plan

*Copyright by designer/architect.*

MASTER BEDROOM
(14'4"x11'8")
+BAY

COVERED PORCH
(10'8"X 12'0")

LAUNDRY ROOM

DINING AREA
(13'4"x10'0")

LIVING ROOM
(16'1"x16'10")

KITCHEN
(9'0"x10'0")

ENTRY

FRONT PORCH
(23'8"X8'0")

*Images provided by designer/architect.*

CAD FILE CAD AVAILABLE

# Plan #521030

**Dimensions:** 41'8" W x 41' D

**Levels:** 2

**Square Footage:** 1,660

**Main Level Sq. Ft.:** 1,034

**Upper Level Sq. Ft.:** 626

**Bedrooms:** 4

**Bathrooms:** 2½

**Foundation:** Crawl space

**Material List Available:** No

**Price Category:** C

## Plan #341284

**Dimensions:** 57'7" W x 26' D
**Levels:** 2
**Square Footage:** 2,384
**Main Level Sq. Ft.:** 960
**Lower Level Sq. Ft:** 1,424
**Bedrooms:** 3
**Bathrooms:** 2½
**Foundation:** Crawl space, slab, basement, or walkout
**Materials List Available:** Yes
**Price Category:** E

Two-story bay windows and wrap-around porch give this traditional home an old-fashioned charm with warmth equal to that inside.

### Features:

- **Family Room:** A fireplace and attached deck make this room ideal for entertaining in any season.
- **Dining Room:** This formal dining room is bathed in sunlight from the bay windows, giving glowing warmth to family meals.
- **Kitchen:** This space fosters the gathering of family and guests alike with its open design and proximity to the breakfast nook and family room. It features plenty of workspace, storage, and a pantry, as well as a raised bar for informal meals on the go.

- **Master Suite:** Separated from the busy first story, this master suite provides tranquility and features a large walk-in closet and full master bath, which features a stall shower and garden tub.
- **Secondary Bedrooms:** Both additional bedrooms boast walk-in closets and are near the second full bathroom and the laundry room. A nearby bonus room could be another bedroom or whatever you choose.

### Main Level Floor Plan

### Upper Level Floor Plan

## Plan #341236

**Dimensions:** 46'4" W x 31'4" D

**Levels:** 2

**Square Footage:** 1,618

**Main Level Sq. Ft.:** 1,046

**Upper Level Sq. Ft:** 572

**Bedrooms:** 3

**Bathrooms:** 2½

**Foundation:** Crawl space, slab, basement, or walkout

**Materials List Available:** Yes

**Price Category:** C

*Images provided by designer/architect.*

This traditional two-story home embraces modern family living.

**Features:**

- **Living Room:** Welcome friends and neighbors into this gracious living room, with its fireplace to add warmth on a cool night. The front-facing large windows will let in plenty of natural light.

- **Kitchen:** This L-shaped kitchen includes a built-in pantry and has room for a breakfast table. The adjacent dining room features French doors to the backyard.

- **Master Suite:** This first-floor master suite is located away from other bedrooms for maximum privacy and includes a walk-in closet and a full master bath with a double vanity.

- **Bonus Space:** This bonus space, located above the master suite, can be finished at a later date. The area would make a perfect game room.

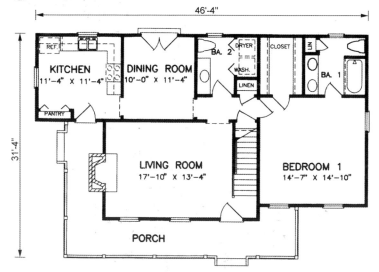

**Main Level Floor Plan**

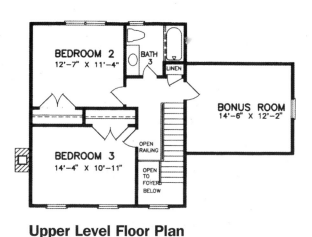

**Upper Level Floor Plan**

*Copyright by designer/architect.*

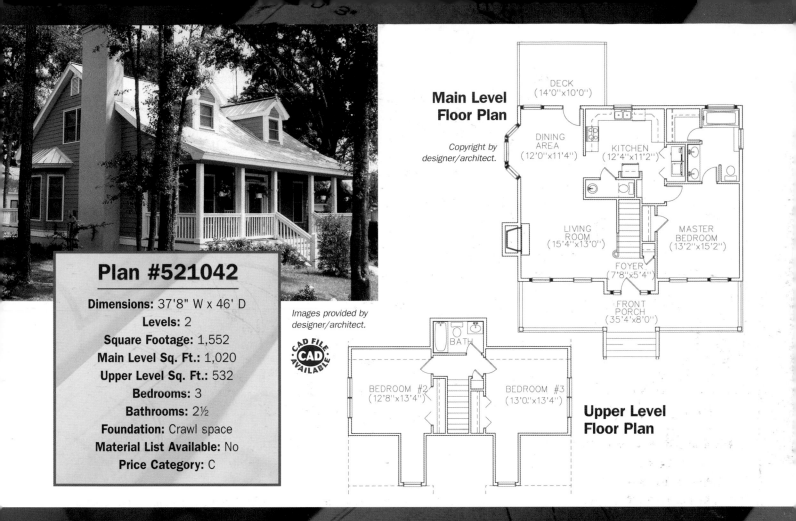

**Main Level Floor Plan**

*Copyright by designer/architect.*

DECK (14'0"x10'0")

DINING AREA (12'0"x11'4")

KITCHEN (12'4"x11'2")

LIVING ROOM (15'4"x13'0")

MASTER BEDROOM (13'2"x15'2")

FOYER (7'8"x5'4")

FRONT PORCH (35'4"x8'0")

BATH

BEDROOM #2 (12'8"x13'4")

BEDROOM #3 (13'0"x13'4")

**Upper Level Floor Plan**

*Images provided by designer/architect.*

**CAD FILE AVAILABLE**

## Plan #521042

**Dimensions:** 37'8" W x 46' D

**Levels:** 2

**Square Footage:** 1,552

**Main Level Sq. Ft.:** 1,020

**Upper Level Sq. Ft.:** 532

**Bedrooms:** 3

**Bathrooms:** 2½

**Foundation:** Crawl space

**Material List Available:** No

**Price Category:** C

**Main Level Floor Plan**

Kit. 12 x11⁰⁶

Bfst. 12 x 13⁶

Grt. rm. 14 x 21³

STORAGE

Gar. 20⁰ x 29⁴

Dn. 12³ x 13⁶

COVERED PORCH

10'-0" CEILING

44'-0"

54'-0"

*Images provided by designer/architect.*

WHIRL POOL

Mbr. 15³ x 13⁶

SKYLIGHT

LIN.

Br. 10⁹ x 12

OPEN TO BELOW

Br. 11 x 10

Br. 10⁸ x 13³

**Upper Level Floor Plan**

*Copyright by designer/architect.*

## Plan #121212

**Dimensions:** 54' W x 44' D

**Levels:** 2

**Square Footage:** 2,219

**Main Level Sq. Ft.:** 1,132

**Upper Level Sq. Ft.:** 1,087

**Bedrooms:** 4

**Bathrooms:** 2½

**Foundation:** Basement; crawl space for fee

**Material List Available:** Yes

**Price Category:** E

## Plan #161116

**Dimensions:** 52'8" W x 45' D
**Levels:** 1
**Square Footage:** 1,442
**Bedrooms:** 3
**Bathrooms:** 2
**Foundation:** Basement
**Material List Available:** Yes
**Price Category:** B

This delightful home offers space-saving convenience and functional living space.

**CAD FILE AVAILABLE**

*Images provided by designer/architect.*

### Features:

- **Great Room:** This gathering area features an over-11-foot-tall ceiling and a corner gas fireplace. A few steps out the back door, and you are on the rear deck.
- **Kitchen:** This fully equipped kitchen offers a counter with seating, dishwasher, and built-in microwave. The garage and laundry areas are conveniently a few steps away.
- **Master Suite:** Split bedrooms offer privacy to this elegant area, which enjoys a 9-ft. ceiling height and large walk-in closet. The master bath boasts a double-bowl vanity and compartmented lavatory and shower area.
- **Bedrooms:** Two secondary bedrooms are located just off the great room and share the second bathroom.

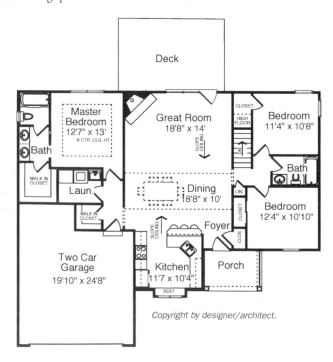

*Copyright by designer/architect.*

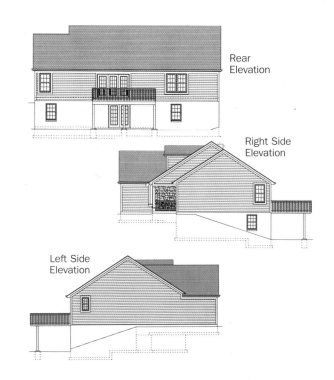

Rear Elevation

Right Side Elevation

Left Side Elevation

## Plan #121014

**Dimensions:** 52' W x 47'4" D
**Levels:** 2
**Square Footage:** 1,869
**Main Level Sq. Ft.:** 1,421
**Upper Level Sq. Ft.:** 448
**Bedrooms:** 3
**Bathrooms:** 2½
**Foundation:** Basement
**Materials List Available:** Yes
**Price Category:** D

*Images provided by designer/architect.*

This compact home is packed with all the amenities you'll need for a gracious lifestyle.

**Features:**

• Ceiling Height: 8 ft. except as noted.

• Great Room: A soaring ceiling and six tall transom-topped windows make this a light and airy spot for entertaining.

• Formal Dining Room: This elegant room is ideal for entertaining dinner guests.

• Breakfast Area: This sunny area shares a see-through fireplace with the great room. It's the perfect place to start the day.

• Master Suite: Here are all the features you expect to find in large luxury homes. Wake up to tall, sloped ceilings, and enjoy the corner whirlpool, separate shower, and vanity. A large walk-in closet provides plenty of wardrobe storage.

• Attached Garage: The garage provides two bays of parking plus plenty of storage space.

**Main Level Floor Plan**

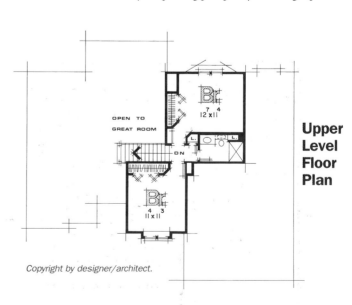

**Upper Level Floor Plan**

*Copyright by designer/architect.*

## Plan #121021

**Dimensions:** 46' W x 48' D
**Levels:** 2
**Square Footage:** 2,270
**Main Level Sq. Ft.:** 1,150
**Upper Level Sq. Ft.:** 1,120
**Bedrooms:** 4
**Bathrooms:** 2½
**Foundation:** Basement
**Materials List Available:** Yes
**Price Category:** E

*This home, as shown in the photograph, may differ from the actual blueprints. For more detailed information, please check the floor plans carefully.*

*Images provided by designer/architect.*

With its wraparound porch, this home evokes the charm of a traditional home.

**Features:**

• Ceiling Height: 8 ft.

• Foyer: The dramatic two-story entry enjoys views of the formal dining room and great room. A second floor balcony overlooks the entry and a plant shelf.

• Formal Dining Room: This gracious room is perfect for family holiday gatherings and for more formal dinner parties.

• Great Room: All the family will want to gather in this comfortable, informal room which features bay windows, an entertainment center, and a see-through fireplace.

• Breakfast Area: Conveniently located just off the great room, the bayed breakfast area features a built-in desk for household bills and access to the backyard.

• Kitchen: An island is the centerpiece of this kitchen. Its intelligent design makes food preparation a pleasure.

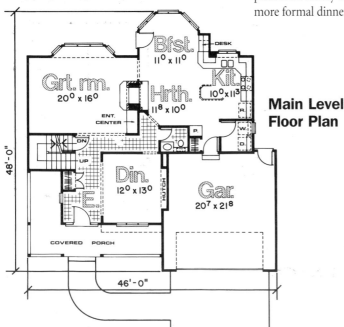

**Main Level Floor Plan**

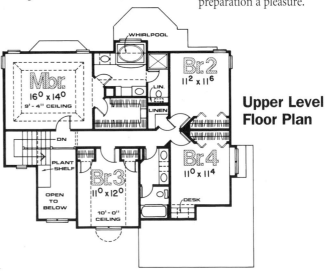

**Upper Level Floor Plan**

*Copyright by designer/architect.*

# Plan #341295

**Dimensions:** 46' W x 58'8" D

**Levels:** 2

**Square Footage:** 2,188

**Main Level Sq. Ft.:** 1,569

**Lower Level Sq. Ft:** 619

**Bedrooms:** 3

**Bathrooms:** 2½

**Foundation:** Crawl space, slab, basement, or walkout

**Materials List Available:** Yes

**Price Category:** D

*Images provided by designer/architect.*

This traditional two-story home includes a covered entry and plenty of space and features for the modern family.

**CAD FILE AVAILABLE** CAD

**Features:**

- **Foyer:** A dramatic entry, the quaint covered porch welcomes guests into this two-story foyer, which includes closet space and a half bathroom.

- **Kitchen:** This L-shaped kitchen features an island and a large pantry. The busy room sits close to the dining room, family room, and breakfast room, providing many choices for mealtime.

- **Deck:** Through the breakfast area is this back deck for barbecues or meals outside.

- **Master Suite:** The vaulted ceilings, walk-in closet, and full master bath with a garden tub make this area the perfect retreat from everyday life.

- **Second Floor:** Both secondary bedrooms feature a large closet and share the second full bathroom. The second floor is open to the first over the foyer and family room, giving the house an attractive sense of freedom.

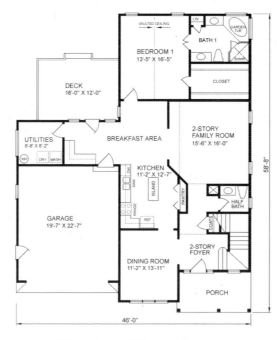

**Main Level Floor Plan**

## Upper Level Floor Plan

*Copyright by designer/architect.*

## Plan #141038

**Dimensions:** 40'4" W x 38' D

**Levels:** 2

**Square Footage:** 1,668

**Main Level Sq. Ft.:** 1,057

**Upper Level Sq. Ft.:** 611

**Bedrooms:** 3

**Bathrooms:** 2½

**Foundation:** Basement with drive-under garage

**Materials List Available:** Yes

**Price Category:** C

*Images provided by designer/architect.*

If you're looking for the ideal plan for a sloping site, this could be the home of your dreams.

**Features:**

- Porch: Set a couple of rockers on this large porch so you can enjoy the evening views.
- Living Room: A handsome fireplace makes a lovely focal point in this large room.
- Dining Room: Three large windows over looking the sundeck flood this room with natural light.

- Kitchen: The U-shaped, step-saving layout makes this kitchen a cook's dream.
- Breakfast Room: With an expansive window area and a door to the sundeck, this room is sure to be a family favorite in any season of the year.
- Master Suite: A large walk-in closet and a private bath with tub, shower, and double vanity complement this suite's spacious bedroom.

**Main Level Floor Plan**

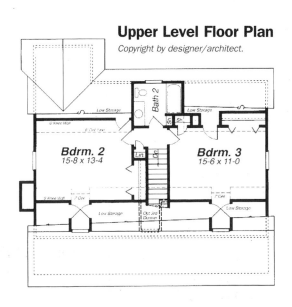

**Upper Level Floor Plan**

*Copyright by designer/architect.*

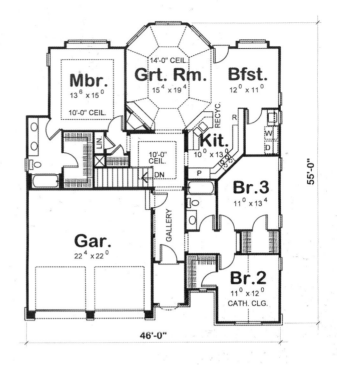

## Plan #121165

**Dimensions:** 46' W x 55' D

**Levels:** 1

**Square Footage:** 1,678

**Bedrooms:** 3

**Bathrooms:** 2

**Foundation:** Basement;
crawl space for fee

**Material List Available:** Yes

**Price Category:** C

*Images provided by designer/architect.*

*This home, as shown in the photograph, may differ from the actual blueprints. For more detailed information, please check the floor plans carefully.*

*Copyright by designer/architect.*

## Plan #181655

**Dimensions:** 44' W x 32' D

**Levels:** 2

**Square Footage:** 1,656

**Main Level Sq. Ft.:** 835

**Upper Level Sq. Ft.:** 821

**Bedrooms:** 3

**Bathrooms:** 2

**Foundation:** Basement

**Material List Available:** Yes

**Price Category:** C

*Images provided by designer/architect.*

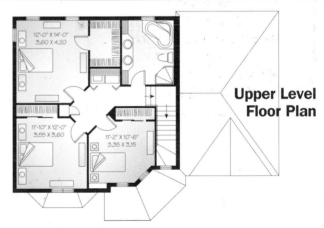

**Upper Level Floor Plan**

**Main Level Floor Plan**

*Copyright by designer/architect.*

## Plan #361443

**Dimensions:** 46' W x 48' D

**Levels:** 2

**Square Footage:** 2,256

**Main Level Sq. Ft.:** 1,173

**Lower Level Sq. Ft:** 1,083

**Bedrooms:** 4

**Bathrooms:** 3

**Foundation:** Crawl space

**Materials List Available:** No

**Price Category:** E

*Images provided by designer/architect.*

This charming country home with beautiful architectural details is designed with modern life in mind.

**Features:**

- Family Room: Full of bright windows and including a fireplace, this is a fine room for family gatherings.

- Kitchen: Housing plenty of workspace and storage, this kitchen also features an eating bar that transitions into the dining room. The utility room sits conveniently between the kitchen and garage.

- Office: Something on which the modern home relies, this spacious office is open to the vaulted entry on one side and a space between the dining room and a full bathroom on the other.

- Second Floor: Here, the master suite opens into a compartmentalized full master bath, with its large shower, tub, dual sinks and walk-in closet. There are also three additional bedrooms, all with large closets, which share a full bathroom.

Main Level Floor Plan

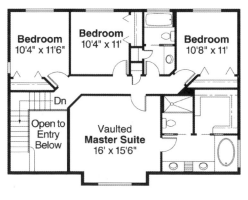

Upper Level Floor Plan

*Copyright by designer/architect.*

# Plan #151016

**Dimensions:** 60'2" W x 39'10" D
**Levels:** 2
**Square Footage:** 1,783;
2,107 with bonus
**Main Level Sq. Ft.:** 1,124
**Upper Level Sq. Ft.:** 659
**Bonus Room Sq. Ft.:** 324
**Bedrooms:** 3
**Bathrooms:** 2½
**Foundation:** Crawl space, slab,
or basement
**CompleteCost List Available:** Yes
**Price Category:** C

*Images provided by designer/architect.*

An open design characterizes this spacious home built for family life and entertaining.

**Features:**

- Great Room: Enjoy the fireplace in this spacious, versatile room.
- Dining Room: Entertaining is easy, thanks to the open design with the kitchen.
- Master Suite: Luxury surrounds you in this suite, with its large walk-in closet, double vanities, and a bathroom with a whirlpool tub and separate shower.

- Upper Bedrooms: Window seats make wonderful spots for reading or relaxing, and a nook between the windows of these rooms is a ready-made play area.
- Bonus Area: Located over the garage, this space could be converted to a home office, a studio, or a game room for the kids.
- Attic: There's plenty of storage space here.

## Bonus Room Above Garage

*Copyright by designer/architect.*

**Main Level Floor Plan**

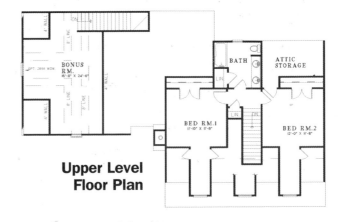

**Upper Level Floor Plan**

## Plan #151204

**Dimensions:** 76'10" W x 53'4" D

**Levels:** 1.5

**Square Footage:** 2,373

**Bedrooms:** 4

**Bathrooms:** 3

**Foundation:** Crawl space or slab

**CompleteCost List Available:** Yes

**Price Category:** E

This spectacular split floor plan blends the warmth of country with classic southern tradition in a detailed porch with round columns on stone pillars.

**CAD FILE AVAILABLE**

*Images provided by designer/architect.*

**Features:**

- **Great Room:** This spacious great room has a built-in media center and a cozy fireplace. The wall of windows, which leads to a breakfast room/kitchen combination, will flood the space with natural light.

- **Master Suite:** This large master suite has access to the column-lined rear porch and is located in its own wing. The master bath is lavish and features a corner whirlpool tub, makeup area, and large walk-in closet.

- **Secondary Bedrooms:** Three additional bedrooms complete the main level of this fine home. Bedrooms 3 and 4 share a Jack-and-Jill bathroom.

- **Bonus Space:** Upstairs you'll find several bonus rooms with creative ceilings and dormer windows. The areas can be finished later to become additional bedrooms or a playroom and home office.

**Main Level Floor Plan**

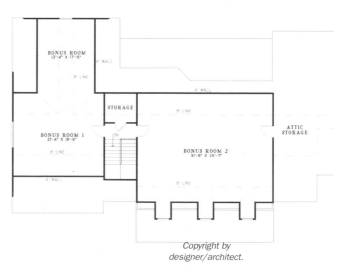

*Copyright by designer/architect.*

**Upper Level Floor Plan**

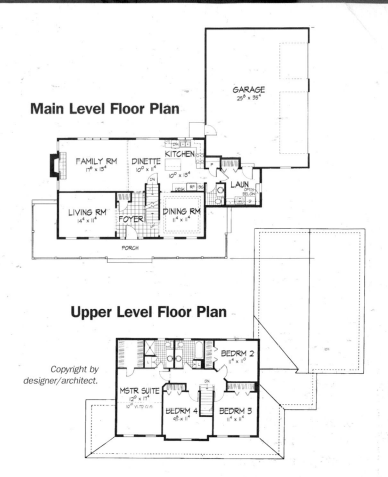

**Main Level Floor Plan**

GARAGE
25⁸ x 35⁴

FAMILY RM
17⁶ x 13⁴

DINETTE
10⁰ x 11

KITCHEN
10⁰ x 13⁴

LAUN

LIVING RM
14⁴ x 11⁴

FOYER

DINING RM
11⁴ x 11

PORCH

*Images provided by designer/architect.*

**Upper Level Floor Plan**

*Copyright by designer/architect.*

BEDRM 2
11⁴ x 11⁰

MSTR SUITE
12⁰ x 17⁴
10⁰ x 10 (x ?)

BEDRM 4
4⁸ x 11⁴

BEDRM 3
11⁴ x 11⁰

## Plan #271070

**Dimensions:** 70'3" W x 60' D

**Levels:** 2

**Square Footage:** 2,144

**Main Level Sq. Ft.:** 1,156

**Upper Level Sq. Ft.:** 988

**Bedrooms:** 4

**Bathrooms:** 2½

**Foundation:** Basement, crawl space

**Materials List Available:** No

**Price Category:** D

---

BEDROOM 2
8'-11"X12'-1"

BEDROOM 3
8'-11"X12'-1"

WASH DRY

UNFINISHED BONUS SPACE

BATH 2

LINENS

CLOSET

BEDROOM 1
13'-6"X11'-1"

BATH 1

**Upper Level Floor Plan**

48'-0"

STOOP

DINING
11'-5"X10'-0"

KITCHEN
11'-5"X12'-1"

REF

36'-0"

LIVING ROOM
13'-6"X19'-5"

BATH 3

GARAGE

FOYER

**Main Level Floor Plan**

*Copyright by designer/architect.*

PORCH

## Plan #341232

**Dimensions:** 48' W x 36' D

**Levels:** 2

**Square Footage:** 1,533

**Main Level Sq. Ft.:** 736

**Upper Level Sq. Ft.:** 797

**Bedrooms:** 3

**Bathrooms:** 2½

**Foundation:** Crawl space, slab, basement or walkout

**Material List Available:** Yes

**Price Category:** C

*Images provided by designer/architect.*

CAD FILE AVAILABLE

## Plan #131001

**Dimensions:** 72'4" W x 32'4" D
**Levels:** 1
**Square Footage:** 1,615
**Bedrooms:** 3
**Bathrooms:** 2
**Foundation:** Crawl space, slab, basement, or walkout
**Materials List Available:** Yes
**Price Category:** D

*Images provided by designer/architect.*

Cathedral ceilings and illuminating skylights add drama and beauty to this practical ranch house.

### Features:

- **Ceiling Height:** 8 ft.

- **Front Porch:** Watch the rain in comfort from the covered front porch.

- **Foyer:** The stone-tiled foyer flows into the living areas.

- **Living Room:** Oriented towards the front of the house, the living room opens to the dining room and shares a lovely three-sided fireplace with the family room.

- **Family Room:** Conveniently located to share the fireplace with the living room, this room is bright and cheery thanks to its skylights as well as the sliding glass doors that open onto the rear patio.

- **Kitchen:** An island makes this sunny room both efficient and attractive.

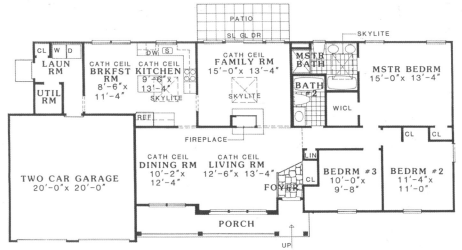

*Copyright by designer/architect.*

- **Breakfast Nook:** Located just off the kitchen, this area can serve double-duty as a spot for kitchen visitors to sit.

- **Dining Room:** The open design between the dining and living rooms adds to the spacious feeling that the cathedral ceiling creates in this area.

- **Laundry Room:** This area opens from the kitchen for convenience.

- **Master Suite:** A walk-in closet makes this room practical, but the master bathroom with a skylight, dual-sink vanity, soaking tub, and separate shower makes it luxurious.

- **Bedrooms:** The two additional bedrooms share a bathroom.

## Upper Level Floor Plan

**Main Level Floor Plan**

*Copyright by designer/architect.*

# Plan #181665

**Dimensions:** 52' W x 31' D

**Levels:** 2

**Square Footage:** 1,740

**Main Level Sq. Ft.:** 873

**Upper Level Sq. Ft.:** 867

**Bedrooms:** 3

**Bathrooms:** 2

**Foundation:** Basement

**Material List Available:** Yes

**Price Category:** C

*Images provided by designer/architect.*

---

## Upper Level Floor Plan

**Main Level Floor Plan**

*Copyright by designer/architect.*

# Plan #341214

**Dimensions:** 56'4" W x 36' D

**Levels:** 2

**Square Footage:** 1,806

**Main Level Sq. Ft.:** 828

**Upper Level Sq. Ft.:** 978

**Bedrooms:** 3

**Bathrooms:** 2½

**Foundation:** Crawl space, slab, basement or walkout

**Material List Available:** Yes

**Price Category:** D

*Images provided by designer/architect.*

**Main Level Floor Plan**

Sundeck 17-6 x 13-6
Brkfst. 8-8 x 15-6
Kit. 11-10 x 10-0
Family 14-10 x 13-6
Dining 11-6 x 13-6
Living 13-6 x 13-6
Lav.
Open Foyer 7-8 x 9-8
Ref
Pant
Cts.
48-0
48-0

© 1995, Jannis Vann & Associates, Inc.

## Plan #141026

**Dimensions:** 48' W x 48' D

**Levels:** 2

**Square Footage:** 1,993

**Main Level Sq. Ft.:** 1,038

**Upper Level Sq. Ft.:** 955

**Bedrooms:** 3

**Bathrooms:** 2½

**Foundation:** Basement

**Materials List Available:** Yes

**Price Category:** D

*Images provided by designer/architect.*

**Upper Level Floor Plan**

Bdrm.2 11-2 x 10-0
Bth.2
Lin
M.Bath
Bdrm.3 11-6 x 13-0
Balcony
Master Bdrm. 13-6 x 17-0
Open To Foyer
Tray Ceil.

*Copyright by designer/architect.*

---

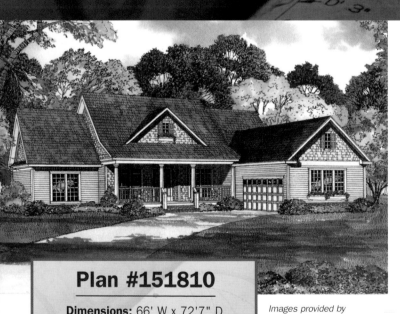

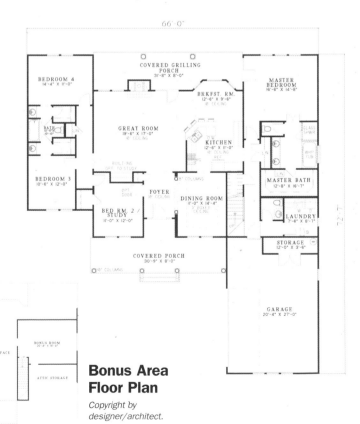

BEDROOM 4 14'-4" X 11'-0"
COVERED GRILLING PORCH 31'-8" X 8'-0"
BRKFST. RM. 12'-6" X 9'-6"
MASTER BEDROOM 16'-6" X 14'-8"
BATH
GREAT ROOM 19'-6" X 17'-0"
KITCHEN 12'-6" X 11'-0"
BEDROOM 3 10'-6" X 12'-0"
MASTER BATH 12'-8" X 16'-7"
FOYER
DINING ROOM 11'-0" X 14'-4"
BED RM. 2 / STUDY 11'-0" X 12'-0"
LAUNDRY 7'-6" X 8'-7"
STORAGE 12'-0" X 3'-6"
COVERED PORCH 30'-9" X 8'-0"
GARAGE 20'-4" X 27'-0"
66'-0"

**Bonus Area Floor Plan**

BONUS ROOM 20'-4" X 8'-4"
FUTURE SPACE
ATTIC STORAGE

*Copyright by designer/architect.*

## Plan #151810

**Dimensions:** 66' W x 72'7" D

**Levels:** 1

**Square Footage:** 2,354

**Bedrooms:** 4

**Bathrooms:** 2½

**Foundation:** Crawl space or slab

**CompleteCost List Available:** Yes

**Price Category:** E

*Images provided by designer/architect.*

CAD FILE AVAILABLE

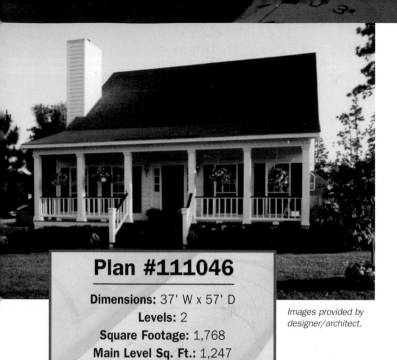

**Main Level Floor Plan**

*Images provided by designer/architect.*

**Upper Level Floor Plan**

*Copyright by designer/architect.*

# Plan #111046

**Dimensions:** 37' W x 57' D

**Levels:** 2

**Square Footage:** 1,768

**Main Level Sq. Ft.:** 1,247

**Upper Level Sq. Ft.:** 521

**Bedrooms:** 3

**Bathrooms:** 2½

**Foundation:** Crawl space

**Materials List Available:** No

**Price Category:** C

*Copyright by designer/architect.*

**Optional Upper Level Floor Plan**

# Plan #151133

**Dimensions:** 66'4" W x 58'7" D

**Levels:** 1

**Square Footage:** 2,029

**Bedrooms:** 3

**Bathrooms:** 2

**Foundation:** Crawl space, slab, or basement

**CompleteCost List Available:** Yes

**Price Category:** D

*Images provided by designer/architect.*

## Plan #141016

**Dimensions:** 64' W x 52' D

**Levels:** 2

**Square Footage:** 2,416

**Main Level Sq. Ft.:** 1,250

**Upper Level Sq. Ft.:** 1,166

**Bedrooms:** 4

**Bathrooms:** 2½

**Foundation:** Basement

**Materials List Available:** Yes

**Price Category:** E

Here is a classic American home with a generous wraparound front porch.

*Images provided by designer/architect.*

**Features:**

- Ceiling Height: 9 ft. unless otherwise noted.

- Formal Dining Room: Located just off the foyer you'll find this inviting dining room, which is perfect for dinner parties of all sizes.

- Formal Living Room: This room is located in close proximity to the dining room, making it easy to usher guests in to dine.

- Family Room: The whole family will want to gather in this spacious area. Columns separate it from the breakfast area while keeping an open feeling across the entire rear of the house.

- Kitchen: This warm and inviting kitchen features corner windows that look into the side yard and a rear screen porch.

- Master Bedroom: This bedroom has a modified cathedral ceiling that highlights a large Palladian window on the rear wall. Access to a second-floor deck creates the perfect master retreat.

**Rear Elevation**

## Main Level Floor Plan

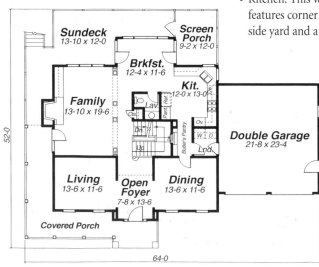

## Upper Level Floor Plan

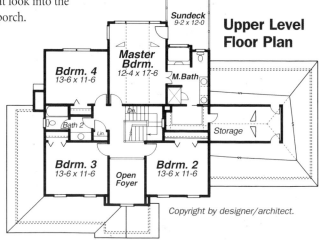

*Copyright by designer/architect.*

## Plan #181314

**Dimensions:** 28' W x 32' D
**Levels:** 2
**Square Footage:** 1,502
**Main Level Sq. Ft.:** 779
**Upper Level Sq. Ft.:** 723
**Bedrooms:** 3
**Bathrooms:** 2
**Foundation:** Basement
**Material List Available:** Yes
**Price Category:** C

Everyone wants to live in a country home with a wraparound porch, don't they?

*Images provided by designer/architect.*

**Features:**

- **Dining Room:** Just off the entry is this formal eating area, which has double swinging doors into the kitchen. The space will feel warm and airy with its two side windows, which fill this space with light.

- **Living Room:** The bay window lights this gathering area, which is just off the entry. The open stairway, which divides this area from the dining room, makes these two rooms feel as one.

- **Kitchen:** This island country kitchen features a lunch counter and a built-in pantry. The space features a laundry area one side and a mudroom on the other.

- **Upper Level:** Three bedrooms and a full bathroom occupy this level. The master bedroom features a dormer to add light and ceiling height.

## Main Level Floor Plan

*Copyright by designer/architect.*

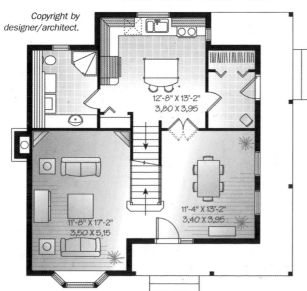

## Upper Level Floor Plan

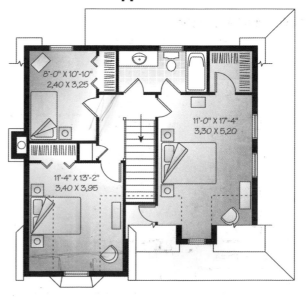

## Plan #151035

**Dimensions:** 37'8" W x 38'4" D
**Levels:** 1.5
**Square Footage:** 1,451
**Main Level Sq. Ft.:** 868
**Upper Level Sq. Ft:** 583
**Bedrooms:** 3
**Bathrooms:** 2
**Foundation:** Crawl space or slab
**CompleteCost List Available:** Yes
**Price Category:** B

*Images provided by designer/architect.*

**Features:**

- Den: The large stone fireplace is the focal point in this gathering area. Located just off the entry porch, the area welcomes you home.

- Kitchen: This efficiently designed kitchen has an abundance of cabinets and counter space. The eat-at counter, open to the den, adds extra space for family and friends.

- Grilling Porch: On nice days, overflow your dinner guests onto this rear covered grilling porch. From the relaxing area you can watch the kids play in the backyard.

- Upper Level: Two bedrooms, with large closets, and a full bathroom occupy this level. The dormers in each of the bedrooms add more space to these rooms.

Country living meets the modern day family in this well designed home.

Kitchen/Den

Porch

Kitchen

Master Bedroom

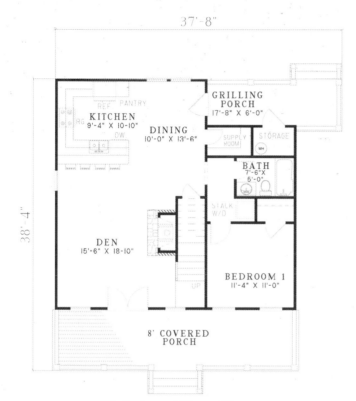

Main Level Floor Plan

Den

Upper Level Floor Plan

Dining Room

# Storage Options for Your Home

One of the great things about moving into a new home is all that new, uncluttered closet space you gain. But if you are like most homeowners, storage of all types will quickly become scarce, especially in a smaller home. Here are some tips for expanding and organizing storage space.

## Shelving Types

Shelving is an easy and economical way to add extra storage space in almost any part of your home—along walls, inside closets, and even in the basement or garage. Building shelves doesn't usually require a lot of skill or specialized tools, so this is one project just about any do-it-yourselfer can handle. And unless you decide to use hardwood—which looks great but costs a bundle—it won't cost a lot to install them either.

Solid wood shelving is the way to go when you want to show off the wood or your work.

Plywood and particleboard offer a couple of advantages when it comes to shelving, though. They cost less than solid wood, and can be bought faced with decorative surfaces. They also come in sheets, which makes them ideal for a really wide

**Home offices** require a mix of storage options: open shelving, drawers, and file cabinets.

shelf. Inexpensive, manufactured storage units ready for assembly often are made from melamine-coated particleboard.

Wood trim will help match your new shelves to the rest of the room or add some interesting detail. Trim is also a handy way to hide seams, gaps, exposed edges of plywood, and other blemishes. You can get trim in either hardwood or softwood. If you plan on finishing a project with stain or sealer, make sure the trim

matches the wood you used for the rest of the project.

## Bracket Options

There are two basic types of ready-to-hang shelving supports: stationary shelf brackets and shelving standards. Stationary brackets come in many sizes and styles, and range from utilitarian to decorative. Shelving standards are slotted metal strips that support various types of shelf brackets.

### Mounting Brackets

For maximum strength, anchor shelf supports to wall studs. If your shelf will carry a light load, you can anchor its supports between studs with mollies or toggle bolts. Attaching supports directly to the studs is always better, though, because sooner or later something heavy will wind up on the shelf. Use masonry anchors to attach shelf supports to brick or concrete. You can also attach shelf supports to a ledger attached to wall studs with 3-inch drywall screws.

**Ready-made shelving,** above, offers a quick alternative to building your own shelves.

**Mud rooms** and areas near the entrance the family uses most should have storage for coats, hats, and boots.

**Shelf Standards.** Metal shelf standards can be mounted directly to walls or, for a more decorative look, you can insert the standards in grooves routed into the wood itself or into hardwood strips.

Cut the standards to fit with a hacksaw, and attach them to wall studs with 3-inch drywall screws. Use a carpenter's level to make sure that both standards are plumb and that the corresponding mounting slots are level. Mount standards 6 inches from the ends of shelving to prevent sagging. For long wall shelves, install standards every 48 inches.

Many kitchen and closet storage systems use wire grids that attach to walls with molded plastic brackets. If you anticipate light loads, you can mount these brackets to drywall using the screws and expansion anchors usually included with such systems. But for heavier loads, use drywall screws to fasten the brackets directly to the wall studs.

## Customized Storage

Built-in storage units are an excellent way to make the most of existing storage space in your home. Ready-made or custom-made built-in shelving units, entertainment centers, kitchen cabinets, medicine cabinets, window seats, and under-bed drawers are not only inexpensive and easy to assemble, they allow you to add a unique, personalized touch to your living spaces.

### Built-in Shelving

A built-in shelving unit can create valuable storage capacity from an overlooked wall space, such as the area between windows or between a door and its adjacent corner. To construct the shelving, you'll need 1×10 or 1×12 lumber for side panels, top and base panels, and shelves; four 2×2 strips for spreaders; trim molding to conceal gaps along the top and bottom of the unit; 12d

common nails and 6d finishing nails. If the unit will be bearing heavy loads, use hardwood boards, and make sure that the shelves span no more than 36 inches. To make installation easier, cut the side pieces an inch shorter than the ceiling height. (This way, you'll be able to tilt the unit into position without scraping the ceiling.) Paint or stain the wood pieces before assembling the unit. Hang the shelves from pegs or end clips inserted into holes drilled in the side pieces.

### Adding Closet Space

What homeowner, even a new homeowner, hasn't complained about having too little closet space? Fortunately, there are almost always ways to find a bit more closet space or to make the closet space you have more efficient. Often, it isn't the space that is lacking but how the space is organized that is the problem. The trick is to find ways to help you organize the space.

**Ventilated closet systems** help keep your belongings neat and within easy reach.

**Organizing Systems.** The easiest and most obvious solution is one of the many commercial closet organizing systems now on the market. There are a number of configurations available, and you can customize most systems to meet your needs. Constructing your own version of a commercial closet organizer is another option. With a combination of shelves and plywood partitions, you can divide a closet into storage zones, with a single clothes pole on one side for full-length garments; double clothes poles on the other side for half-length garments like jackets, skirts, or slacks; a column of narrow shelves between the two for folded items or shoes; and one or more closet-wide shelves on top.

**Before designing** a closet system, above, inventory all of the items you want to store in the closet.

**Metal shelf standards** can provide a quick solution for creating shelving in areas where it is needed.

## Cedar Closets

Both solid cedar boards and composite cedar panels have only moderate resistance to insects, and are used more for their pleasant aroma and appearance. The sheets of pressed red and tan particles are no less aromatic than solid wood, but the panels are 40 to 50 percent less expensive, and are easier to install. Solid boards require more carpentry work, and are likely to produce a fair amount of waste unless you piece the courses and create more joints. To gain the maximum effect, every inside surface should be covered, including the ceiling and the back of the door. The simplest option is to use ¼-inch-thick panels, which are easy to cut into big sections that cover walls in one or two pieces. Try to keep cedar seams in boards or panels from falling over drywall seams. No stain, sealer, or clear finish is needed; just leave the wood raw. The cedar aroma will fade over the years as natural oils crystallize on the surface. But you can easily regenerate the

order direct: 1-800-523-6789

**For garages and basements,** you'll find a combination of shelving and hanging hooks keeps tools and equipment organized, opposite.

**Storage for basements,** garages, and workshops, opposite bottom, should include a cabinet that locks for storage of dangerous chemicals.

**Specialized storage** accessories, such as the sports storage system shown at right, not only keeps items organized but they also keep them in ready-to-play condition.

scent from the panels by scuffing the surface with fine sandpaper.

## Ideas for Basements, Garages, and Workshops

Workshops and other utility areas such as garages, attics, and basements can benefit from storage upgrades as much as any other room in the home—perhaps even more so, as utility areas are prone to clutter. Convenience, flexibility, and safety are the things to keep in mind when reorganizing your work space. Try to provide storage space for tools and hardware as near as possible to where they'll be used. In addition to a sturdy workbench, utility shelving

is a mainstay in any workshop. You can buy ready-to-assemble units or make your own using ¾-inch particleboard or plywood shelves and ¾ × 1½-inch (1×2) hardwood stock for cleats (nailed to the wall), ribs (nailed to the front underside of the shelves), and vertical shelf supports.

**DIY Utility Storage.** Don't forget about pegboard. To make a pegboard tool rack, attach washers to the back of the pegboard with hot glue, spacing the washers to coincide with wall studs. Position the pegboard so that the rear washers are located over studs. Drive drywall screws through finish washers and the pegboard into studs. (Use masonry anchors for concrete walls.)

Finally, try to take advantage of any oth-

erwise wasted space. The area in your garage above your parked car is the ideal spot for a U-shaped lumber storage rack, made of 1×4 stock and connecting plates. The space in front of the car could be used for a storage cabinet or even a workbench.

**Instant Storage.** To utilize the overhead space in your garage, build deep storage platforms supported by ledgers screwed to wall studs and threaded rods hooked to ceiling joists or rafters. You can also hang tools from the walls by mounting pegboard. You can buy sets with a variety of hooks and brackets for tools. For small items, such as jars of nails, make shallow shelves by nailing 1×4 boards between the exposed studs.

**Suit storage** to your needs. The narrow pullout pantry above is located between the refrigerator and a food-preparation area. Notice how you can access the shelves from both sides of the pantry when it is extended.

# Kitchen Storage

The type of storage in a kitchen is almost as important as the amount. Some people like at least a few open shelves for displaying attractive china or glassware; others want absolutely everything tucked away behind doors.

What are your storage needs? The answer depends partly on your food shopping habits and partly on how many pots, pans, and other pieces of kitchen equipment you have or would like to have. A family that goes food shopping several times a week and prepares mostly fresh foods needs more refrigerator space, less freezer capacity, and fewer cabinets than a family that prefers packaged or prepared foods and makes only infrequent forays to the local supermarket.

## Planning

To help clarify your needs, mentally walk yourself through a typical meal and list the utensils used to prepare food, where you got them, and your progress throughout the work area. And don't limit yourself to full-scale meals. Much kitchen work is devoted to preparing snacks, reheating leftovers, and making lunches for the kids to take to school.

**Food Preparation.** During food preparation, the sink and stove come into use. Some families rely heavily on the microwave for reheating. Using water means repeated trips to the sink, so that area might be the best place to keep a steamer, salad spinner, and coffee and tea canisters, as well as glassware and cups. Near the stove you may want storage for odd-shaped items such as a fish poacher or wok. You can hang frequently used pans and utensils from a convenient rack; stow other items in cabinets so that they do not collect grease.

**During the Meal.** When the food is ready, you must take it to the table. If the eating space is nearby, a work counter might turn into a serving counter. If the dining space is in another room, a pass-through facilitates serving.

**Storage accessories,** such as the pullout pot holder above, come as options from some cabinet manufacturers, or you can install them later yourself. Notice how the side rails hold the pot lids in place. The cabinet below features space for small baskets.

**After the Meal.** When the meal ends, dishes must go from the table to the sink or dishwasher, and leftovers to storage containers and the refrigerator. Now the stove and counters need to be wiped down and the sink scoured. When the dishwasher finishes its cycle, everything must be put away.

**Open versus Closed Storage.** Shelves, pegboards, pot racks, cup hooks, magnetic knife racks, and the like put your utensils on view, which is a good way to personalize your kitchen.

But open storage has drawbacks. Items left out in the open can look messy unless they are kept neatly arranged. Another option is to install glass doors on wall cabinets. This handily solves the dust problem but often costs more than solid doors.

## Plan #181151

**Dimensions:** 50' W x 46' D
**Levels:** 2
**Square Footage:** 2,283
**Main Level Sq. Ft.:** 1,274
**Second Level Sq. Ft.:** 1,009
**Bedrooms:** 3
**Bathrooms:** 2½
**Foundation:** Basement
**Materials List Available:** Yes
**Price Category:** E

• **Kitchen:** This efficient and well-designed kitchen has double sinks and offers a separate eating area for those impromptu family meals.

• **Master Bedroom:** This master retreat has a walk-in closet and its own sumptuous bath.

• **Home Office:** Whether you work at home or just need a place for the family computer and keeping track of family finances, this home office fills the bill.

Multiple porches, stately columns, and arched multi-paned windows adorn this country home.

**CAD FILE AVAILABLE**

### Features:

• Ceiling Height: 8 ft. unless otherwise noted.

• Great Room: The second-floor mezzanine overlooks this great room. With its soaring ceiling, this dramatic room is the centerpiece of a spacious and flowing design that is just as suited to entertaining as it is to family life.

• Dining Area: Guests will naturally flow into this dining area when it is time to eat. After dinner they can step directly out onto the porch to enjoy coffee and dessert when the weather is fair.

Front View

## Main Level Floor Plan

21'-0" X 20'-8"
6,30 X 6,20

17'-0" X 11'-8"
5,10 X 3,50

9'-8" X 8'-8"
2,90 X 2,60

9'-0" X 10'-0"
2,70 X 3,00

10'-0" X 12'-0"
3,00 X 3,60

9'-8" X 9'-4"
2,90 X 2,80

12'-0" X 20'-8"
3,60 X 6,20

46'-0"
13,8 m

50'-0"
15,0 m

## Upper Level Floor Plan

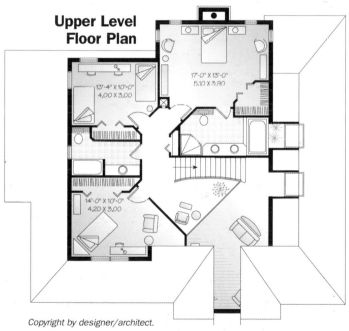

13'-4" X 10'-0"
4,00 X 3,00

17'-0" X 13'-0"
5,10 X 3,90

14'-0" X 10'-0"
4,20 X 3,00

*Copyright by designer/architect.*

## SMARTtip

### Coping Chair Rails

If the teeth of your rasp tend to break out thin edges of the cope, try wrapping the rasp with sandpaper to make fine adjustments.

Dining Room

Living Room

Master Bath

## Plan #151408

**Dimensions:** 34'4" W x 48'4" D
**Levels:** 1.5
**Square Footage:** 1,544
**Main Level Sq. Ft.:** 1,031
**Upper Level Sq. Ft.:** 513
**Bedrooms:** 3
**Bathrooms:** 2
**Foundation:** Crawl space
**CompleteCost List Available:** Yes
**Price Category:** C

*Images provided by designer/architect.*

This cozy cottage will make the perfect year-round or weekend getaway home.

**Features:**

• Great Room: Enter this large room from the entry porch. Feel the warmth from the stone fireplace rising up through the vaulted ceiling.

• Kitchen: The L-shaped design and large island make this kitchen ideal for daily meals or entertaining.

• Dining Room: This dining room has a door to the rear grilling porch and is open to the kitchen, giving it a large, open feeling.

• Loft: This area has an ample amount of storage, plus a third bedroom and full bathroom.

**Upper Level Floor Plan**

**Main Level Floor Plan**

*Copyright by designer/architect.*

## Plan #121037

**Dimensions:** 46' W x 47'10" D
**Levels:** 2
**Square Footage:** 2,292
**Main Level Sq. Ft.:** 1,158
**Upper Level Sq. Ft.:** 1,134
**Bedrooms:** 4
**Bathrooms:** 2½
**Foundation:** Basement
**Materials List Available:** Yes
**Price Category:** E

*Images provided by designer/architect.*

This convenient and comfortable home is filled with architectural features that set it apart.

**Features:**

- Ceiling Height: 8 ft. unless otherwise noted.
- Foyer: You'll know you have arrived when you enter this two-story area highlighted by a decorative plant shelf and a balcony.
- Great Room: Just beyond the entry is the great room where the warmth of the two-sided fireplace will attract family and friends to gather. A bay window offers a more intimate place to sit and converse.
- Hearth Room: At the other side of the fireplace, the hearth offers a cozy spot for smaller gatherings or a place to sit alone and enjoy a book by the fire.
- Breakfast Area: With sunlight streaming into its bay window, the breakfast area offers the perfect spot for informal family meals.
- Master Suite: This private retreat is made more convenient by a walk-in closet. It features its own tub and shower.

### Main Level Floor Plan

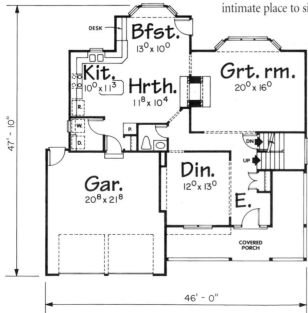

### Upper Level Floor Plan

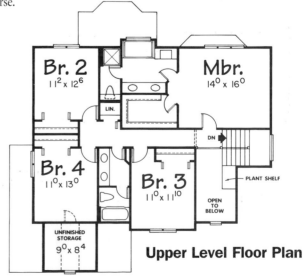

*Copyright by designer/architect.*

## Plan #351036

**Dimensions:** 78' W x 46' D
**Levels:** 1
**Square Footage:** 1,799
**Bedrooms:** 3
**Bathrooms:** 2½
**Foundation:** Crawl space or slab
**Materials List Available:** Yes
**Price Category:** D

This beautifully styled home has everything your family needs.

**CAD FILE AVAILABLE**

### Features:

- **Great Room:** There is cozy fireplace in the corner of this room, plus a view out to the grilling porch.

- **Kitchen:** This country kitchen with island and raised bar will keep family and friends close but out of the work triangle.

- **Master Suite:** This suite is well appointed with a jetted tub, dual vanities, a separate walk-in shower, and large closets.

- **Bonus Room:** This optional bonus room over the garage may serve as a fourth bedroom, game room, or office.

*Images provided by designer/architect.*

### Optional Bonus Area Floor Plan

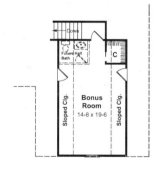

*Copyright by designer/architect.*

Rear View

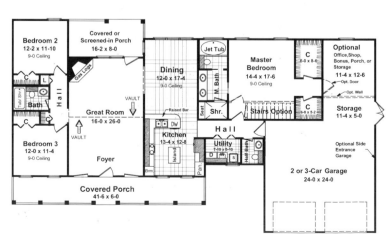

# Plan #141037

**Dimensions:** 40'4" W x 44' D
**Levels:** 2
**Square Footage:** 1,735
**Main Level Sq. Ft.:** 1,045
**Upper Level Sq. Ft.:** 690
**Bedrooms:** 3
**Bathrooms:** 2½
**Foundation:** Basement with drive under garage
**Materials List Available:** No
**Price Category:** C

*Images provided by designer/architect.*

The contemporary design features inside this traditional-looking home will delight you.

**Features:**

- **Living Room:** The open floor plan adds an airy feeling to this spacious room, but you'll be cozy by the handsome fireplace.

- **Dining Room:** Natural light pours into this room, which looks out to the sundeck.

- **Kitchen:** The angled bar adds to the convenient layout here that speeds your tasks.

- **Breakfast Room:** With large windows and a door to the deck, this room will be a gathering spot.

- **Master Suite:** The large bedroom is complemented by a walk-in closet and bath with corner tub, separate shower, and double vanity.

- **Upper Floor:** The sitting area is a lovely feature on this floor, which has two large bedrooms, a bath, extra storage space, and a linen closet.

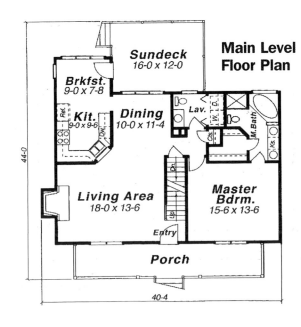

**Main Level Floor Plan**

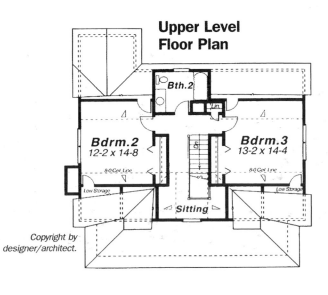

**Upper Level Floor Plan**

*Copyright by designer/architect.*

## Plan #351049

**Dimensions:** 78' W x 49'6" D

**Levels:** 1

**Square Footage:** 2,004

**Bedrooms:** 3

**Bathrooms:** 2½

**Foundation:** Crawl space or slab

**Materials List Available:** Yes

**Price Category:** E

*Images provided by designer/architect.*

A traditional brick ranch is a perfect addition to any neighborhood.

**Features:**

- Foyer: A dramatic entry with a 10-ft.-high ceiling welcomes you to this home. The convenient coat closet is close by.

- Great Room: A vaulted ceiling adds grandeur to this gathering area. The corner fireplace will take the chill off on cool nights. Windows with a view of the backyard bring in plenty of natural light.

- Master Suite: This expansive master suite features a vaulted ceiling in the master bedroom and large his and her walk-in closets. The master bath boasts an oversize jetted tub, 4-ft.-square shower, and plenty of counter space.

- Storage: A "flex space" on the first floor and a bonus room over the garage further enhance the floor plan. The garage is oversized for full-size vehicles.

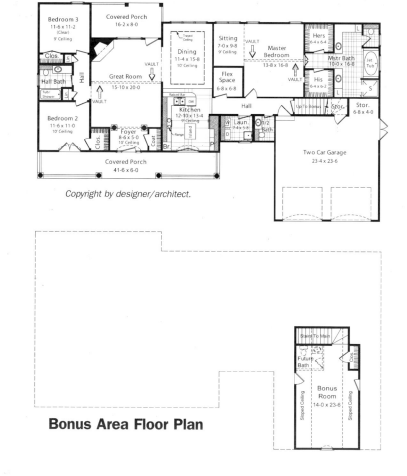

*Copyright by designer/architect.*

**Bonus Area Floor Plan**

## Plan #441023

**Dimensions:** 60' W x 42' D
**Levels:** 2
**Square Footage:** 2,500
**Main Level Sq. Ft.:** 1,319
**Lower Level Sq. Ft:** 1,181
**Bedrooms:** 4
**Bathrooms:** 2½
**Foundation:** Crawl space; slab or basement for fee
**Materials List Available:** No
**Price Category:** E

Symmetry is the order of the day in this plan. Cedar shingles and stone accents further the attraction.

*CAD FILE AVAILABLE*

### Features:

- **Kitchen:** This island kitchen boasts an open floor plan, sharing space with the breakfast nook and the family room. A convenient butler's pantry connects the dining room and the service hall to the kitchen.

- **Master Suite:** The vaulted ceiling is the highlight of this master suite. The master bath is worthy of note, as it contains a huge walk-in closet, separate shower, spa tub, and compartmented toilet.

- **Secondary Bedrooms:** Two large bedrooms are located on the upper level in close proximity to the master suite. They enjoy natural light from the large windows and adequate-sized closets.

- **Bonus Room:** This bonus space over the garage can become a fifth bedroom, a game room, or home office space in the future.

Rear Elevation

### Main Level Floor Plan

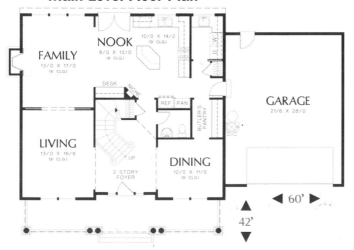

### Upper Level Floor Plan

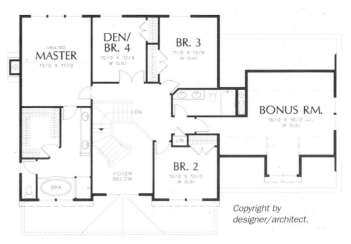

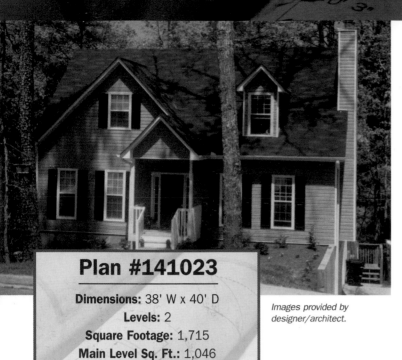

**Main Level Floor Plan**

38-0

32-0

8-0

Deck 16-0 x 12-0

Skylights

Breakfast

Kitchen 9-0 x 9-6

Dining Area 9-10 x 11-4

Bath

W D

M. Bath

Living Area 18-0 x 13-6

Master Bedroom 15-6 x 13-6

© 1989

Porch

*Images provided by designer/architect.*

**Upper Level Floor Plan**

Bath

Bedroom 2 15-8 x 13-4

Down

Bedroom 3 15-6 x 11-0

*Copyright by designer/architect.*

## Plan #141023

**Dimensions:** 38' W x 40' D

**Levels:** 2

**Square Footage:** 1,715

**Main Level Sq. Ft.:** 1,046

**Upper Level Sq. Ft.:** 669

**Bedrooms:** 3

**Bathrooms:** 2½

**Foundation:** Basement

**Materials List Available:** Yes

**Price Category:** C

---

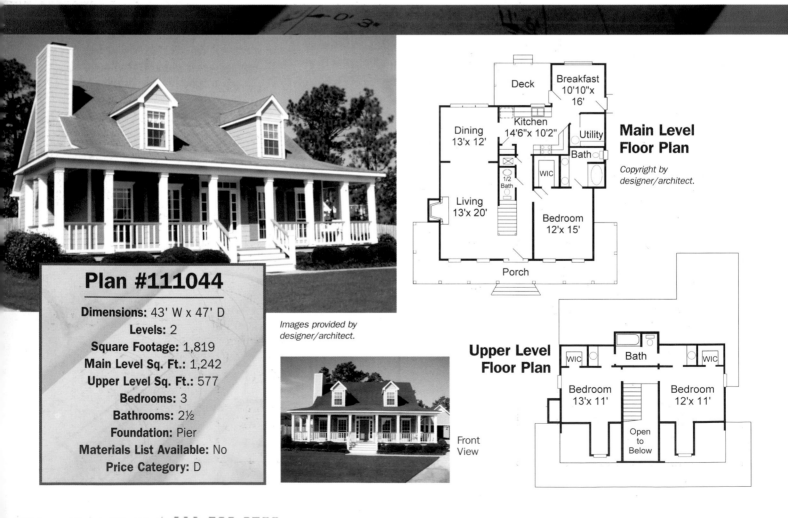

**Main Level Floor Plan**

*Copyright by designer/architect.*

Deck

Breakfast 10'10"x 16'

Kitchen 14'6"x 10'2"

Dining 13' 12'

Utility

Bath

WIC

1/2 Bath

Living 13'x 20'

Bedroom 12'x 15'

Porch

*Images provided by designer/architect.*

Front View

**Upper Level Floor Plan**

WIC

Bath

WIC

Bedroom 13'x 11'

Bedroom 12'x 11'

Open to Below

## Plan #111044

**Dimensions:** 43' W x 47' D

**Levels:** 2

**Square Footage:** 1,819

**Main Level Sq. Ft.:** 1,242

**Upper Level Sq. Ft.:** 577

**Bedrooms:** 3

**Bathrooms:** 2½

**Foundation:** Pier

**Materials List Available:** No

**Price Category:** D

## Main Level Floor Plan

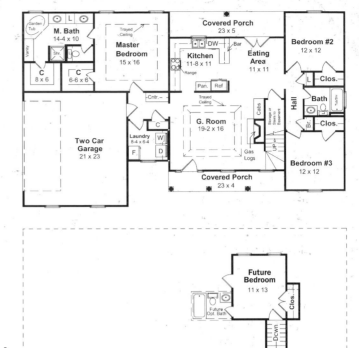

**M. Bath** 14-4 x 10

Garden Tub

Vanity

**Master Bedroom** 15 x 16

Trayed Ceiling

C 8 x 6

C 6-6 x 6

**Covered Porch** 23 x 5

**Kitchen** 11-8 x 11

DW Bar

Range

Pan. Ref

**Eating Area** 11 x 11

**Bedroom #2** 12 x 12

Clos.

**Bath**

Clos.

**Two Car Garage** 21 x 23

**Laundry** 8-4 x 6-4

C

W
D

Trayed Ceiling

**G. Room** 19-2 x 16

Cabs

Storage or Stairs to Basement

UP

Gas Logs

Hall

**Bedroom #3** 12 x 12

**Covered Porch** 23 x 4

**Future Bedroom** 11 x 13

Future Opt. Bath

Clos.

Dcwn

# Plan #351041

**Dimensions:** 64' W x 50' D

**Levels:** 2

**Square Footage:** 1,800

**Main Level Sq. Ft.:** 1,639

**Upper Level Sq. Ft.:** 161

**Bedrooms:** 3

**Bathrooms:** 2

**Foundation:** Crawl space, slab, or basement

**Material List Available:** Yes

**Price Category:** E

*Images provided by designer/architect.*

## Upper Level Floor Plan

*Copyright by designer/architect.*

---

**Bedroom 3** 11-6 x 12-8 (Clear) 9' Ceiling

**Covered Porch** 13-8 x 13-0

**Patio** 18-8 x 9-4

**Bath** 7-6 x 5-8

Gas Logs

9-0 Clg. Ht.
10-0 Clg. Ht.

**Dining** 11-4 x 15-8 10' Ceiling

**Sitting** 7-0 x 9-8 9' Ceiling

VAULT

**Master Bedroom** 13-8 x 16-8

VAULT

Clos. 6-4 x 6-2

L

**Mstr Bath** 10-0 x 16-8

Jet Tub

**Media Room** 7-6 x 4-2

Built-In

**Great Room** 15-10 x 20-0

VAULT

**Flex Space** 6-8 x 6-8

Clos. 6-4 x 6-2

**Bath** 7-6 x 5-2

Hall

VAULT

Raised Bar

Hall

L

**Stor.** 6-8 x 4-0

**Bedroom 2** 11-6 x 13-6 10' Ceiling

Clos.

**Foyer** 8-6 x 5-0 10' Ceiling

Coat

**Kitchen** 12-10 x 13-4 9' Ceiling

Island

DW

**Laun.** 6-10 x 8-0

**Half Bath** 5-0 x 8-0

Up To Bonus

Stor.

**Two Car Garage** 23-4 x 23-6

**Covered Porch** 41-6 x 6-0

Open Storage

*Copyright by designer/architect.*

Stairs To Main

Future Bath

Clos.

**Bonus Room** 14-0 x 23-6

Sloped Ceiling

Sloped Ceiling

## Bonus Area Floor Plan

# Plan #351067

**Dimensions:** 78' W x 58'6" D

**Levels:** 1

**Square Footage:** 2,200

**Bedrooms:** 3

**Bathrooms:** 3½

**Foundation:** Crawl space or slab

**Material List Available:** Yes

**Price Category:** F

*Images provided by designer/architect.*

**Main Level Floor Plan**

SIDE PORCH

MASTER BEDROOM (12'4"x11'8")

DINING AREA (11'4"x10'0")

LIVING ROOM (16'4"x16'10")

KITCHEN (9'0"x10'0")

ENTRY

FRONT PORCH

BEDROOM #2 (10'0"x11'8")

ATTIC STORAGE

BEDROOM #3 (10'0"x11'6")

**Upper Level Floor Plan**

*Copyright by designer/architect.*

Front View

## Plan #521056

**Dimensions:** 36'8" W x 41' D

**Levels:** 2

**Square Footage:** 1,400

**Main Level Sq. Ft.:** 953

**Upper Level Sq. Ft.:** 447

**Bedrooms:** 3

**Bathrooms:** 2½

**Foundation:** Crawl space

**Material List Available:** No

**Price Category:** B

*Images provided by designer/architect.*

**CAD FILE AVAILABLE**

---

## Plan #461149

**Dimensions:** 28' W x 61' D

**Levels:** 1

**Square Footage:** 1,116

**Bedrooms:** 3

**Bathrooms:** 2

**Foundation:** Crawl space or slab; basement for fee

**Material List Available:** No

**Price Category:** B

*Images provided by designer/architect.*

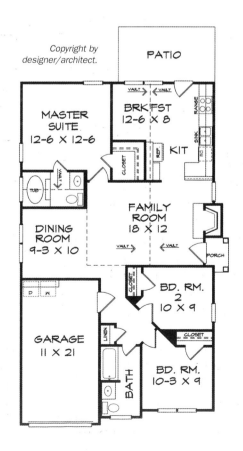

*Copyright by designer/architect.*

PATIO

MASTER SUITE 12-6 X 12-6

BRK FST 12-6 X 8

KIT

FAMILY ROOM 18 X 12

DINING ROOM 9-3 X 10

PORCH

BD. RM. 2 10 X 9

GARAGE 11 X 21

BATH

BD. RM. 10-3 X 9

**Main Level Floor Plan**

*Copyright by designer/architect.*

NOOK
11/0 X 9/0 +/-
(9' CLG.)

FAMILY
15/8 X 12/8
(9' CLG.)

DEN
9/8 X 10/4
(9' CLG.)

DINING
11/0 X 10/0
(9' CLG.)

GARAGE
19/0 X 19/6 +

VAULTED
LIVING
13/0 X 12/0

43'

◀ 40' ▶

*Images provided by designer/architect.*

**Upper Level Floor Plan**

VAULTED
MASTER
14/4 X 12/8

BR. 2
11/4 X 10/0

VAULTED
BR. 3
10/0 X 11/0

PLANT SHELF

**CAD FILE AVAILABLE**

Rear Elevation

## Plan #441020

**Dimensions:** 43' W x 40' D

**Levels:** 2

**Square Footage:** 1,994

**Main Level Sq. Ft.:** 1,112

**Upper Level Sq. Ft.:** 882

**Bedrooms:** 3

**Bathrooms:** 2½

**Foundation:** Crawl space or slab; basement for fee

**Material List Available:** No

**Price Category:** D

---

*Copyright by designer/architect.*

DECK
(17'0"x6'0")

LIVING ROOM
16'4"x21'4")

DINING AREA

KITCHEN
(16'4"x10'6")

FOYER

FRONT PORCH
(8'0"x19'8")

SCREENED PORCH
(21'0"x11'4")

MASTER BEDROOM
(15'4"x12'0")

BEDROOM #2
(12'8"x12'0")

BEDROOM #3
(10'8"x13'0")

**CAD FILE AVAILABLE**

*Images provided by designer/architect.*

*This home, as shown in the photographs, may differ from the actual blueprints. For more detailed information, please check the floor plans carefully.*

## Plan #521040

**Dimensions:** 42'2" W x 57' D

**Levels:** 1

**Square Footage:** 1,555

**Bedrooms:** 3

**Bathrooms:** 2½

**Foundation:** Slab

**Material List Available:** No

**Price Category:** C

Front View

Rear View

**Main Level Floor Plan**

GRILLING PORCH
29'-0" X 8'-0"

BATH
8'-0" X 5'-0"

DINING / KITCHEN
15'-8" X 9'-0"

MASTER BEDROOM
8'-6" X 14'-10"

GREAT ROOM
15'-8" X 11'-4"

COVERED PORCH
29'-0" X 8'-0"

30' 6"

37' 0"

LOFT
16'-0" X 10'-0"

BEDROOM 2
8'-6" X 12'-0"

**Upper Level Floor Plan**

*Copyright by designer/architect.*

# Plan #151182

**Dimensions:** 30'6" W x 37' D

**Levels:** 1½

**Square Footage:** 975

**Main Level Sq. Ft.:** 616

**Upper Level Sq. Ft.:** 359

**Bedrooms:** 2

**Bathrooms:** 1

**Foundation:** Crawl space, slab; basement or walkout basement available for fee)

**CompleteCost List Available:** Yes

**Price Category:** A

*Images provided by designer/architect.*

**CAD FILE AVAILABLE**

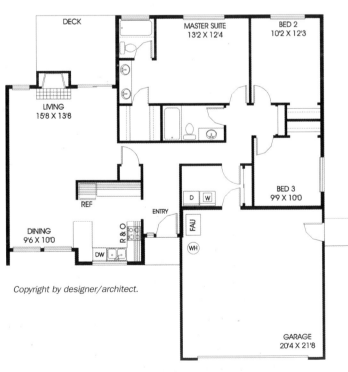

DECK

MASTER SUITE
13'2 X 12'4

BED 2
10'2 X 12'3

LIVING
15'8 X 13'8

REF

ENTRY

FAU

BED 3
9'9 X 10'0

DINING
9'6 X 10'0

D W

R & O

DW

WH

GARAGE
20'4 X 21'8

*Copyright by designer/architect.*

# Plan #501093

**Dimensions:** 46' W x 50' D

**Levels:** 1

**Square Footage:** 1,286

**Bedrooms:** 3

**Bathrooms:** 2

**Foundation:** Crawl space

**Material List Available:** Yes

**Price Category:** B

*Images provided by designer/architect.*

## Plan #111010

**Dimensions:** 34' W x 38' D

**Levels:** 3

**Square Footage:** 1,804

**Main Level Sq. Ft.:** 731

**Upper Level Sq. Ft.:** 935

**Third Level Sq.Ft.:** 138

**Bedrooms:** 3

**Bathrooms:** 3

**Foundation:** Piers

**Materials List Available:** No

**Price Category:** D

### Third Level Floor Plan

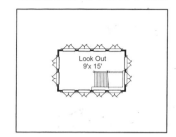

Look Out
9'x 15'

*Images provided by designer/architect.*

Side View

### Main Level Floor Plan

Deck
14'x 10'

Kitchen
10'6"x 13'9"

Dining
9'x 13'8"

Living
14'x 19'

Screen
Porch
19'6"x 10'

*Copyright by designer/architect.*

Master
Bedroom
18'6"x 15'

Bedroom
11'6"x 11'

Bedroom
12'x 10'

### Upper Level Floor Plan

---

## Plan #181313

**Dimensions:** 28' W x 28' D

**Levels:** 2

**Square Footage:** 1,568

**Main Level Sq. Ft.:** 784

**Upper Level Sq. Ft.:** 784

**Bedrooms:** 3

**Bathrooms:** 1½

**Foundation:** Basement

**Material List Available:** Yes

**Price Category:** C

*Images provided by designer/architect.*

9'-4" X 10'-8"
2,80 X 3,20

10'-0" X 16'-0"
3,00 X 4,80

5'-0" X 8'-4"
1,50 2,50

16'-0" X 12'-0"
4,80 X 3,60

28'-0"
8,4 m

### Main Level Floor Plan

28'-0"
8,4 m

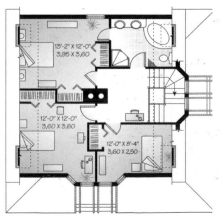

13'-2" X 12'-0"
3,95 X 3,60

12'-0" X 12'-0"
3,60 X 3,60

12'-0" X 12'-0"
3,60 X 3,60

12'-0" X 8'-4"
3,60 X 2,50

### Upper Level Floor Plan

*Copyright by designer/architect.*

# Plan #491001

**Dimensions:** 24' W x 36' D
**Levels:** 2
**Square Footage:** 582
**Main Level Sq. Ft.:** 384
**Lower Level Sq. Ft:** 198
**Bedrooms:** 1
**Bathrooms:** 1
**Foundation:** Crawl space
**Materials List Available:** Yes
**Price Category:** A

This economical, compact floor plan is perfectly suited for a narrow lot and would minimize the environmental impact on any piece of property.

**Features:**

- Wraparound Porch: This area incorporates the front entry porch and the rear deck. This outdoor space will give you a 360-degree view of the great outdoors.

- Living Area: Even though it's reduced to bare essentials, the living area boasts a two-story-high vaulted ceiling. The living area window wall maximizes all the available views and floods the room with natural light.

- Loft: Designed as a sleeping loft, this area can be used for whatever you desire. The area is large enough to be divided in two.

- Bathroom: An efficient bathroom is located on the main level. Located just off the kitchen, it features a vanity, lavatory, and standup shower.

**Main Level
Floor Plan**

**Upper Level
Floor Plan**

## Plan #141041

**Dimensions:** 43' W x 45' D
**Levels:** 1.5
**Square Footage:** 1,821
**Main Level Sq. Ft.:** 1,166
**Upper Level Sq. Ft.:** 655
**Bedrooms:** 3
**Bathrooms:** 2
**Foundation:** Basement
**Materials List Available:** No
**Price Category:** D

This home is perfect for those who want a year-round lakeside haven that is large enough for friends and family as well.

**Features:**

• Outdoor Spaces: The first-story wraparound porch is perfect for enjoying warm nights with crickets for company. Second-story balconies bring in summer breezes and provide the ideal place for stargazing.

• Living Room: This two-story living room creates architectural interest and gives the cozy cottage an elegant expansion.

• Kitchen: Perfect for the budding and expert chef alike, this large area has plenty of workspace and storage. For easy transitions, the kitchen opens directly into the window-flanked, sunlit dining room.

• Master Suite: This expansive area allows the owner to enjoy one-story living while guests enjoy the privacy of a second floor to themselves. It has an entry to the porch, a walk-in closet, and a compartmentalized full master bath with dual sinks, a large tub, and a separate shower stall.

• Second Floor: Two parallel bedrooms include individual balconies and plenty of closet space. They share the second full bathroom and a view of the rest of the home from the open living room.

• Basement: An unfinished basement and an attached double garage provide space for hobbies, storage, and leisure. The rustic cottage upstairs might descend into a cool entertainment area, complete with a pool table and large-screen TV.

## Main Level Floor Plan

## Upper Level Floor Plan

## Basement Level Floor Plan

*Copyright by designer/architect.*

# Plan #111047

**Dimensions:** 36' W x 54' D
**Levels:** 2
**Square Footage:** 1,863
**Main Level Sq. Ft.:** 1,056
**Upper Level Sq. Ft.:** 807
**Bedrooms:** 4
**Bathrooms:** 3
**Foundation:** Pier
**Materials List Available:** No
**Price Category:** D

Designed for a coastline, this home is equally appropriate as a year-round residence or a vacation retreat.

**Features:**

- Orientation: The rear-facing design gives you an ocean view and places the most attractive side of the house where beach-goers can see it.

- Entryway: On the waterside, a large deck with a covered portion leads to the main entrance.

- Carport: This house is raised on piers that let you park underneath it and that protect it from water damage during storms.

- Living Room: A fireplace, French doors, and large windows grace this room, which is open to both the kitchen and the dining area.

- Master Suite: Two sets of French doors open to a balcony on the ocean side, and the suite includes two walk-in closets and a fully equipped bath.

**Main Level Floor Plan**

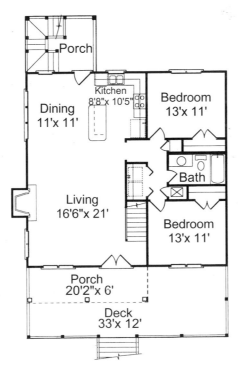

Porch

Dining 11'x 11'

Kitchen 8'8"x 10'5"

Bedroom 13'x 11'

Bath

Living 16'6"x 21'

Bedroom 13'x 11'

Porch 20'2"x 6'

Deck 33'x 12'

**Upper Level Floor Plan**

Ma. Bath

Bath

Master Bedroom 16'6"x 19'

Bedroom 13'x 13'

Balcony 20'2"x 6'

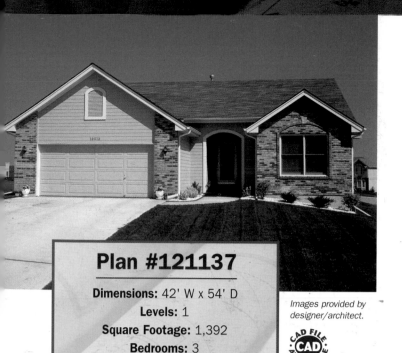

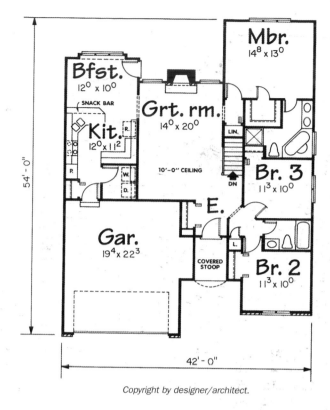

## Plan #121137

**Dimensions:** 42' W x 54' D

**Levels:** 1

**Square Footage:** 1,392

**Bedrooms:** 3

**Bathrooms:** 2

**Foundation:** Basement; crawl space for fee

**Material List Available:** Yes

**Price Category:** B

*Images provided by designer/architect.*

**CAD FILE AVAILABLE**

*Copyright by designer/architect.*

## Plan #431003

**Dimensions:** 34' W x 36' D

**Levels:** 2

**Square Footage:** 1,330

**Main Level Sq. Ft.:** 1,030

**Upper Level Sq. Ft.:** 300

**Bedrooms:** 2

**Bathrooms:** 1

**Foundation:** Crawl space or basement

**Material List Available:** Yes

**Price Category:** B

*Images provided by designer/architect.*

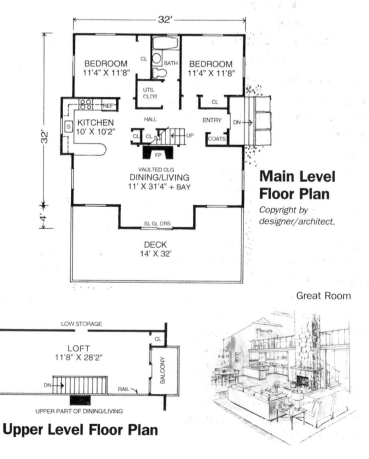

**Main Level Floor Plan**

*Copyright by designer/architect.*

**Great Room**

**Upper Level Floor Plan**

## Plan #271051

**Dimensions:** 30' W x 44'8" D
**Levels:** 2
**Square Footage:** 1,920
**Main Level Sq. Ft.:** 1,210
**Upper Level Sq. Ft.:** 710
**Bedrooms:** 3
**Bathrooms:** 2
**Foundation:** Crawl space or walkout
**Materials List Available:** Yes
**Price Category:** D

Dramatic windows soar to the peak of this vacation home, offering unlimited views of the outdoor scenery.

**Features:**

- Living Room: This spacious living room, with its 26-ft. vaulted ceiling, boasts a cozy fireplace. The sliding glass doors open to the wraparound deck, while the wall of windows fill the space with natural light.

- Secluded Bedroom: This main-floor bedroom has convenient access to the full bathroom and two large closets.

- Upper Level: Going up the U-shaped stairs brings you to this level, where you are greeted by an open loft, a full bathroom and two bedrooms. Each bedroom has two large closets and a window with a view of the backyard.

- Lower Level: The daylight basement provides a versatile recreation room that has another fireplace, a garage and shop area, and a service room for lots of storage.

*Images provided by designer/architect.*

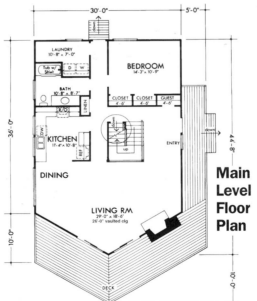

**Main Level Floor Plan**

*Copyright by designer/architect.*

**Upper Level Floor Plan**

**Garage Level Floor Plan**

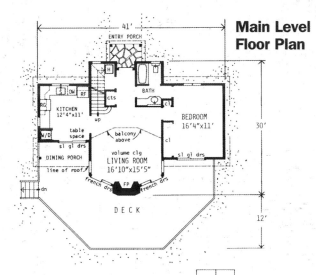

**Main Level Floor Plan**

## Plan #431004

**Dimensions:** 41' W x 30' D

**Levels:** 2

**Square Footage:** 1,156

**Main Level Sq. Ft.:** 810

**Upper Level Sq. Ft.:** 346

**Bedrooms:** 2

**Bathrooms:** 2

**Foundation:** Crawl space

**Material List Available:** Yes

**Price Category:** B

*Images provided by designer/architect.*

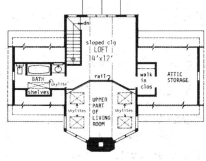

**Upper Level Floor Plan**

*Copyright by designer/architect.*

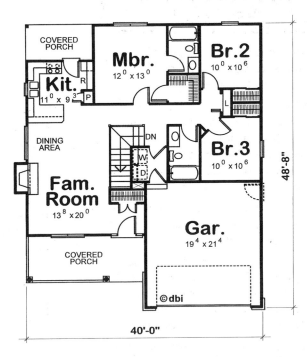

## Plan #121144

**Dimensions:** 40' W x 48'8" D

**Levels:** 1

**Square Footage:** 1,195

**Bedrooms:** 3

**Bathrooms:** 2

**Foundation:** Basement; crawl space for fee

**Material List Available:** Yes

**Price Category:** B

*Images provided by designer/architect.*

**CAD FILE AVAILABLE**

*Copyright by designer/architect.*

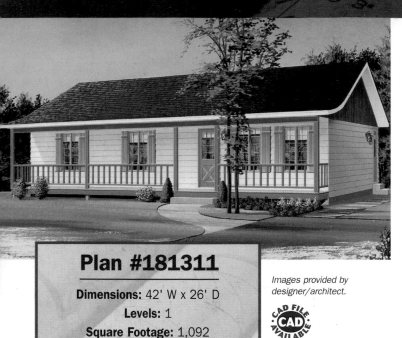

*Copyright by designer/architect.*

*Images provided by designer/architect.*

26'-0"
7,8 m

11'-4" X 12'-0"
3,40 X 3,60

8'-0" X 12'-0"
2,40 X 3,60

12'-4" X 12'-0"
3,70 X 3,60

11'-4" X 9'-8"
3,40 X 2,90

10'-4" X 8'-8"
3,10 X 2,60

16'-0" X 12'-4"
4,80 X 3,70

42'-0"
12,6 m

Rear Elevation

## Plan #181311

**Dimensions:** 42' W x 26' D

**Levels:** 1

**Square Footage:** 1,092

**Bedrooms:** 3

**Bathrooms:** 1

**Foundation:** Basement

**Material List Available:** Yes

**Price Category:** B

CAD FILE AVAILABLE

---

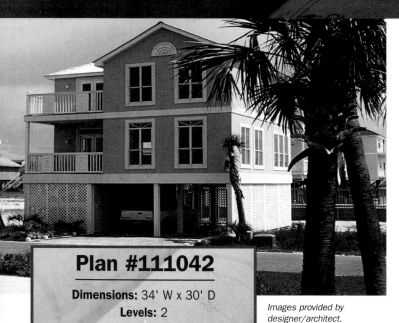

*Images provided by designer/architect.*

## Plan #111042

**Dimensions:** 34' W x 30' D

**Levels:** 2

**Square Footage:** 1,779

**Main Level Sq. Ft.:** 907

**Upper Level Sq. Ft.:** 872

**Bedrooms:** 3

**Bathrooms:** 2½

**Foundation:** Pier

**Materials List Available:** No

**Price Category:** C

Kitchen
13'x 11'6"

Utility

Sunroom
9'6"x 11'6"

1/2 Ba.

Dining
14'x 10'

Living
19'x 17'6"

Porch
14'x 8'

**Main Level Floor Plan**

Bedroom
11'x 9'4"

Bath

Master Bath

WIC

*Copyright by designer/architect.*

Bedroom
11'x 9'2"

Master Bedroom
19'x 13'4"

Balcony
14'x 8'

**Upper Level Floor Plan**

## Plan #361042

**Dimensions:** 47' W x 30' D
**Levels:** 2
**Square Footage:** 1,246
**Main Level Sq. Ft.:** 918
**Upper Level Sq. Ft.:** 328
**Bedrooms:** 1
**Bathrooms:** 1
**Foundation:** Crawl space
**Material List Available:** No
**Price Category:** B

*Images provided by designer/architect.*

**CAD FILE AVAILABLE**

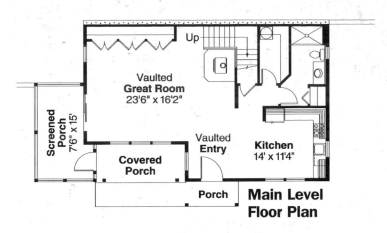

**Main Level Floor Plan**

- Up
- Vaulted **Great Room** 23'6" x 16'2"
- Screened Porch 7'6" x 15'
- Vaulted Entry
- Kitchen 14' x 11'4"
- Covered Porch
- Porch

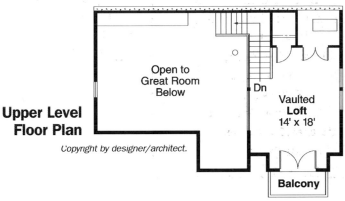

**Upper Level Floor Plan**

- Open to Great Room Below
- Dn
- Vaulted **Loft** 14' x 18'
- Balcony

*Copyright by designer/architect.*

---

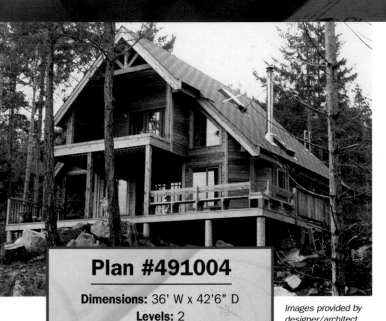

## Plan #491004

**Dimensions:** 36' W x 42'6" D
**Levels:** 2
**Square Footage:** 1,154
**Main Level Sq. Ft.:** 672
**Upper Level Sq. Ft.:** 482
**Bedrooms:** 2
**Bathrooms:** 2
**Foundation:** Crawl space
**Material List Available:** Yes
**Price Category:** B

*Images provided by designer/architect.*

Front View

**Main Level Floor Plan**

36'-0"
42'-6"

- WINDOW SEAT
- 13' VAULTED CLG.
- LIV./DIN. 23' x 9'4" & 14'6"
- WOOD STOVE
- 8'10" x 8'
- GUEST 10'8" x 9'

*Copyright by designer/architect.*

**Upper Level Floor Plan**

- STUDIO 15'4" x 11'8" 13' VAULTED CLG.
- OPEN
- BED RM. 15' x 9' 10' VAULTED CLG.

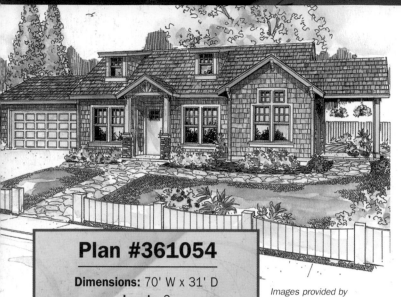

# Plan #361054

**Dimensions:** 70' W x 31' D

**Levels:** 2

**Square Footage:** 1,363

**Main Level Sq. Ft.:** 1,110

**Upper Level Sq. Ft.:** 253

**Bedrooms:** 2

**Bathrooms:** 1

**Foundation:** Crawl space

**Material List Available:** No

**Price Category:** B

*Images provided by designer/architect.*

**CAD FILE AVAILABLE**

**CAD**

**Bonus Area Floor Plan**

*Copyright by designer/architect.*

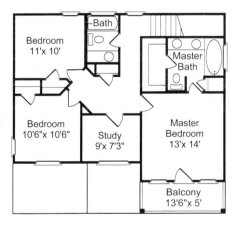

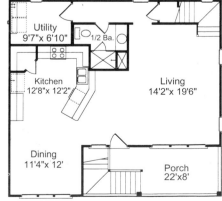

# Plan #111041

**Dimensions:** 34' W x 32' D

**Levels:** 2

**Square Footage:** 1,743

**Main Level Sq. Ft.:** 912

**Upper Level Sq. Ft.:** 831

**Bedrooms:** 3

**Bathrooms:** 3

**Foundation:** Pier

**Materials List Available:** No

**Price Category:** C

*Images provided by designer/architect.*

**Upper Level Floor Plan**

**Main Level Floor Plan**

*Copyright by designer/architect.*

## Plan #131058

**Dimensions:** 53' W x 36' D
**Levels:** 1.5
**Square Footage:** 1,648
**Main Level Sq. Ft.:** 1,191
**Upper Level Sq. Ft.:** 457
**Bedrooms:** 3
**Bathrooms:** 2
**Foundation:** Walkout basement
**Material List Available:** Yes
**Price Category:** D

This rustic multilevel cabin offers an impressive wraparound deck.

**Features:**

- **Great Room:** The vaulted ceiling in this gathering area gives the space an open and airy feeling. The fireplace, flanked by sliding glass doors, adds a focal point to the room.

- **Kitchen:** This massive country kitchen, with its peninsula and fireplace, adds a cozy feeling to the home. The snack bar adds additional seating space for overflow from the main table.

- **Master Bedroom:** Located on the main level for convenience, this bedroom has access to the main bathroom. The large closet is a welcome feature.

- **Upper Level:** This area holds two bedrooms and the second full bathroom. The skylight above the stairwell floods the area with natural light.

Great Room

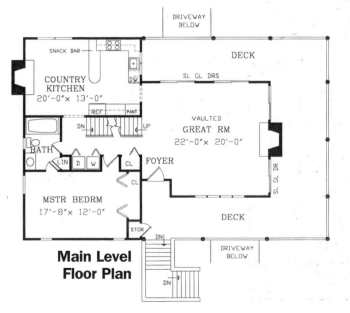

**Main Level Floor Plan**

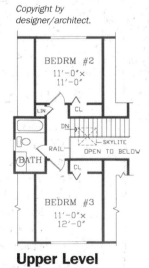

**Upper Level Floor Plan**

*Images provided by designer/architect.*

## Plan #361032

**Dimensions:** 50' W x 40' D

**Levels:** 2

**Square Footage:** 2,017

**Main Level Sq. Ft.:** 1,295

**Upper Level Sq. Ft:** 722

**Bedrooms:** 3

**Bathrooms:** 2

**Foundation:** Crawl space or basement

**Materials List Available:** No

**Price Category:** D

The two-level deck on this house gives you plenty of space to enjoy beautiful weather.

**Features:**

• Living Room: Take your coat off and relax in this living room in front of the cozy fireplace. The ceiling slopes up to the second level, giving the gathering area an airy feeling.

• Kitchen: This peninsula kitchen features a raised bar that's open into the dining room. The built-in pantry is a much-welcome bonus.

• Master Suite: Located on the upper level for privacy, this retreat boasts a large sleeping area with sliding glass doors to the upper deck. The master bathroom will pamper you with a walk-in closet, soaking tub and a stall shower.

• Secondary Bedrooms: Two main floor bedrooms feature a view of the backyard and are in close proximity to the laundry room.

## Main Level Floor Plan

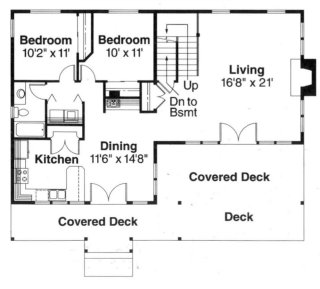

## Upper Level Floor Plan

*Copyright by designer/architect.*

## Plan #271048

**Dimensions:** 60' W x 32'6" D
**Levels:** 2
**Square Footage:** 2,143
**Main Level Sq. Ft.:** 1,200
**Upper Level Sq. Ft.:** 943
**Bedrooms:** 4
**Bathrooms:** 3
**Foundation:** Crawl space, basement
**Materials List Available:** No
**Price Category:** D

With a nod to historical architecture, this authentic Cape Cod home boasts a traditional exterior with an updated floor plan.

**Features:**

- Living Room: This spacious area is warmed by an optional fireplace and merges with the dining room.

- Kitchen: Efficient and sunny, this walk-through kitchen handles almost any task with aplomb.

- Family Room: The home's second optional fireplace can be found here, along with a smart log-storage bin that can be loaded from the garage. Sliding-glass-door access to a backyard patio is a bonus.

- Guest Bedroom: Private access to a bath and plenty of room to relax make this bedroom a winner.

- Master Suite: Amenities abound in the master bedroom, including two closets, a separated dressing spot, and a dormer as a sitting area.

*Images provided by designer/architect.*

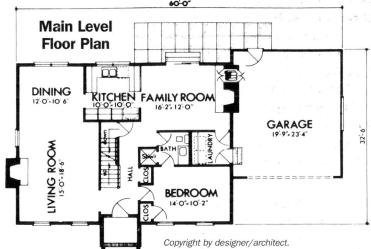

*Copyright by designer/architect.*

# Plan #151750

**Dimensions:** 67'6" W x 43' D

**Levels:** 1.5

**Square Footage:** 2,482

**Main Level Sq. Ft.:** 1,504

**Upper Level Sq. Ft:** 978

**Bedrooms:** 5

**Bathrooms:** 3

**Foundation:** Crawl space

**CompleteCost List Available:** Yes

**Price Category:** E

*Images provided by designer/architect.*

Abe Lincoln grew up in a log home before he became president; maybe your children, one day, can say the same.

**Features:**

- **Great Room:** This gathering room, with its stone fireplace, greets you as you enter the home. The dining room is close by for smooth flow between both rooms.

- **Kitchen:** This centrally located kitchen makes life in the house flow smoothly. On one side is the laundry room and the other is the dining room.

- **Bedrooms:** Three bedrooms are located on the main level. Two secondary bedrooms share a common bathroom. The master suite has a private master bath with an oversize tub.

- **Upper Level:** Bedrooms 4 and 5 occupy this area and share a full bathroom. Two dormers add additional living space to both bedrooms.

## Main Level Floor Plan

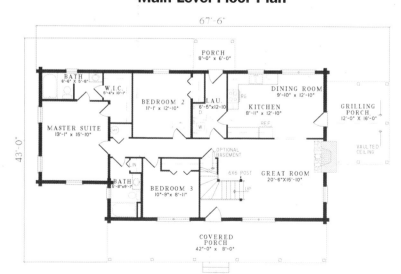

## Upper Level Floor Plan

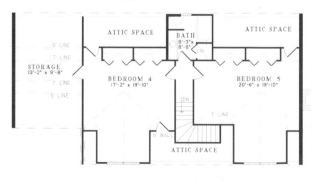

*Copyright by designer/architect.*

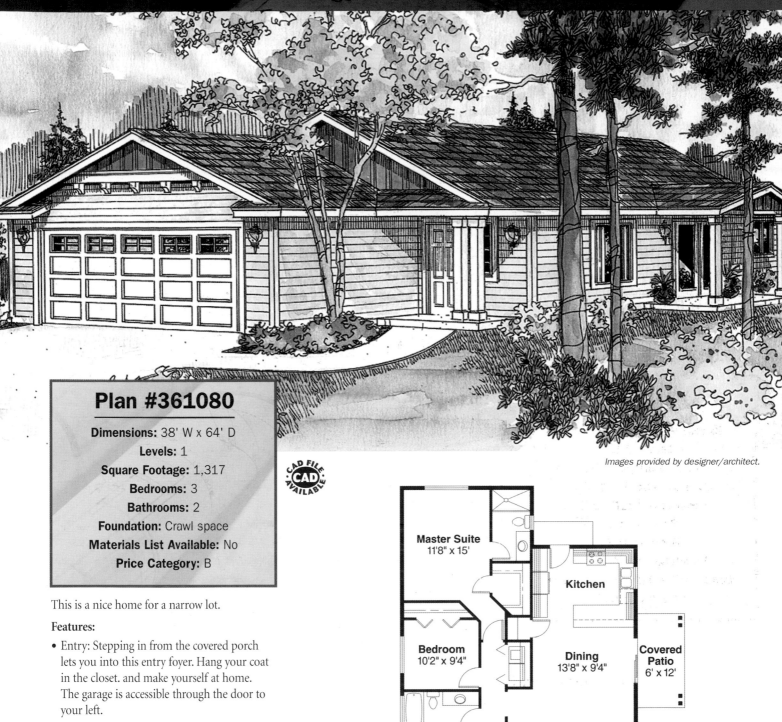

## Plan #361080

**Dimensions:** 38' W x 64' D

**Levels:** 1

**Square Footage:** 1,317

**Bedrooms:** 3

**Bathrooms:** 2

**Foundation:** Crawl space

**Materials List Available:** No

**Price Category:** B

CAD FILE AVAILABLE

*Images provided by designer/architect.*

This is a nice home for a narrow lot.

**Features:**

- Entry: Stepping in from the covered porch lets you into this entry foyer. Hang your coat in the closet. and make yourself at home. The garage is accessible through the door to your left.

- Living Room: The main gathering area of the home, this living room has plenty of wall space to accommodate any furniture layout. Open to the dining room and kitchen, this area has an airy feeling.

- Kitchen: This well-designed, efficiently sized kitchen has plenty of cabinets and counter space. The raised bar will add more seating to the dining room.

- Master Suite: Featuring an adequately sized sleeping area and a generous walk-in closet, this space is ready for you to decorate. The master bath boasts an oversize stall shower.

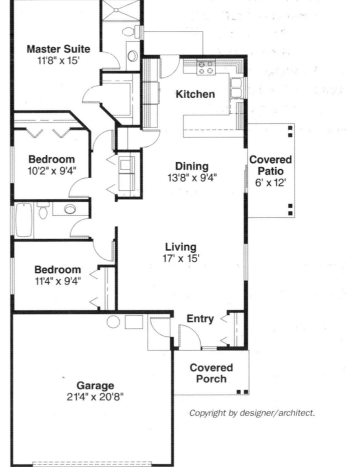

Master Suite
11'8" x 15'

Kitchen

Bedroom
10'2" x 9'4"

Dining
13'8" x 9'4"

Covered Patio
6' x 12'

Bedroom
11'4" x 9'4"

Living
17' x 15'

Entry

Garage
21'4" x 20'8"

Covered Porch

*Copyright by designer/architect.*

## Main Level Floor Plan

17'-8" X 13'-8"
5,30 X 4,10

15'-8" X 11'-0"
4,70 X 3,30

10'-8" X 11'-8"
3,20 X 3,50

15'-8" X 15'-4"
4,70 X 4,60

31'-4"
9,4 m

38'-0"
11,4 m

# Plan #181630

**Dimensions:** 38' W x 31'4" D
**Levels:** 2
**Square Footage:** 2,098
**Main Level Sq. Ft.:** 1,092
**Upper Level Sq. Ft.:** 1,006
**Bedrooms:** 3
**Bathrooms:** 1½
**Foundation:** Basement
**Material List Available:** Yes
**Price Category:** D

*Images provided by designer/architect.*

## Upper Level Floor Plan

13'-8"/11'-8" X 21'-8"
4,10/3,50 X 6,50

11'-8" X 10'-0"
3,50 X 3,00

11'-8" X 12'-0"
3,50 X 3,60

*Copyright by designer/architect.*

---

12'-0" X 14'-4"
3,60 X 4,30

12'-0" X 26'-8"
3,60 X 8,00

12'-0" X 12'-4"
3,60 X 3,70

12'-0" X 15'-0"
3,60 X 4,50

28'-0"
8,4 m

## Main Level Floor Plan

40'-0"
12 m

# Plan #181558

**Dimensions:** 40' W x 28' D
**Levels:** 2
**Square Footage:** 2,460
**Main Level Sq. Ft.:** 1,241
**Upper Level Sq. Ft.:** 1,219
**Bedrooms:** 4
**Bathrooms:** 1
**Foundation:** Basement
**Material List Available:** Yes
**Price Category:** E

*Images provided by designer/architect.*

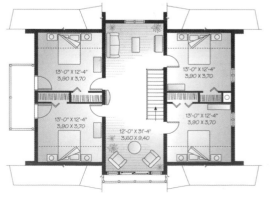

## Upper Level Floor Plan

13'-0" X 12'-4"
3,90 X 3,70

13'-0" X 12'-4"
3,90 X 3,70

13'-0" X 12'-4"
3,90 X 3,70

12'-0" X 31'-4"
3,60 X 9,40

13'-0" X 12'-4"
3,90 X 3,70

*Copyright by designer/architect.*

## Plan #101015

**Dimensions:** 28' W x 46' D
**Levels:** 2
**Square Footage:** 1,647
**Main Level Sq. Ft.:** 1,288
**Upper Level Sq. Ft.:** 359
**Bedrooms:** 2
**Bathrooms:** 1
**Foundation:** Slab
**Materials List Available:** No
**Price Category:** C

This comfortable vacation retreat has handsome board-and-batten siding with stone accents..

**CAD FILE AVAILABLE**

**Features:**

• Ceiling Height: 20 ft. unless otherwise noted.

• Front Porch: This delightful front porch is perfect for spending relaxing vacation time in an old-fashioned rocker or porch swing.

• Great Room: From the porch you'll enter this enormous great room, where the whole family will enjoy spending time together under its 20-ft. vaulted ceiling.

• Kitchen: Within the great room is this open kitchen. An island provides plenty of food-preparation space, and there's a breakfast bar for casual vacation meals. The large pantry area provides space for a stacked washer and dryer.

• Bath: Also located downstairs is a compartmented bath with a 2-ft.-8-in. door that allows wheelchair access.

• Loft: Upstairs is an enormous loft with an 11-ft. ceiling. Use it to augment the two downstairs bedrooms or for recreation space.

### Main Level Floor Plan

### Upper Level Floor Plan

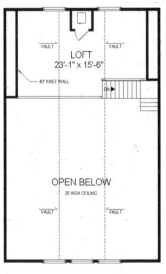

## Plan #401019

**Dimensions:** 34' W x 32' D
**Levels:** 1½
**Square Footage:** 1,256
**Main Level Sq. Ft.:** 898
**Upper Level Sq. Ft.:** 358
**Bedrooms:** 3
**Bathrooms:** 1½
**Foundation:** Crawl space
**Materials List Available:** Yes
**Price Category:** B

A surrounding sun deck and expansive window wall capitalize on vacation-home views in this design. The full-height windows flood the living and dining rooms with abundant natural light and bring attention to the high vaulted ceilings.

**Features:**

- **Living Room:** A woodstove in this room warms cold winter nights.

- **Kitchen:** This efficient U-shaped kitchen has ample counter and cupboard space. Behind it is a laundry room and rear entrance.

- **Master Bedroom:** Located on the first floor, this main bedroom has a large wall closet.

- **Bedrooms:** Two family bedrooms are on the second floor and have use of a half-bath.

### Main Level Floor Plan

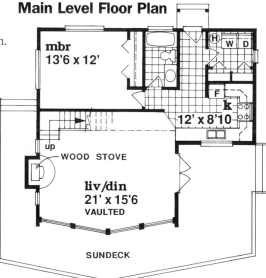

*Copyright by designer/architect.*

### Upper Level Floor Plan

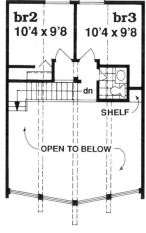

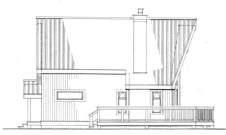

Left Side Elevation

Rear Elevation

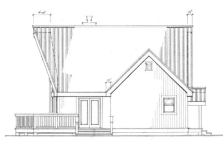

Right Side Elevation

## Main Level Floor Plan

SUNDECK  
GREENHOUSE WINDOW

BR3  
9' x 10'

BR2  
9' x 10'2"

KIT.  
10' x 10'4"

SKYLIGHTS

DIN. RM.  
11'6" x 8'8"  
16'11" VAULTED CLG.

FOYER  
16'11" VAULTED CLG.

LIV. RM.  
13'6" x 12'4"  
16'11" VAULTED CLG.

DN

UP

COVERED PORCH

28'-0"

46'-0"

*Images provided by designer/architect.*

## Plan #491003

**Dimensions:** 46' W x 28' D

**Levels:** 2

**Square Footage:** 1,235

**Main Level Sq. Ft.:** 893

**Upper Level Sq. Ft.:** 342

**Bedrooms:** 3

**Bathrooms:** 2

**Foundation:** Crawl space

**Material List Available:** Yes

**Price Category:** B

### Upper Level Floor Plan

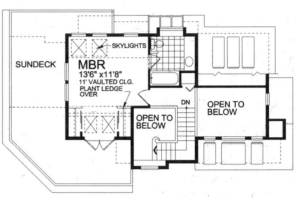

SUNDECK

SKYLIGHTS

MBR  
13'6" x11'8"  
11' VAULTED CLG.  
PLANT LEDGE  
OVER

OPEN TO BELOW

DN

OPEN TO BELOW

*Copyright by designer/architect.*

---

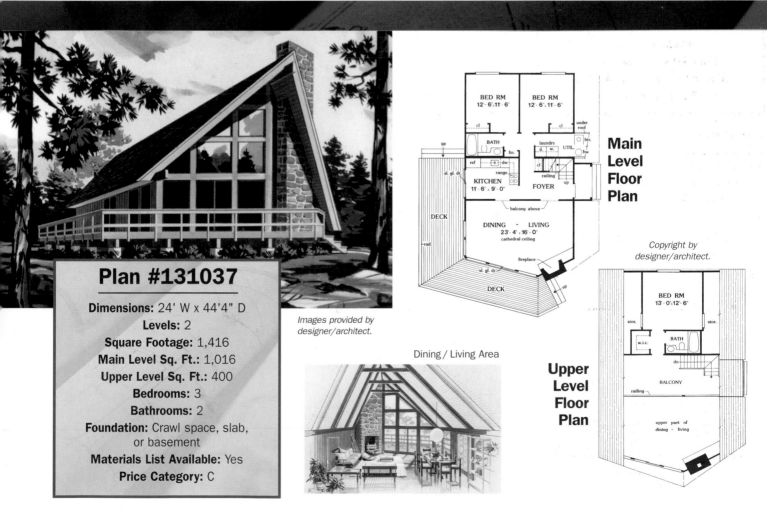

## Plan #131037

**Dimensions:** 24' W x 44'4" D

**Levels:** 2

**Square Footage:** 1,416

**Main Level Sq. Ft.:** 1,016

**Upper Level Sq. Ft.:** 400

**Bedrooms:** 3

**Bathrooms:** 2

**Foundation:** Crawl space, slab, or basement

**Materials List Available:** Yes

**Price Category:** C

*Images provided by designer/architect.*

### Main Level Floor Plan

BED RM  
12'-6":11'-6"

BED RM  
12'-6":11'-6"

under roof

up

BATH

lin.

laundry

UTIL

htr.

hw

ref

s

dw

railing

cl

d

w

KITCHEN  
11'-6" x 9'-0"

range

FOYER

up

DECK

rail

balcony above

DINING ~ LIVING  
23'-4" x 16'-0"  
cathedral ceiling

fireplace

sl. gl. dr.

up

DECK

*Copyright by designer/architect.*

### Dining / Living Area

### Upper Level Floor Plan

BED RM  
13'-0":12'-6"

stor.

stor.

w.i.c.

BATH

dn

BALCONY

railing

upper part of dining ~ living

*Images provided by designer/architect.*

## Plan #151760

**Dimensions:** 48' W x 34' D
**Levels:** 2
**Square Footage:** 2,296
**Main Level Sq. Ft.:** 1,684
**Upper Level Sq. Ft:** 612
**Bedrooms:** 3
**Bathrooms:** 2½
**Foundation:** Crawl space
**CompleteCost List Available:** Yes
**Price Category:** E

This rustic log home features an 8-ft.-deep wraparound porch, which is perfect for enjoying cool fall evenings.

**Features:**

- Great Room: This gathering area features a vaulted ceiling and a handcrafted staircase leading to the upper level. The stone fireplace adds warmth and atmosphere to the area.

- Kitchen: A few steps away from the great room is this L-shaped kitchen, which is open to the dining room. The laundry area is close by, with the washer and dryer nicely tucked into a closet.

- Master Suite: This main-level master suite has a large walk-in closet and has plenty of wall space for multiple furniture plans. The private master bath is an added bonus.

- Secondary Bedrooms: These two additional bedrooms are located upstairs and have adequate closet space. The second full bathroom, which they share, boasts a contemporary skylight and a full linen closet.

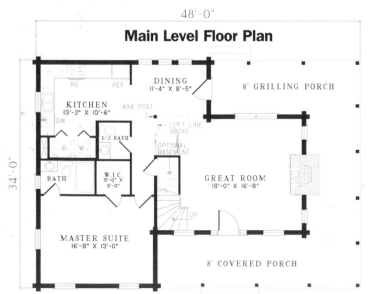

**Main Level Floor Plan**

48'-0"

34'-0"

RG  REF
DINING 11'-4" X 8'-5"
8' GRILLING PORCH
KITCHEN 13'-2" X 10'-6"
6x6 POST
DW
1/2 BATH
LOFT LINE ABOVE
OPTIONAL BASEMENT
D  W
BATH
W.I.C. 5'-0" X 5'-0"
GREAT ROOM 18'-0" X 16'-8"
UP
MASTER SUITE 16'-8" X 13'-0"
8' COVERED PORCH

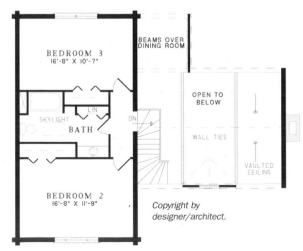

**Upper Level Floor Plan**

BEDROOM 3 16'-8" X 10'-7"
BEAMS OVER DINING ROOM
OPEN TO BELOW
SKYLIGHT
LIN
BATH
DN
WALL TIES
VAULTED CEILING
BEDROOM 2 16'-8" X 11'-9"

*Copyright by designer/architect.*

# Plan #491008

**Dimensions:** 36' W x 50'6" D
**Levels:** 2
**Square Footage:** 1,644
**Main Level Sq. Ft.:** 955
**Upper Level Sq. Ft.:** 689
**Bedrooms:** 2
**Bathrooms:** 2
**Foundation:** Crawl space
**Materials List Available:** Yes
**Price Category:** C

This sweet cabin-style home has everything you want and need to relax in a cozy retreat.

**Features:**

• Outdoor Space: The wraparound porch welcomes neighbors for a spell of calm conversation or quiet stargazing.

• Great Room: Warmed by a romantic wood stove and with half of the room sunlit and spanning both stories, this great room is sure to enchant you and your guests.

• Kitchen: An efficient space, this kitchen has enough workspace and storage to keep even the expert chef happy. Warm, inviting scents will drift over the breakfast bar and fill the home.

• Second Floor: This is a space that is entirely your own. The master bedroom sits away from the din of daily life so you have peace and quiet, day or night. A full bathroom and a studio, to be molded to your needs, means having everything you need within arm's reach.

## Main Level Floor Plan

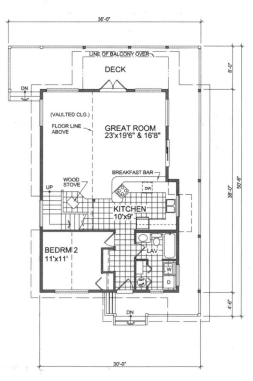

## Upper Level Floor Plan

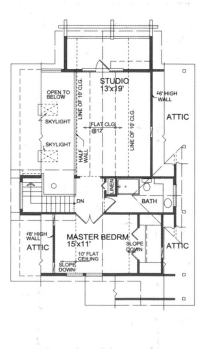

## Plan #151757

**Dimensions:** 54' W x 53' D
**Levels:** 2
**Square Footage:** 2,206
**Main Level Sq. Ft.:** 1,576
**Upper Level Sq. Ft:** 630
**Bedrooms:** 3
**Bathrooms:** 2½
**Foundation:** Crawl space
**CompleteCost List Available:** Yes
**Price Category:** E

Simplify your life with this magnificent log home.

*Images provided by designer/architect.*

**Features:**

- **Great Room:** Family and friends will naturally gather in this two-story room, with its dramatic wall of windows. The stone fireplace is the focal point of the space.

- **Kitchen:** This efficiently designed island kitchen boasts an abundance of cabinets and counter space. The built-in pantry is an added bonus.

- **Master Suite:** Located on the main level for privacy and convenience, this master suite features a French door leading to the rear deck. The master bath will pamper you with dual sinks and a whirlpool bath.

- **Upper Level:** A stairway up from the great room leads to this level, which has two bedrooms and the second full bathroom. There is also attic access from this level.

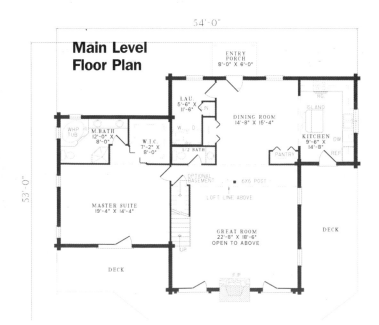

*Copyright by designer/architect.*

## Plan #451063

**Dimensions:** 40' W x 40' D
**Levels:** 2
**Square Footage:** 2,368
**Main Level Sq. Ft.:** 1,600
**Upper Level Sq. Ft:** 768
**Bedrooms:** 3
**Bathrooms:** 2½
**Foundation:** Slab or walkout
**Materials List Available:** No
**Price Category:** E

A beautiful log home, like this one, would be perfect for a large wooded lot or in any neighborhood.

**CAD FILE AVAILABLE**

**Features:**

- Great Room: French doors make the passage from the front deck into this gathering area seamless. The two-story-high ceiling gives this space an open and airy feeling.

- Kitchen: This efficiently designed food-preparation area waits for the family chef to make a culinary masterpiece. The raised bar adds a welcomed seating area to the breakfast nook.

- Master Suite: This main-level retreat features a magnificent sleeping area and a large walk-in closet. The master bath boasts a compartmentalized lavatory, stall shower, and whirlpool tub.

- Secondary Bedrooms: Two bedrooms are located on the upper level; each has a walk-in closet, and the second full bathroom is close by.

- Lower Level: This open space can be finished as you like, or use it for storage space.

### Main Level Floor Plan

### Upper Level Floor Plan

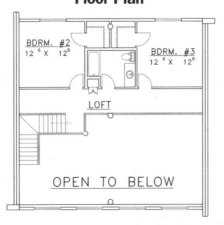

### Garage Level Floor Plan

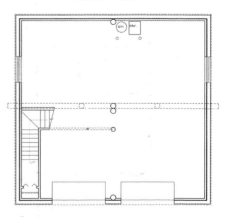

## Plan #491005

**Dimensions:** 36' W x 44'6" D

**Levels:** 2

**Square Footage:** 1,333

**Main Level Sq. Ft.:** 768

**Upper Level Sq. Ft.:** 565

**Bedrooms:** 2

**Bathrooms:** 2

**Foundation:** Crawl space

**Material List Available:** Yes

**Price Category:** B

### Main Level Floor Plan

6'-0"  24'-0"  6'-0"

8'-0"

16' VAULTED CLG.

GREAT ROOM
23' x 10'2" x& 16'6"

32'-0"

WOOD STOVE

KIT
8'6" x 6'

GUEST
10'8' x 11'

4'-6"

W D

*Images provided by designer/architect.*

### Upper Level Floor Plan

RAILING

OPEN

STUDIO
15'4' x13'4'
13' VAULTED CLG.

DN

BED RM.
15' x 11'
10' VAULTED CLG.

*Copyright by designer/architect.*

Rear View

---

## Plan #131008

**Dimensions:** 45'4" W x 36'4" D

**Levels:** 1

**Square Footage:** 1,299

**Bedrooms:** 3

**Bathrooms:** 2

**Foundation:** Crawl space, basement

**Materials List Available:** Yes

**Price Category:** C

*Images provided by designer/architect.*

DECK

MUD RM
laundry
w. d.

DINING

cathedral ceiling

KITCHEN
12'-10'x 8'-6'

bench

sl. gl. dr.

shr.
s.
dw

BATH

MASTER
BED RM
14'-4' x 12'-10'

DECK

sl. gl. dr.

LIVING RM
24' x 15'

ref.

BATH

high beam

htr.

HALL

lin.

sl. gl. dr.

heat-circulating
fireplace

hw

FOYER

BED RM
11' x 9'

BED RM
12'-4' x 10'-6'

DECK

*Copyright by designer/architect.*

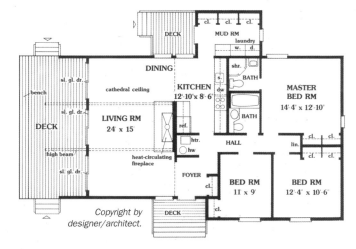

Rear View

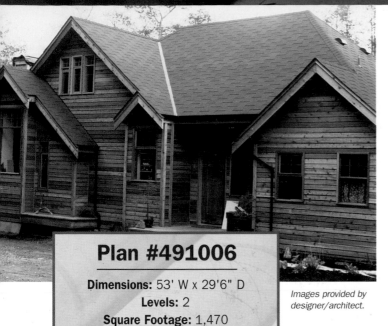

## Main Level Floor Plan

SUNDECK

DINING
14' x 12'
16'11" VAULTED CLG.

BR.
11' x 12'4"
10' VAULTED CLG.

LIVING
16' x 15'
16'11" VAULTED CLG.

FOYER

SEAT

SITTING

COVERED PORCH

LDR

10'-0"

29'-6"

53'-0"

4'-0"

*Images provided by designer/architect.*

## Plan #491006

**Dimensions:** 53' W x 29'6" D

**Levels:** 2

**Square Footage:** 1,470

**Main Level Sq. Ft.:** 1,130

**Upper Level Sq. Ft.:** 340

**Bedrooms:** 2

**Bathrooms:** 2

**Foundation:** Crawl space

**Material List Available:** Yes

**Price Category:** B

Front View

BALCONY

BR.
12'2" x 10'
10' VAULTED CLG.

LOFT
VAULTED

OPEN TO BELOW

RAILING

RAILING

PLANT LEDGE

OPEN

UP

DN

## Upper Level Floor Plan

*Copyright by designer/architect.*

---

50'-0"

FRENCH DOORS

KITCHEN
15'-4" X 15'-6"

PANTRY · LAU CHUTE

DUMB WAITER

W. LAU.
8'-0" X 5'-10"

GREAT RM.
14'-4" X 27'-0"

BATH
11'-6" X 6'-0"

4" STEP DOWN

ISLAND / BAR

DESK

MW OVEN

SUN RM.
6'-10" X 27'-0"

4" STEP DOWN

BEDROOM 2
11'-8" X 8'-0"

BEDROOM 3
11'-6" X 11'-2"

28'-0"

8'-0" DECK

## Main Level Floor Plan

*Images provided by designer/architect.*

## Plan #151299

**Dimensions:** 50' W x 28' D

**Levels:** 2

**Square Footage:** 2,143

**Main Level Sq. Ft.:** 1,400

**Upper Level Sq. Ft.:** 743

**Bedrooms:** 3

**Bathrooms:** 2

**Foundation:** Crawl space or slab

**CompleteCost List Available:** Yes

**Price Category:** D

CAD FILE AVAILABLE
CAD

Rear View

DUMB WAITER

REF

GLASS SHWR

MASTER BATH
10'-2" X 6'-6"

WHP TUB

KNEE SPACE

SEAT

LIN

OPEN TO GREAT RM.

MASTER SUITE
27'-10" X 13'-4"

SKYLIGHTS

RAIL

FRENCH DOOR

LAMINATED BEAMS

SKYLIGHTS

FIREPLACE

BALCONY DECK
8'-0" X 28'-0"

OFFICE
7'-8" X 6'-0"

## Upper Level Floor Plan

*Copyright by designer/architect.*

# Plan #151755

**Dimensions:** 50' W x 38' D
**Levels:** 2
**Square Footage:** 2,389
**Main Level Sq. Ft.:** 1,486
**Upper Level Sq. Ft:** 903
**Bedrooms:** 3
**Bathrooms:** 2
**Foundation:** Crawl space
**CompleteCost List Available:** Yes
**Price Category:** E

*Images provided by designer/architect.*

Windows and French doors enhance this beautiful log home, while three of its sides are wrapped with sun decks.

**Features:**

- Kitchen: This corner kitchen is open to the dining room and the great room and will function perfectly for family meals or a large get-together.

- Master Suite: Located on the main level for privacy and convenience, this master suite features a French door leading onto the rear deck and a walk-in closet. The master bath boasts dual sinks and a whirlpool bath.

- Loft: This will be a perfect place to relax with a book and with a view down into the great room; you are never too far from the family.

- Secondary Bedrooms: Two bedrooms are located on the upper level and share the second full bathroom. Bedroom 3 boasts a walk-in closet and its own access to the bathroom.

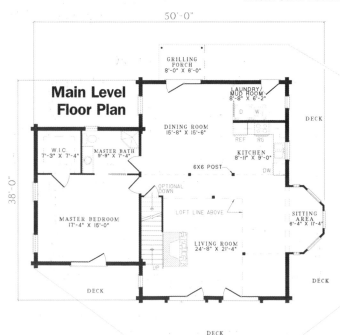

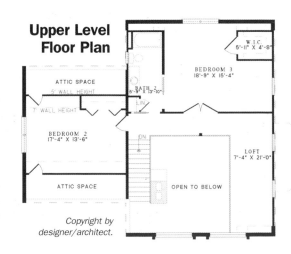

*Copyright by designer/architect.*

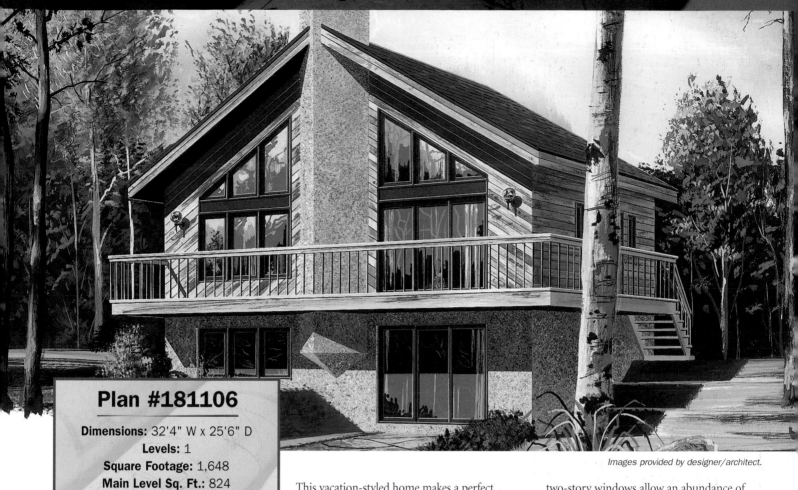

## Plan #181106

**Dimensions:** 32'4" W x 25'6" D
**Levels:** 1
**Square Footage:** 1,648
**Main Level Sq. Ft.:** 824
**Lower Level Sq. Ft.:** 824
**Bedrooms:** 3
**Bathrooms:** 2
**Foundation:** Basement or walkout
**Materials List Available:** Yes
**Price Category:** C

This vacation-styled home makes a perfect year-round residence, giving the feeling of the great outdoors.

**Features:**

- **Porch:** This porch occupies the front and one side of the home, providing plenty of room to relax with family and friends.
- **Family Room:** The cathedral ceiling in this family room extends into the kitchen. The two-story windows allow an abundance of light into this area.
- **Kitchen:** This L-shaped kitchen features an eating area and a triple sliding glass door onto the front deck. The fireplace, which it shares with the family room, will warm this area on cold mornings.
- **Lower Level:** Two bedrooms and a den with a woodstove highlight this area. The full bathroom has room for the washer and dryer.

## Lower Level Floor Plan

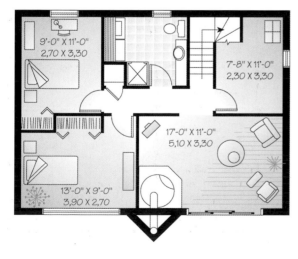

9'-0" X 11'-0"
2,70 X 3,30

7'-8" X 11'-0"
2,30 X 3,30

17'-0" X 11'-0"
5,10 X 3,30

13'-0" X 9'-0"
3,90 X 2,70

## Main Level Floor Plan

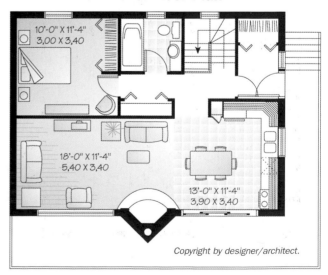

10'-0" X 11'-4"
3,00 X 3,40

18'-0" X 11'-4"
5,40 X 3,40

13'-0" X 11'-4"
3,90 X 3,40

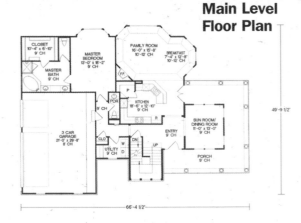

## Main Level Floor Plan

## Plan #121160

**Dimensions:** 66'4" W x 49'9" D

**Levels:** 1.5

**Square Footage:** 2,188

**Main Level Sq. Ft.:** 1,531

**Upper Level Sq. Ft.:** 657

**Bedrooms:** 3

**Bathrooms:** 2½

**Foundation:** Slab; basement for fee

**Materials List Available:** Yes

**Price Category:** D

*Images provided by designer/architect.*

## Upper Level Floor Plan

Front View

*Copyright by designer/architect.*

## Plan #111040

**Dimensions:** 37' W x 52' D

**Levels:** 2

**Square Footage:** 1,650

**Main Level Sq. Ft.:** 1,122

**Upper Level Sq. Ft.:** 528

**Bedrooms:** 4

**Bathrooms:** 2

**Foundation:** Pier

**Materials List Available:** No

**Price Category:** C

*Images provided by designer/architect.*

## Main Level Floor Plan

## Upper Level Floor Plan

*Copyright by designer/architect.*

## Upper Level Floor Plan

*Copyright by designer/architect.*

BEDROOM 2
9'-10" X 14'-0"

BEDROOM 3
9'-10" X 14'-0"

BATH

LOFT
26'-0" X 8'-8"

OPEN TO BELOW

## Main Level Floor Plan

DECK
26'-6" X 8'-0"

MASTER SUITE
15'-8" X 14'-6"

MASTER BATH

KITCHEN
12'-4" X 11'-0"

DINING
12'-0" X 12'-0"

GREAT ROOM
26'-0" X 20'-0"

MEDIA CENTER

8' DECK

**CAD FILE AVAILABLE**

*Images provided by designer/architect.*

Rear View

## Plan #151316

**Dimensions:** 47' W x 63' D

**Levels:** 2

**Square Footage:** 2,054

**Main Level Sq. Ft.:** 1,413

**Upper Level Sq. Ft.:** 641

**Bedrooms:** 3

**Bathrooms:** 2½

**Foundation:** Crawl space, slab, basement or walkout

**CompleteCost List Available:** Yes

**Price Category:** D

---

## Main Level Floor Plan

STOR

BEDRM #2
12' 0" X 10'-0"

BEDRM #1
12'-0" X 12'-4"

STOR

CL

PORCH
9'-2" X 13'-6"

BATH

SHWR

KITCHEN
7'-0" X 10'-0"

SCREENED PORCH

BBQ

STOR

VAULTED
GREAT RM
24'-4" X 14'-0"

UP

SL GL DRS

OPT DECK

*Images provided by designer/architect.*

## Upper Level Floor Plan

*Copyright by designer/architect*

BEDRM #3
10'-0" X 16'-0"

WOOD DECK

BATH

WICL

BALC/LOFT
10'-0" X 10'-6"

DN

RAIL

UPPER GREAT RM

## Plan #131056

**Dimensions:** 40' W x 54' D

**Levels:** 1.5

**Square Footage:** 1,396

**Main Level Sq. Ft.:** 964

**Upper Level Sq. Ft.:** 432

**Bedrooms:** 3

**Bathrooms:** 2

**Foundation:** Slab or basement

**Materials List Available:** Yes

**Price Category:** C

Rear View

*Images provided by designer/architect.*

## Plan #151758

**Dimensions:** 40' W x 36' D
**Levels:** 1.5
**Square Footage:** 1,725
**Main Level Sq. Ft.:** 1,120
**Upper Level Sq. Ft:** 605
**Bedrooms:** 3
**Bathrooms:** 2
**Foundation:** Crawl space
**CompleteCost List Available:** Yes
**Price Category:** C

Here, you have found a traditional log home plan with a full covered porch and a simple yet refined floor plan.

**Features:**

- Living Room: As you enter the home from the covered porch, this gathering area welcomes you. Feel the heat coming from the fireplace as you shake off the cold.

- Kitchen: This peninsula kitchen is open to the dining room and the living room, giving the feeling of one open space. Step out the back door, and you can enjoy the great outdoors.

- Bedrooms: Two bedrooms are located on the main level and share the main bathroom, which is located close by. The hallway closet, which holds the washer and dryer, is just a few steps away.

- Upper Level: Up the L-shaped stairs brings you to the loft with an overview of the living room below. Bedroom 3 and the second full bathroom are also located on this level.

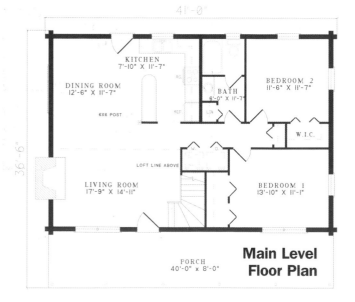

**Main Level Floor Plan**

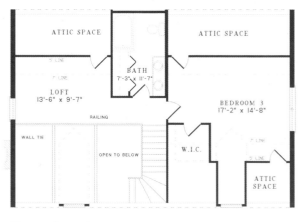

**Upper Level Floor Plan**

*Copyright by designer/architect.*

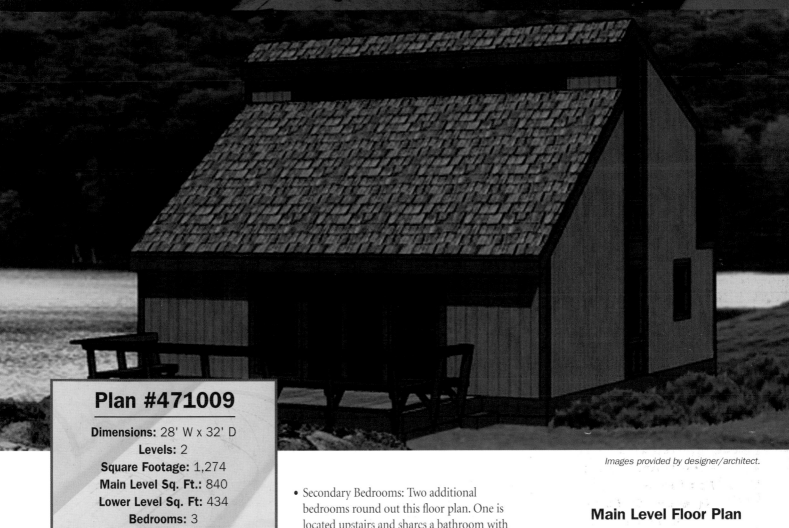

## Plan #471009

**Dimensions:** 28' W x 32' D
**Levels:** 2
**Square Footage:** 1,274
**Main Level Sq. Ft.:** 840
**Lower Level Sq. Ft:** 434
**Bedrooms:** 3
**Bathrooms:** 2
**Foundation:** Crawl space
**Materials List Available:** No
**Price Category:** B

*Images provided by designer/architect.*

This contemporary cabin has all the features you will need for a weekend getaway or a year-round residence.

**Features:**

- **Living Room:** This gathering area features a sloping ceiling up to the second story. The sliding glass doors open onto the rear deck.

- **Kitchen:** Conveniently located near the entry, this U-shaped kitchen has an abundance of cabinets and a counter, which is open to the dining room. Just a few steps away is the main-floor bathroom, to which the main level bedroom has access.

- **Master Suite:** Located on the second floor, this retreat boasts a private deck. The large walk-in closet and access to the shared bathroom make this area perfect.

- **Secondary Bedrooms:** Two additional bedrooms round out this floor plan. One is located upstairs and shares a bathroom with the master suite, while the other is on the main level.

### Main Level Floor Plan

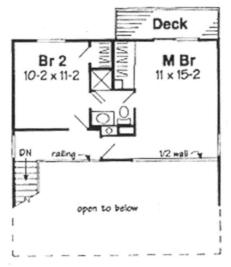

**Upper Level Floor Plan**

*Copyright by designer/architect.*

# Plan #451121

**Dimensions:** 85'8" W x 51' D
**Levels:** 2
**Square Footage:** 2,157
**Main Level Sq. Ft.:** 1,827
**Upper Level Sq. Ft:** 330
**Bedrooms:** 2
**Bathrooms:** 2
**Foundation:** Slab with insulated concrete forms
**Materials List Available:** No
**Price Category:** D

This rustic-looking home is perfect for empty nesters or a young family, with room for expansion when needed.

**CAD FILE AVAILABLE**

**Features:**

- **Great Room:** The foyer opens into this large two-story gathering area boasting an elegant fireplace. The wall of windows floods the area with natural light.

- **Master Suite:** Just off the foyer is this retreat, which displays desirable features such as sliding glass doors to the front deck and a romantic fireplace. The master bath includes dual vanities, a stall shower, and a compart-mentalized lavatory.

- **Guest Suite:** Also located on the main level, this area boasts a large closet and is in close proximity to the main full bathroom.

- **Loft:** Walk up the stairs into this quaint area with a view to the great room below. Put a couch in front of the large window, and enjoy sunlight warmth as you read your favorite book.

- **Garage:** Enjoy the space of this oversized three-car garage, which has one door to the front and another to the rear deck. A perfect place for parking the cars, there is even room for some "boy toys."

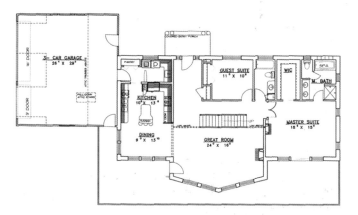

**Main Level Floor Plan**

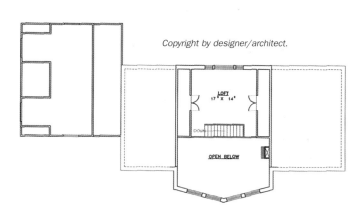

**Upper Level Floor Plan**

# Plan #321025

**Dimensions:** 28' W x 28' D

**Levels:** 1

**Square Footage:** 914

**Bedrooms:** 2

**Bathrooms:** 1

**Foundation:** Basement, walkout

**Materials List Available:** Yes

**Price Category:** A

This cute little home's great layout packs in an abundance of features.

**Features:**

- Living Room: The cozy fireplace in this open, welcoming room invites you to relax awhile.

- Dining Room: This area has a bay window and is open to the kitchen and the living room.

- Kitchen: This compact kitchen has everything you'll need, including a built-in pantry.

- Master Bedroom: Generously sized, with a large closet, this room has a private door into the common bathroom.

- Bedroom: This secondary bedroom can also be used as a home office.

*Images provided by designer/architect.*

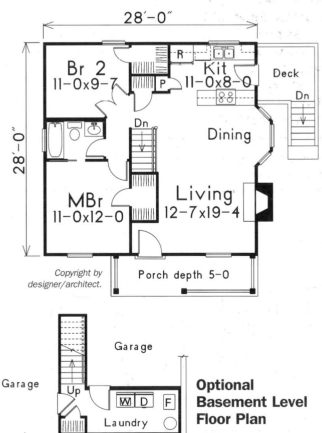

*Copyright by designer/architect.*

**Optional Basement Level Floor Plan**

# Plan #491007

**Dimensions:** 36' W x 50'6" D

**Levels:** 2

**Square Footage:** 2,414

**Main Level Sq. Ft.:** 864

**Upper Level Sq. Ft.:** 686

**Lower Level Sq. Ft.:** 864

**Bedrooms:** 3

**Bathrooms:** 1½

**Foundation:** Basement

**Material List Available:** Yes

**Price Category:** E

**Upper Level Floor Plan**

*Copyright by designer/architect.*

*Images provided by designer/architect.*

CAD FILE AVAILABLE — CAD

**Main Level Floor Plan**

Front View

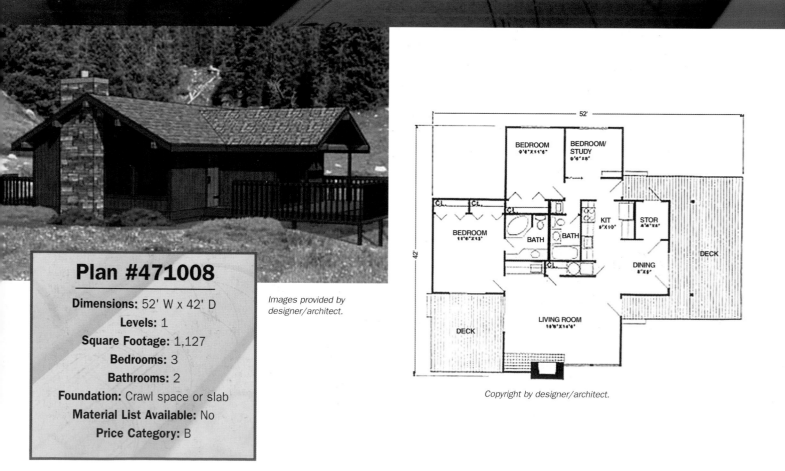

# Plan #471008

**Dimensions:** 52' W x 42' D

**Levels:** 1

**Square Footage:** 1,127

**Bedrooms:** 3

**Bathrooms:** 2

**Foundation:** Crawl space or slab

**Material List Available:** No

**Price Category:** B

*Images provided by designer/architect.*

*Copyright by designer/architect.*

# Plan #281002

**Dimensions:** 54' W x 33' D
**Levels:** 2
**Square Footage:** 1,859
**Main Level Sq. Ft.:** 959
**Second Level Sq. Ft.:** 900
**Bedrooms:** 3
**Bathrooms:** 2½
**Foundation:** Basement
**Materials List Available:** Yes
**Price Category:** D

This lovely three-bedroom home has the layout and amenities you need for comfortable living.

## Features:

- Ceiling Height: 8 ft. unless otherwise noted.
- Foyer: Guests will walk through the lovely and practical front porch into this attractive foyer, with its vaulted ceiling.

- Living/Dining Room: Family and friends will be drawn to the warmth of the cozy, convenient gas fireplace in this combination living/dining room.

- Master Suite: You'll enjoy retiring at the end of the day to this luxurious master suite. It has a private sitting area with built-in storage for your books and television. Relax in the bath under its skylight.

- Kitchen: At the center of the main floor you will find this kitchen, with its eating nook that takes full advantage of the view and is just the right size for family meals.

- Deck: This large deck is accessible from the master suite, eating nook, and living/dining room.

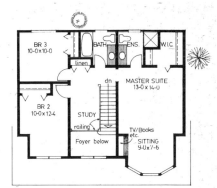

**Upper Level Floor Plan**

**Main Level Floor Plan**

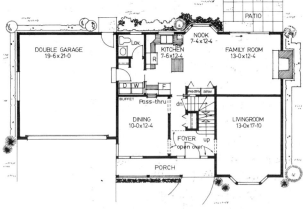

## Plan #281015

**Dimensions:** 32' W x 48' D
**Levels:** 2
**Square Footage:** 1,660
**Main Level Sq. Ft.:** 964
**Upper Level Sq. Ft.:** 696
**Bedrooms:** 4
**Bathrooms:** 2½
**Foundation:** Basement
**Materials List Available:** Yes
**Price Category:** C

You'll love the gracious features and amenities in this charming home, which is meant for a narrow lot.

**Features:**

- Foyer: This two-story foyer opens into the spacious living room.

- Living Room: The large bay window in this room makes a perfect setting for quiet times alone or entertaining guests.

- Dining Room: The open flow between this room and the living room adds to the airy feeling.

- Family Room: With a handsome fireplace and a door to the rear patio, this room will be the heart of your home.

- Kitchen: The U-shaped layout, pantry, and greenhouse window make this room a joy.

- Master Suite: The bay window, large walk-in closet, and private bath make this second-floor room a true retreat.

*Images provided by designer/architect.*

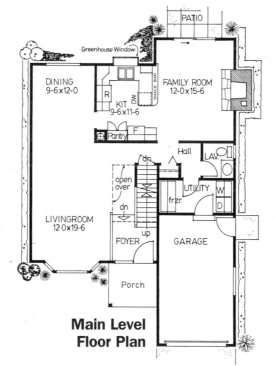

**Main Level
Floor Plan**

**Upper Level
Floor Plan**

*Copyright by
designer/architect.*

Rear
Elevation

Left Side Elevation

Right Side Elevation

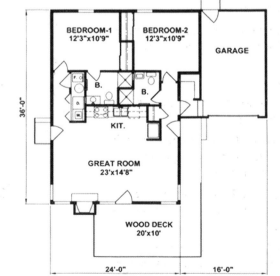

## Plan #471002

**Dimensions:** 38' W x 26' D

**Levels:** 1

**Square Footage:** 835

**Bedrooms:** 2

**Bathrooms:** 2

**Foundation:** Crawl space or slab

**Material List Available:** No

**Price Category:** A

*Images provided by designer/architect.*

*Copyright by designer/architect.*

## Plan #471003

**Dimensions:** 40' W x 36' D

**Levels:** 1

**Square Footage:** 920

**Bedrooms:** 2

**Bathrooms:** 2

**Foundation:** Crawl space

**Material List Available:** Yes

**Price Category:** A

*Images provided by designer/architect.*

*Copyright by designer/architect.*

## Plan #451065

**Dimensions:** 33' W x 52' D

**Levels:** 1

**Square Footage:** 1,811

**Main Level Sq. Ft.:** 1,232

**Lower Level Sq. Ft.:** 579

**Bedrooms:** 3

**Bathrooms:** 2½

**Foundation:** Walkout, insulated concrete form

**Material List Available:** No

**Price Category:** D

**Main Level Floor Plan**

Images provided by designer/architect.

**CAD FILE AVAILABLE**

**Garage Level Floor Plan**

Copyright by designer/architect.

## Plan #451105

**Dimensions:** 36' W x 56' D

**Levels:** 1

**Square Footage:** 2,059

**Main Level Sq. Ft.:** 1,344

**Lower Level Sq. Ft.:** 715

**Bedrooms:** 3

**Bathrooms:** 2½

**Foundation:** Slab, insulated concrete form

**Material List Available:** No

**Price Category:** D

**CAD FILE AVAILABLE**

Images provided by designer/architect.

Rear View

**Main Level Floor Plan**

Copyright by designer/architect.

**Garage Level Floor Plan**

## Plan #111021

**Dimensions:** 34' W x 44' D
**Levels:** 2
**Square Footage:** 2,221
**Main Level Sq. Ft.:** 1,307
**Upper Level Sq. Ft.:** 914
**Bedrooms:** 4
**Bathrooms:** 3
**Foundation:** Pier
**Materials List Available:** No
**Price Category:** E

If you've got a view you want to admire, choose this well-designed home, with its comfortable front porch and spacious second-floor balcony.

**Features:**

- Porch: Double doors open to both the living and dining rooms for complete practicality.

- Living Room: The spacious living room anchors the open floor plan in this lovely home.

- Dining Room: Natural light pours into this room from the large front windows.

- Kitchen: An angled snack bar that's shared with the dining room doubles as a large counter.

- Master Suite: Double doors lead from the bedroom to the balcony. The bath includes a tub, separate shower, and double vanity.

- Sitting Area: This quiet area is nestled into a windowed alcove between the study and the master suite.

### Main Level Floor Plan

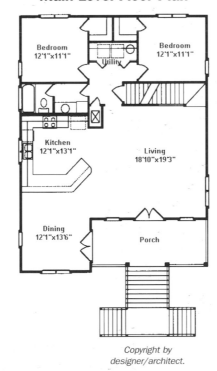

Copyright by
designer/architect.

### Upper Level Floor Plan

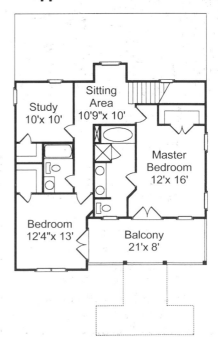

## Plan #111013

**Dimensions:** 33' W x 59' D

**Levels:** 1

**Square Footage:** 1,606

**Bedrooms:** 3

**Bathrooms:** 2

**Foundation:** Slab

**Materials List Available:** No

**Price Category:** C

*Images provided by designer/architect.*

This is the home you have been looking for to fit on that narrow building lot.

**Features:**

- Living Room: Entering this home from the front porch, you arrive in this gathering area. The corner fireplace adds warmth and charm to the area.

- Kitchen: This island kitchen features two built-in pantries and is open to the breakfast room. The oversize laundry room is close by and has room for the large items the kitchen needs to store.

- Master Suite: Located toward the rear of the home to give some extra privacy, this suite boasts a large sleeping area. The master bath has amenities such as his and her walk-in closets, dual vanities, and a whirlpool tub.

- Rear Porch: Just off the breakfast room is this covered rear porch with storage area. On nice days you can sit outside in the shaded area and watch the kids play outside.

*Copyright by designer/architect.*

## Plan #451249

**Dimensions:** 52' W x 54'8" D
**Levels:** 2
**Square Footage:** 2,281
**Main Level Sq. Ft.:** 1,436
**Upper Level Sq. Ft.:** 845
**Bedrooms:** 3
**Bathrooms:** 3
**Foundation:** Walkout basement
**Materials List Available:** No
**Price Category:** E

This is the perfect house for a sloping lot, perhaps with a mountain view.

**CAD FILE AVAILABLE**

**Features:**

- **Entry:** The covered front porch welcomes you to the lovely home; in the foyer, you'll find a coat closet and a half bathroom.

- **Kitchen:** As you leave the foyer and arrive in this open kitchen, you'll be impressed by all of the cabinets and counter space. The raised bar is open to the dining room. The built-in pantry is a much-welcome bonus.

- **Master Suite:** This main-level oasis is separated from the other bedrooms, which are located upstairs. The French doors open from the sleeping area onto the rear deck. The two walk-in closets are the perfect size. The master bath boasts a stall shower, oversized tub, and his and her vanities.

- **Upper Level:** Two secondary bedrooms with nicely sized closets share a full bathroom.

The loft area, with a view down into the great room, will be the perfect area to relax.

- **Lower Level:** This future space may have a wet bar, recreation room, full bathroom, and office space. The French door to the lower patio will be a welcome breath of fresh air.

Front/Side View

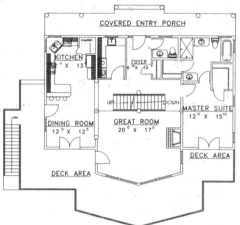

**Main Level Floor Plan**

**Basement Level Floor Plan**

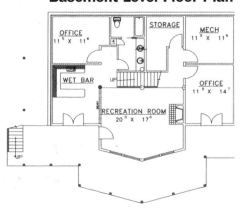

**Upper Level Floor Plan**

## Plan #111049

**Dimensions:** 60' W x 50' D

**Levels:** 2

**Square Footage:** 2,205

**Main Level Sq. Ft.:** 1,552

**Upper Level Sq. Ft.:** 653

**Bedrooms:** 3

**Bathrooms:** 2

**Foundation:** Pier

**Materials list available:** No

**Price Code:** E

This stately beach home offers many waterfront views.

*Images provided by designer/architect.*

**Features:**

- Ceiling Height: 8 ft.

- Entrance: This home features raised stairs, with two wings that lead to the central staircase.

- Front Porch: This area is 110 square feet.

- Living Room: This huge room features a wood-burning fireplace and large windows, and it leads to the rear covered porch and a spacious deck. It is also open to the kitchen and dining area.

- Kitchen: This room has ample counter space

and an island that is open to the dining area.

- Master Suite: This upper level room has a large balcony. This balcony is a perfect place to watch the sun set over the beach. This room also a walk-in closet.

- Master Bath: This room has all the modern amenities, with separate vanities, large corner tub and walk-in shower.

- Lower Level Bedrooms: These rooms each have a walk in closet and share a bathroom.

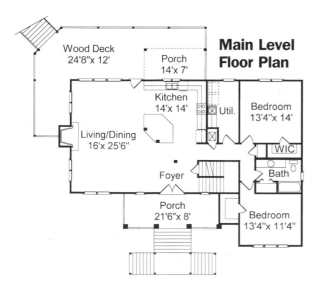

**Main Level Floor Plan**

Wood Deck 24'8"x 12'
Porch 14'x 7'
Kitchen 14'x 14'
Util.
Bedroom 13'4"x 14'
Living/Dining 16'x 25'6"
WIC
Bath
Foyer
Porch 21'6"x 8'
Bedroom 13'4"x 11'4"

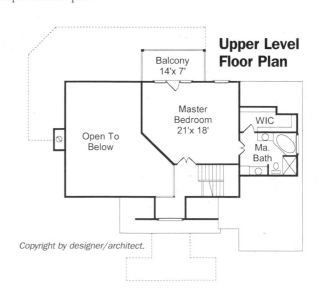

**Upper Level Floor Plan**

Balcony 14'x 7'
Master Bedroom 21'x 18'
WIC
Open To Below
Ma. Bath

*Copyright by designer/architect.*

Rear View

## SMARTtip

### Removing Carpet Stains in Kid's Rooms

Kids will be kids, and so accidents will happen. The cardinal rule for removing a stain from carpeting is to always clean up a spot or spill immediately, using white cloths or paper towels. Blot, never rub or scrub, a stain. Work from the outer edge in toward the center of the spot, and then follow up with clean water to remove any residue of the stain. Blot up any moisture remaining from the cleanup by layering white paper towels over the spot and weighing them down with a heavy object.

To remove a water-soluble stain, blot as much of it as possible with white paper towels that have been dampened with cold water. If necessary, mix a solution of 1¼ teaspoon of clear, mild, nonbleach laundry detergent with 32 ounces of water, and then spray it lightly onto the spot. Blot it repeatedly with white paper towels. Rinse it with a spray of clean water; then blot it dry.

To treat soils made by urine or vomit, mix equal parts of white vinegar and water, and blot it onto the spot with white paper towels; then clean with detergent solution.

To remove an oil-based stain, blot as much of it as you can; then apply a nonflammable spot remover made specifically for grease, oil, or tar to a clean, white paper towel. Don't apply the remover directly to the carpet, or you may damage the backing. Blot the stain with the treated towel. Wear rubber gloves to protect your hands. Use this method for stains caused by crayons, cosmetics, ink, paint, and shoe polish.

For spots made by cola, chocolate, or blood, apply a solution of 1 tablespoon of ammonia and 1 cup of water to the stain; then go over it with the detergent solution. Do not use ammonia on a wool carpet. Try an acid stain remover—lemon juice or white vinegar diluted with water.

To remove chewing gum or candle wax, try freezing the spot with ice cubes, and then gently scrape off the gum or wax with a blunt object. Follow this with a vacuuming. If this doesn't work, apply a commercial gum remover to the area, following the manufacturer's directions.

## Plan #121004

**Dimensions:** 55'4" W x 48' D

**Levels:** 1

**Square Footage:** 1,666

**Bedrooms:** 3

**Bathrooms:** 2

**Foundation:** Basement

**Materials List Available:** Yes

**Price Category:** C

An efficient floor plan and plenty of amenities create a luxurious lifestyle.

**Features:**

• Ceiling Height: 8 ft. except as noted.

• Entry: Enjoy summer breezes on the porch; then step inside the entry where sidelights and an arched transom create a bright, cheery welcome.

• Great Room: The 10-ft. ceiling and the transom-topped windows flooding the room with light provide a sense of spaciousness. The fireplace adds warmth and style.

• Dining Room: You'll usher your guests into this room located just off the great room.

• Breakfast Area: Also located off the great room, the breakfast area offers another dining option.

• Master Suite: The master bedroom is highlighted by a tray ceiling and a large walk-in closet. Luxuriate in the private bath with its sunlit whirlpool, separate shower, and double vanity.

*Images provided by designer/architect.*

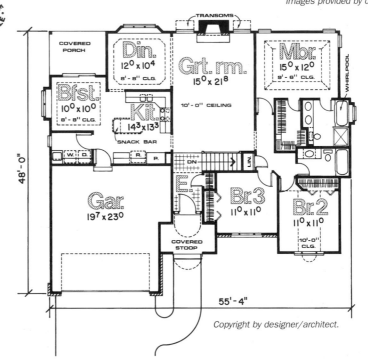

*Copyright by designer/architect.*

## SMARTtip

### Carpeting

Install the best underlayment padding available, as well as the highest grade of carpeting you can afford. This will guarantee a feeling of softness beneath your feet and protect your investment for years to come by reducing wear and tear on the carpet.

# Plan #151805

**Dimensions:** 67'2" W x 50' D

**Levels:** 1

**Square Footage:** 1,777

**Bedrooms:** 3

**Bathrooms:** 2

**Foundation:** Crawl space or slab

**CompleteCost List Available:** Yes

**Price Category:** C

*Images provided by designer/architect.*

This brick home with arched windows gives an elegant look to any neighborhood.

**Features:**

- **Foyer:** The entrance to your home sets to mood for the entire house. This foyer features a coat closet and is open to the dining room.

- **Great Room:** Friends and family will love to gather in this great space near the fireplace. The large rear windows allow an abundance of natural light into the room.

- **Master Suite:** This escape is located at the rear of the home for privacy. The 9-ft.-high boxed ceiling in the sleeping area adds an elegant feel. The master bath boasts a generous amount of space, with its whirlpool tub and two walk-in closets.

- **Garage:** A side-loading garage allows the front of the home to be free of the large door. There is room for two cars plus a storage area.

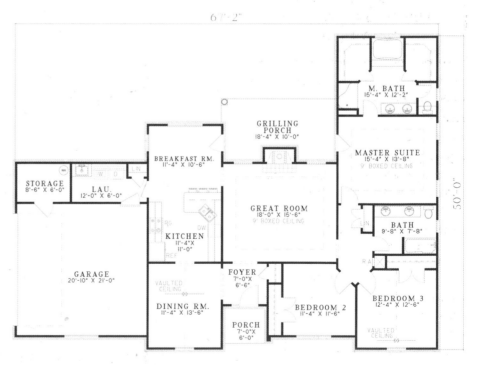

*Copyright by designer/architect.*

## Plan #121003

**Dimensions:** 76' W x 55'4" D

**Levels:** 1

**Square Footage:** 2,498

**Bedrooms:** 4

**Bathrooms:** 2½

**Foundation:** Basement

**Materials List Available:** Yes

**Price Category:** E

*Images provided by designer/architect.*

Repeated arches bring style and distinction to the interior and exterior of this spacious home.

**Features:**

- Ceiling Height: 8 ft. except as noted.

- Den: A decorative volume ceiling helps make this spacious retreat the perfect place to relax after a long day.

- Formal Living Room: The decorative volume ceiling carries through to the living room that invites large formal gatherings.

- Formal Dining Room: There's plenty of room for all the guests to move into this gracious formal space that also features a decorative volume ceiling.

- Master Suite: Retire to this suite with its glamorous bayed whirlpool, his and her vanities, and a walk-in closet.

- Optional Sitting Room: With the addition of French doors, one of the bedrooms can be converted into a sitting room for the master suite.

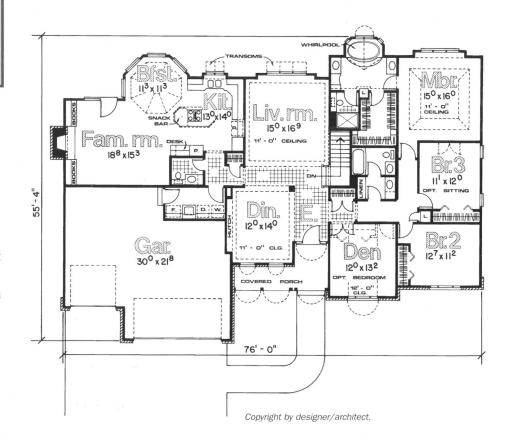

*Copyright by designer/architect.*

## Plan #131063

**Dimensions:** 61' W x 66' D

**Levels:** 1

**Square Footage:** 1,996

**Bedrooms:** 3

**Bathrooms:** 2½

**Foundation:** Crawl space, slab, or basement

**Materials List Available:** Yes

**Price Category:** E

This fabulous ranch home provides everything you have wanted in a house–in a modest and affordable size.

**Features:**

- Formal Space: Just off the entry are the formal dining room and parlor, both with stepped ceilings. The parlor might also be used as a home office.

- Master Suite: Separated from the secondary bedrooms, this large suite features a tray ceiling and bay window in the sleeping area. The master bath boasts his and her vanities and a compartmentalized lavatory.

- Secondary Bedrooms: Two additional bedrooms are tucked away behind the garage. The second full bathroom is located close by, just off the breakfast room.

- Bonus Area: This upper level could hold two future bedrooms and a Jack-and-Jill bathroom. Bedroom #5 features a space-adding dormer.

*Images provided by designer/architect.*

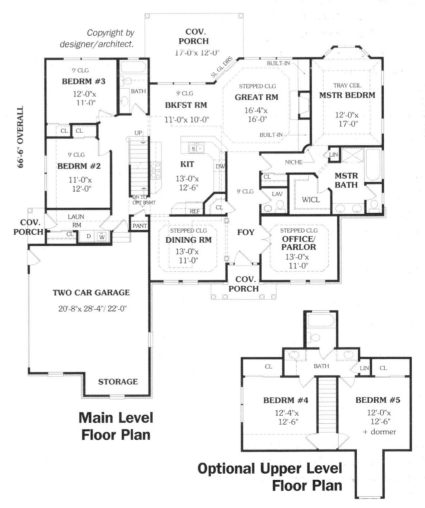

**Main Level Floor Plan**

**Optional Upper Level Floor Plan**

*Images provided by designer/architect.*

## Plan #131064

**Dimensions:** 74' W x 47' D

**Levels:** 1

**Square Footage:** 1,783

**Bedrooms:** 3

**Bathrooms:** 2

**Foundation:** Crawl space, slab, or basement

**Material List Available:** Yes

**Price Category:** D

High ceilings and a flowing, open, interior distinguish this charming, country-style ranch.

**Features:**

- **Great Room:** This large gathering area boasts a stepped ceiling and a beautiful fireplace. There are built-in cabinets on either side of the fireplace, which would be a perfect entertainment center.

- **Dining Room:** Accented with columns and a stepped ceiling, this dining room is able to handle all formal gatherings. Open to the foyer and the great room, the area allows friends and family to have easy access to the rest of the house.

- **Kitchen:** This island kitchen boasts an abundance of cabinet and counter space. The adjoining breakfast room's large windows flood the space with natural light.

- **Master Suite:** This private retreat boasts a large sleeping area with a tray ceiling. The master bath features his and her vanities, a second walk-in closet, and a compartmentalized toilet area.

- **Bedrooms:** Two secondary bedrooms with walk-in closets share a common full bathroom.

**Rear Elevation**

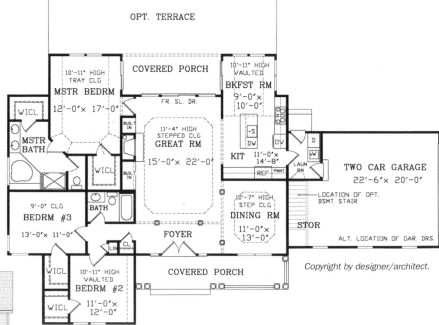

*Copyright by designer/architect.*

## Plan #151761

**Dimensions:** 39' W x 41'8" D

**Levels:** 1

**Square Footage:** 1,092

**Bedrooms:** 2

**Bathrooms:** 1

**Foundation:** Crawl space

**CompleteCost List Available:** Yes

**Price Category:** B

Images provided by designer/architect.

This log home has a simple straight-lined design featuring a front covered porch, perfect for stargazing and a cup of hot chocolate.

**Features:**

• Front Porch: This covered porch, with plenty of room for relaxing, runs the full width of the home.

• Entry: This cozy entry leads to the open floor plan, with its spacious great room, kitchen, and large dining room.

• Kitchen: This kitchen has ample counter and cabinet space and is open to the dining room. Nearby is the grilling porch with columns for lazy summer afternoons.

• Bedrooms: The two bedrooms are surprisingly large for a home of this size. They share the common bathroom, which has dual vanities.

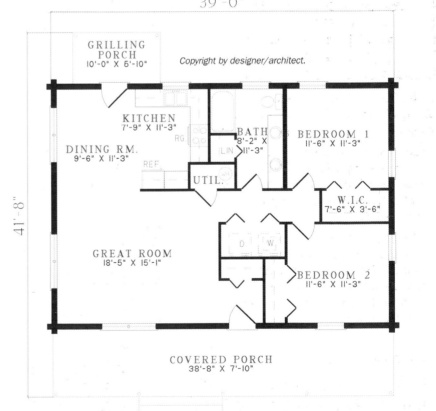

39'-0"

41'-8"

GRILLING PORCH 10'-0" X 5'-10"

Copyright by designer/architect.

KITCHEN 7'-9" X 11'-3"

DINING RM. 9'-6" X 11'-3"

BATH 8'-2" X 11'-3"

BEDROOM 1 11'-6" X 11'-3"

UTIL.

W.I.C. 7'-6" X 3'-6"

GREAT ROOM 18'-5" X 15'-1"

BEDROOM 2 11'-6" X 11'-3"

COVERED PORCH 38'-8" X 7'-10"

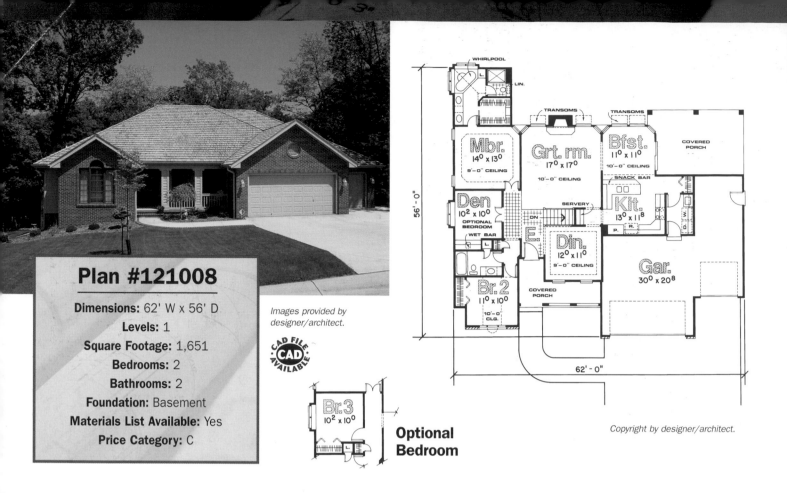

# Plan #121008

**Dimensions:** 62' W x 56' D

**Levels:** 1

**Square Footage:** 1,651

**Bedrooms:** 2

**Bathrooms:** 2

**Foundation:** Basement

**Materials List Available:** Yes

**Price Category:** C

*Images provided by designer/architect.*

**CAD FILE AVAILABLE**

**Optional Bedroom**

*Copyright by designer/architect.*

# Plan #181490

**Dimensions:** 48' W x 29' D

**Levels:** 2

**Square Footage:** 1,849

**Main Level Sq. Ft.:** 866

**Upper Level Sq. Ft.:** 983

**Bedrooms:** 3

**Bathrooms:** 1½

**Foundation:** Basement

**Material List Available:** Yes

**Price Category:** D

*Images provided by designer/architect.*

**CAD FILE AVAILABLE**

**Main Level Floor Plan**

**Upper Level Floor Plan**

*Copyright by designer/architect.*

## Plan #511014

**Dimensions:** 75'2" W x 50'6" D

**Levels:** 1

**Square Footage:** 2,054

**Bedrooms:** 3

**Bathrooms:** 2

**Foundation:** Crawl space or slab

**Material List Available:** No

**Price Category:** D

*Images provided by designer/architect.*

**CAD FILE AVAILABLE**

*Copyright by designer/architect.*

## Plan #511015

**Dimensions:** 61'6" W x 59' D

**Levels:** 1

**Square Footage:** 2,079

**Bedrooms:** 3

**Bathrooms:** 2

**Foundation:** Crawl space or slab

**Material List Available:** No

**Price Category:** D

*Images provided by designer/architect.*

**CAD FILE AVAILABLE**

*Copyright by designer/architect.*

# Plan #341153

**Dimensions:** 31'4" W x 32'8" D

**Levels:** 2

**Square Footage:** 1,224

**Main Level Sq. Ft.:** 652

**Upper Level Sq. Ft:** 572

**Bedrooms:** 3

**Bathrooms:** 1½

**Foundation:** Crawl space, basement, or walkout

**Materials List Available:** Yes

**Price Category:** B

A transitional two-story design with a style all its own, this home is one that is sure to be admired.

**Features:**

- **Covered Porch:** On a nice evening, pull up a chair and relax with family and friends on this porch. From this area you can enter the home through the kitchen or the living room.

- **Living Room:** A great place to relax, this living room welcomes you home. There is plenty of wall space, offering numerous ways to lay out your furniture.

*Images provided by designer/architect.*

- **Kitchen:** The L-shaped design allows room for a table in this kitchen, saving the dining room for formal gatherings. There is a powder room and laundry area nearby.

- **Upper Level:** Three adequately sized bedrooms share this level with the single full bathroom.

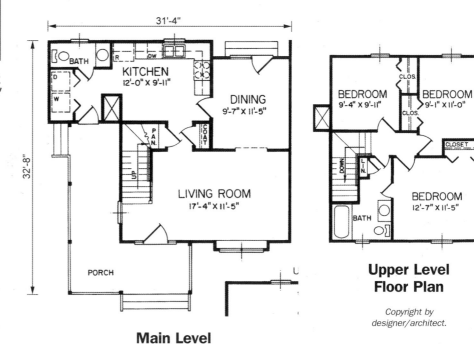

**Main Level
Floor Plan**

**Upper Level
Floor Plan**

*Copyright by
designer/architect.*

## Plan #121050

**Dimensions:** 64' W x 50' D

**Levels:** 1

**Square Footage:** 1,996

**Bedrooms:** 2

**Bathrooms:** 2

**Foundation:** Basement

**Materials List Available:** Yes

**Price Category:** D

This compact design includes features usually reserved for larger homes and has styling that is typical of more-exclusive home designs.

### Features:

- **Entry:** As you enter this home, you'll see the formal living and dining rooms—both with special ceiling detailing—on either side.

- **Great Room:** Located in the rear of the home for convenience, this great room is likely to be your favorite spot. The fireplace is framed by transom-topped windows, so you'll love curling up here, no matter what the weather or time of day.

- **Kitchen:** Ample counter and cabinet space make this kitchen a dream in which to work.

- **Master Suite:** A tray ceiling and lovely corner windows create an elegant feeling in the bedroom, and two walk-in closets make it easy to keep this space tidy and organized. The private bath has a skylight, corner whirlpool tub, and two separate vanities.

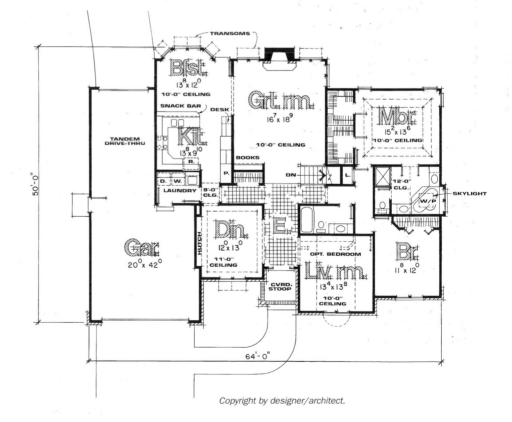

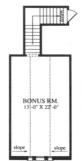

## Plan #511021

**Dimensions:** 65'9" W x 49'10" D

**Levels:** 1

**Square Footage:** 1,821

**Bedrooms:** 3

**Bathrooms:** 2

**Foundation:** Crawl space or slab

**Material List Available:** No

**Price Category:** D

*Images provided by designer/architect.*

**Bonus Area Floor Plan**

*Copyright by designer/architect.*

## Plan #521023

**Dimensions:** 68'4" W x 59'4" D

**Levels:** 1

**Square Footage:** 2,038

**Bedrooms:** 3

**Bathrooms:** 3

**Foundation:** Crawl space

**Material List Available:** No

**Price Category:** D

*Images provided by designer/architect.*

**CAD FILE AVAILABLE**

*Copyright by designer/architect.*

## Plan #521052

**Dimensions:** 54' W x 52'8" D

**Levels:** 1

**Square Footage:** 1,460

**Bedrooms:** 3

**Bathrooms:** 2

**Foundation:** Slab

**Material List Available:** No

**Price Category:** B

*Images provided by designer/architect.*

*Copyright by designer/architect.*

## Plan #421016

**Dimensions:** 56'8" W x 53' D

**Levels:** 2

**Square Footage:** 2,431

**Main Level Sq. Ft.:** 1,394

**Upper Level Sq. Ft.:** 1,037

**Bedrooms:** 4

**Bathrooms:** 2½

**Foundation:** Crawl space, slab, or basement

**Material List Available:** No

**Price Category:** E

*Images provided by designer/architect.*

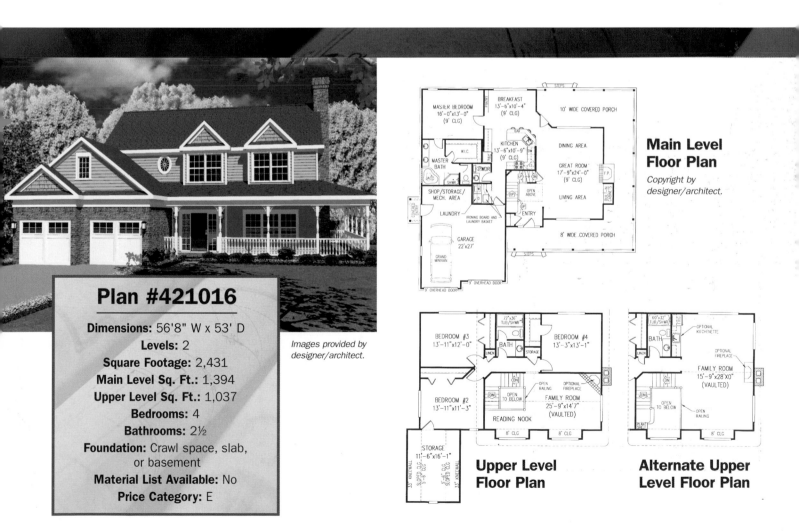

### Main Level Floor Plan

*Copyright by designer/architect.*

### Upper Level Floor Plan

### Alternate Upper Level Floor Plan

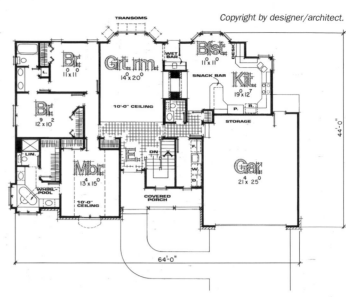

Copyright by designer/architect.

## Plan #121051

**Dimensions:** 64' W x 44' D
**Levels:** 1
**Square Footage:** 1,808
**Bedrooms:** 3
**Bathrooms:** 2½
**Foundation:** Basement
**Materials List Available:** Yes
**Price Category:** D

*Images provided by designer/architect.*

## SMARTtip

## Cutting Molding

Using an bench-top table saw and a simple plywood jig is a safe, efficient, and foolproof way to cut many trim members at angles of less than 45 degrees.

## Plan #181722

**Dimensions:** 68'8" W x 41'8" D
**Levels:** 1
**Square Footage:** 1,883
**Bedrooms:** 3
**Bathrooms:** 2
**Foundation:** Basement
**Material List Available:** Yes
**Price Category:** D

*Images provided by designer/architect.*

CAD FILE AVAILABLE

Copyright by designer/architect.

# Plan #151762

**Dimensions:** 57'8" W x 63'8" D
**Levels:** 2
**Square Footage:** 2,402
**Main Level Sq. Ft.:** 2,128
**Upper Level Sq. Ft:** 274
**Bedrooms:** 2
**Bathrooms:** 2
**Foundation:** Crawl space
**CompleteCost List Available:** Yes
**Price Category:** E

*Images provided by designer/architect.*

A log home will bring you back to a simpler time, and living here would help simplify your life.

## Features:

- **Loft:** Walk up the stairs to this cozy loft area with a view down into the great room. This will be the perfect spot to sit a read a book.

- **Kitchen:** This U-shaped kitchen with an island is large enough for all of the chefs in the family to help make the meals. Off of this kitchen is the mudroom, which has ample closet space and access to the garage via the gabled breezeway.

- **Master Suite:** Located for privacy on the opposite side of the home from the secondary bedroom, this suite boasts French doors with access to the rear deck. The master bath pampers you with a whirlpool tub and dual vanities.

- **Laundry Room:** A U-shaped counter helps this laundry room take care of the "dirty work."

**Main Level Floor Plan**

**Loft Area Floor Plan**

*Copyright by designer/architect.*

## Plan #161118

**Dimensions:** 70'2" W x 50'8" D
**Levels:** 1
**Square Footage:** 2,154
**Main Level Sq. Ft.:** 1,483
**Lower Level Sq. Ft:** 671
**Bedrooms:** 3
**Bathrooms:** 3
**Foundation:** Basement or walkout
**Materials List Available:** Yes
**Price Category:** D

This home was designed to provide private spaces for each household member.

CAD FILE CAD AVAILABLE

*Images provided by designer/architect.*

**Features:**

- Kitchen: This U-shaped kitchen, with its counter seating, and the adjacent dining area are fully equipped for formal or informal gatherings. The glass door leads to the rear deck.

- Master Suite: Separated from the secondary bedrooms for privacy, this master suite will be your oasis. The master bath boasts a walk-in closet, dual vanities, and a linen closet.

- Secondary Bedrooms: Two additional family bedrooms share a the second full bathroom in common.

- Lower Level: A future recreation room, the third full bathroom, and bedroom 4 can be finished to your liking. There is also plenty of storage space.

Rear Elevation

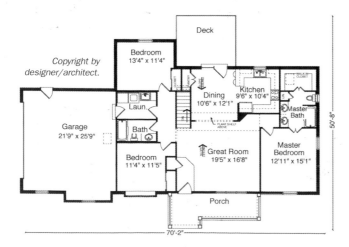

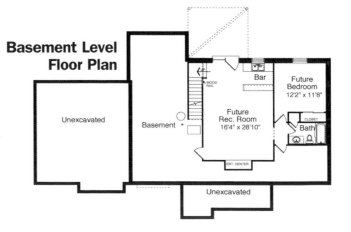

## Plan #321037

**Dimensions:** 78'8" W x 50'6" D

**Levels:** 1

**Square Footage:** 2,397

**Bedrooms:** 3

**Bathrooms:** 2

**Foundation:** Basement or walkout

**Materials List Available:** Yes

**Price Category:** E

Come home to this three-bedroom stucco home with arched windows.

**Features:**

- **Dining Room:** Just off the entry is this formal room, with its vaulted ceiling.

- **Great Room:** This large room has a vaulted ceiling and a fireplace.

- **Kitchen:** A large pantry and an abundance of counter space make this kitchen a functional work space.

- **Master Suite:** This suite has a large walk-in closet and a private bath.

- **Bedrooms:** The two additional bedrooms share a common bathroom.

*Images provided by designer/architect.*

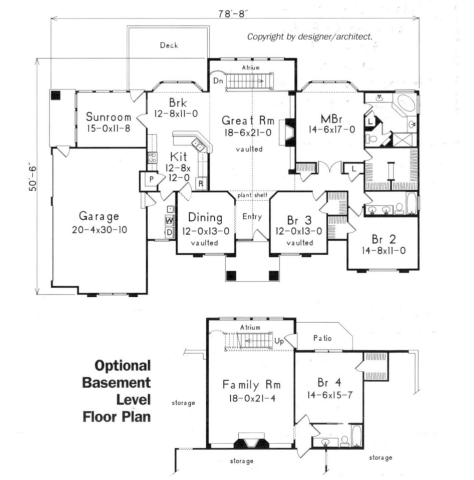

**Optional Basement Level Floor Plan**

## Plan #391059

**Dimensions:** 68' W x 46' D
**Levels:** 1
**Square Footage:** 2,020
**Bedrooms:** 3
**Bathrooms:** 2½
**Foundation:** Basement
**Materials List Available:** Yes
**Price Category:** C

*Images provided by designer/architect.*

A small porch and inviting entry draw folks inside to a central dining room with elegant ceiling treatment.

**Features:**

- **Kitchen:** This clever kitchen with island boasts a corner-window breakfast area with the aura of a café.

- **Great Room:** This room with fireplace heads out to a large deck.

- **Bedrooms:** Two secondary bedrooms share a full bath.

- **Master Suite:** This area (with tiled tub and dual vanities) is located on the opposite side of the house from the living areas for more intimacy.

*Copyright by designer/architect.*

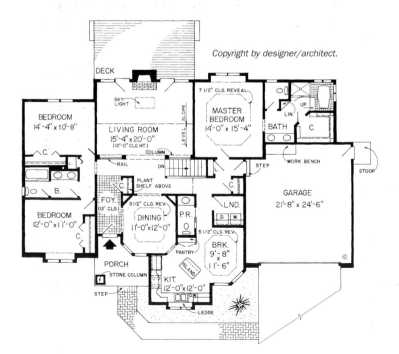

Front View/Side View

Rear View

## Plan #121092

**Dimensions:** 65'4" W x 52'8" D

**Levels:** 1

**Square Footage:** 1,887

**Bedrooms:** 3

**Bathrooms:** 2½

**Foundation:** Basement

**Materials List Available:** Yes

**Price Category:** D

*Images provided by designer/architect.*

This is the design if you want a home that will be easy to expand as your family grows.

**Features:**

- **Entry:** Both the dining room and great room are immediately accessible from this lovely entry.

- **Great Room:** The transom-topped bowed windows highlight the spacious feeling here.

- **Gathering Room:** Also with an angled ceiling, this room has a fireplace as well as built-in

entertainment center and bookcases.

- **Dining Room:** This elegant room features a 13-ft. boxed ceiling and majestic window around which you'll love to decorate.

- **Kitchen:** Designed for convenience, this kitchen includes a lovely angled ceiling and gazebo-shaped breakfast area.

- **Basement:** Use the plans for finishing a family room and two bedrooms when the time is right.

### Main Level Floor Plan

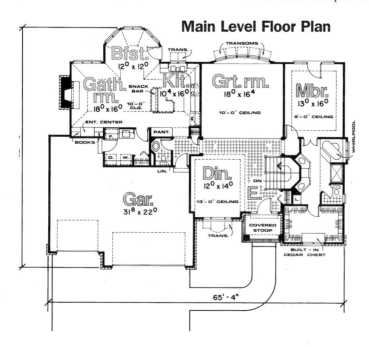

### Lower Level Floor Plan

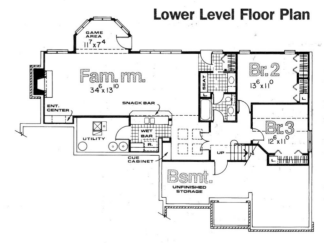

*Copyright by designer/architect.*

## Plan #121074

**Dimensions:** 68'8" W x 47'8" D
**Levels:** 2
**Square Footage:** 2,486
**Main Level Sq. Ft.:** 1,829
**Upper Level Sq. Ft.:** 657
**Bedrooms:** 4
**Bathrooms:** 2½
**Foundation:** Basement
**Materials List Available:** Yes
**Price Category:** E

*Images provided by designer/architect.*

Enjoy the natural light that streams through the many lovely windows in this well-designed home.

**Features:**

• Living Room: This room is sure to be your family's headquarters, thanks to the lovely 15-ft. ceiling, stacked windows, central location, and cozy fireplace.

• Dining Room: A boxed ceiling adds formality to this well-positioned room.

• Kitchen: The island cooktop in this kitchen is so large that it includes a snack bar area. A pantry gives ample storage space, and a built-in desk—where you can set up a computer station or a record-keeping area—adds efficiency.

• Master Suite: For the sake of privacy, this master suite is located on the opposite side of the home from the other living areas. You'll love the roomy bedroom and luxuriate in the private bath with its many amenities.

## Main Level Floor Plan

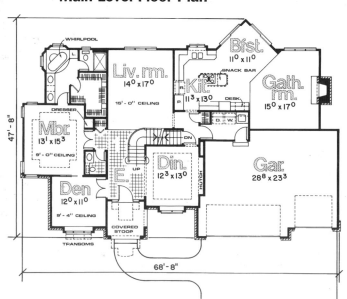

## Upper Level Floor Plan

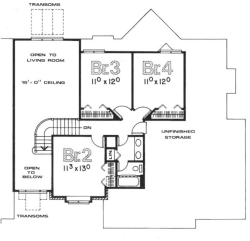

*Copyright by designer/architect.*

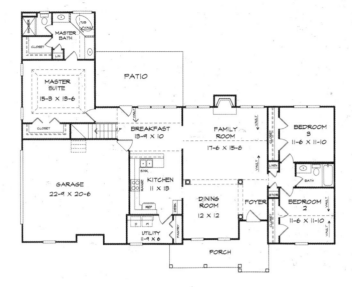

## Plan #461032

**Dimensions:** 67'6" W x 36' D

**Levels:** 1

**Square Footage:** 1,799

**Bedrooms:** 3

**Bathrooms:** 2

**Foundation:** Slab; crawl space or basement for fee

**Material List Available:** No

**Price Category:** *C*

*Images provided by designer/architect.*

*Copyright by designer/architect.*

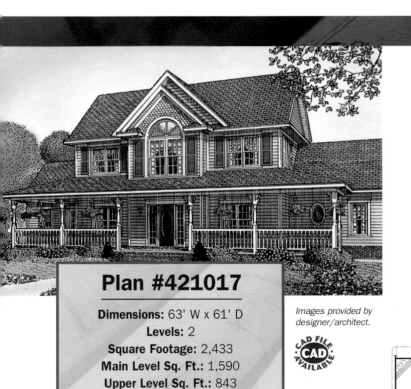

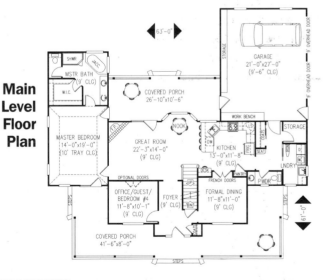

**Main Level Floor Plan**

## Plan #421017

**Dimensions:** 63' W x 61' D

**Levels:** 2

**Square Footage:** 2,433

**Main Level Sq. Ft.:** 1,590

**Upper Level Sq. Ft.:** 843

**Bedrooms:** 4

**Bathrooms:** 2½

**Foundation:** Crawl space, slab, or basement

**Materials List Available:** Yes

**Price Category:** E

*Images provided by designer/architect.*

**CAD FILE AVAILABLE**

**Optional Great Room Floor Plan**

**Upper Level Floor Plan**

*Copyright by designer/architect.*

This article was reprinted from *Ultimate Guide to Basements, Attics, and Garages* (Creative Homeowner 2006).

# The Ultimate Garage

For years, most homeowners have used their garages for parking cars and storing stuff that doesn't fit anywhere else or is overflow from other parts of the house. Or they have taken that valuable floor space and turned it into another master suite or family room.

Rather than using your garage as a scaled-down storage unit or new living space that looks like the rest of the house, consider making it into a high-end recreational space that is improved but at the same time more garage-like. If you like working on cars, why not create a state-of-the-art car-restoration studio? Maybe you'd prefer a furniture-making shop that will be the envy of every craftsman in town, or a big home gym.

Part of what's driving this change is the availability of new storage products designed specifically for the garage. But simple common sense plays a bigger role. Most two-car garages occupy about 500 square feet of space, and that's space that already has a foundation under it, a floor in it, walls around it, a roof over it, and very easy access for big and heavy items through the overhead doors. In these times of high real estate costs, you can't find 500 nearly habitable square feet for less money anywhere.

**A total garage makeover,** above, costs some money, especially if you choose high-end cabinets and flooring. But the results look great, create accessible storage for all the essentials, and even leave room for the cars, at least for the time being.

**Modular storage systems,** below, that include both cabinets and wall-hung options can accommodate just about everything that most people need to store.

# Storage Systems

If you want to make the most out of the garage space you have, then you have to figure out how much space is actually available. It's no good to create a plan that calls for your expensive garden tractor to be banished suddenly to the elements, when you know you want to keep it inside.

Start by waiting for a few days of good weather. Then place everything you want to keep in the garage in the driveway. Start putting things into the garage, starting with the biggest (your cars, if you plan to keep them inside) and moving down in size. You'll quickly see this as the zero-sum game that it is. For every box of old lawn ornaments you keep, that's one less piece of exercise equipment for your new home gym or power tool for your workshop. In this case, being ruthless is a virtue. Either get

rid of nonessentials or find a new place to store them.

Once the essentials are back in place, you have defined the true available space with which you have to work. Now is the time to start looking for storage systems. You'll find two basic options: a cabinet-based system and a wall-hung system. Both are designed to make the most out of vertical storage.

The main difference between the two is the amount of floor space each occupies. For example, the typical base cabinet will measure about 24 inches deep, which makes it hard to fit alongside a car and still have room to open the cabinet or the car door. On the other hand, the average perforated hardboard wall system projects only a few inches into the room.

Because of their different virtues, a combination of the two basic systems makes sense for filling the needs of most people.

**Perforated hardboard,** above, is the granddaddy of all wall storage systems. The material contains holes into which you put metal hooks. It works as well today as it did 50 years ago.

**Some storage systems,** above, blend cabinets with traditional open shelving. This shelving is very versatile and avoids the expense of cabinet doors.

**Modular cabinet systems,** like those shown above, make for very flexible storage, particularly when mounted on casters. The layout can change easily when your needs change.

**Many ceiling-mounted storage units,** above, are available. Some have doors like this one, others are open. Large specialty units can even fit above overhead garage doors.

## Cabinet Systems

A good cabinet system is best defined by how it works, not by how it looks. If you have specialty items that are difficult to store, like some sporting goods, make sure that you find a cabinet that will handle the job. Probably the best—and the most expensive—way to get a good cabinet system is to have a cabinet dealer outfit your garage for you. However, you can do the same thing by figuring out what cabinet sizes you need and then buying knockdown units at a home center.

Another option is to buy one of the new modular garage storage systems. These systems have a big selection of different base and wall cabinets, often with a caster-mounting option so you can easily reposition the units when your needs change. Some of these manufacturers also offer wall-hung storage systems that complement their cabinets.

When looking at different cabinet lines, be sure to check for specialty units that hang from the ceiling. Some are just simple boxes with clever hanging hardware.

## SMARTtip

### Increasing Your Mobility

Not everything in a garage is best stored permanently against a wall. Woodworking equipment and exercise machines are just two kinds of hardware that come to mind. These things need more space when they're being used and need much less when they're not. The logical solution is to mount them on casters so they're easy to move.

Sometimes the base of heavy-duty tools comes with holes for installing casters, but usually you'll have to create some way to mount them. This can take some time and often a lot of creativity. But once things are rolling you'll be happy you made the effort.

Casters come in different sizes and with different mounting hardware. Some simply swivel while others swivel and can be locked in place. Because you'll almost always need four casters for anything you want to move, it's a good idea to put a combination of two swivel and two locking casters on each item. This yields good maneuverability and locking capability, and at less cost than putting locking casters on each corner.

But others are designed to make use of the entire space above your garage doors.

## Wall Systems

Traditional perforated hardboard is still going strong today because it's inexpensive, easy to install, and works well. But now consumers have a lot of other choices.

The most basic alternative is a shelving system that hangs from standards attached to the wall. One popular version of this is the steel-wire systems originally designed for organizing closets. With a wide variety of shelves, drawers, and compartments, you should be able to store most of what you need.

Another alternative is a slat-wall storage system. These slotted plastic panels are screwed directly to the garage wall, and then hooks are placed in the slots to support just about whatever you have. The system is very flexible and can easily change as your storage requirements change.

Steel-grid systems are also available. The open-grid panels are attached to the wall, and hooks and brackets are clipped onto the grid. The grids themselves are pretty inexpensive. But as with most of the wall storage systems, the cost of the hooks and brackets can add up quickly.

**Easy-to-install and inexpensive,** above, steel-wire storage systems, originally designed for closets and kitchens, work just as well in the garage.

**Wall-hung metal shelving,** below, is a quick and clean way to get stuff off the floor. Most systems have wall-mounted standards and adjustable shelf brackets.

## Flooring Options

Most garage floors are made of concrete, which is a wonderful building material. It's hard and durable, and it can carry a tremendous amount of weight without breaking. In other words, it's perfect for garage floors. When properly installed, the only problems concrete will give you are cosmetic: it stains easily, and it's uncomfortable—standing on concrete for a long time hurts your feet and legs. Even when concrete is clean, though, some people find its appearance boring. In recent years, these people have been drawn to a number of different flooring treatments that make concrete look as good as it works.

## Upgrading Concrete

The most common way to improve your concrete floor is to paint it. Until the last few years, this choice was often disappointing. The paint didn't bond well to the concrete and was damaged when hot tires were parked on it. But new garage floor paints, available at home centers, are designed to work much better. One good system has two parts. First you apply an epoxy paint; then you sprinkle colored paint chips over the fresh surface. When the floor dries, the chips provide extra traction to make the concrete much less slippery.

The high-end garage-conversion people tend to favor floor coverings rather than coatings. One popular option is floor pads. These come in rolls, often 6 feet wide, that are installed in much the same way as

**Garage floors,** right, have requirements that differ from other floors in your home. Standard paints won't hold up, but speciality finishes can provide an attractive, durable floor.

**Specialty floor paint,** far right, creates a clean, attractive surface for any garage floor. Proper preparation is essential for the paint to bond successfully to the concrete.

sheet acrylic flooring, though no adhesive is used. The material floats on the floor, and any seams are taped together. Many colors and textures are available.

Plastic floor tiles are another high-end option. They usually come in 12-inch interlocking squares and require no adhesive or tape. You lay out, measure, and cut these tiles much as you would vinyl tiles for the bathroom or kitchen. The tiles will take longer to install than the roll pads, but the work is easier and the tiles are thicker than the pads, so you'll get more cushioning if that's important to you.

Neither the pads nor the tiles are cheap, especially if you cover the entire floor of a two-car garage. Expect to pay at least $1,000 to do the job yourself. But then, nothing can change the look of your garage as dramatically as a bright red or yellow floor.

## Garage Mechanicals

If you plan to use your garage a lot during cold weather, you will want some heat; and if you want heat, you're going to want insulation unless you've got money to burn. Some newer garages are built with insulation in place and finished with dry-

**Brightly colored floor tiles,** above, laid in a clever pattern make a strong design statement. No one could confuse this floor with a boring concrete slab.

wall, but many garages aren't. Make the space more livable by adding insulation and weatherstripping the door.

Choosing your heat source can be complicated because so many different options are available. If your garage is attached to your house and your furnace has the extra capacity, a heating contractor can often run a heat duct from your house to the garage.

## SMARTtip

### Keeping Your Floor Clean

Your new floor may look great when you're done installing it, but a short trip on a muddy road or a day spent driving on salty winter highways can make it look pretty bad once you get home. If you are fortunate enough to have a floor drain, you can just wait until your cars drip dry and then hose down the floor and let the drain take the dirty water away.

On a coated or uncoated floor without a drain, a 3-foot-wide floor squeegee is a great help. Hose down the floor; then use the squeegee to push the water out through the garage door openings. The squeegee also works for grooved floor pads, but not as well on modular floor tiles. Traditional tools, a floor mop and bucket, are required for those.

You also have space-heating options. Probably the most practical choice is an electric-resistance heater, either a standard model or a convection unit that includes a fan to circulate the warmed air quicker. These heaters have no open flame, so they can't ignite flammable fumes that might be present in your garage. And they put no combustion byproducts (carbon monoxide and water vapor) into the air. But in most areas, electricity is more expensive than natural gas or heating oil. Space heaters using other fuels are available in many different designs—most are vented; some are ventless. A local heating equipment supplier can explain your options.

## Ventilation

Your garage ventilation needs are directly proportional to how much your activities foul the air. In warm climates, opening the overhead doors and using a floor fan to keep fresh air moving through should do the trick. But if

**Ventilation and lighting,** left, can help make what was once a dank, uninviting space livable and inviting.

you keep your garage heated, you'll need active ventilation.

You'll probably find more ventilation options than heating options if you really need to clean a lot of air. The most common solution is to install an electric exhaust fan in the garage wall or on the roof. These units are rated by how much air they can move per minute (abbreviated as cfm, cubic feet of air per minute). The air they remove is replaced by fresh air coming into the building from air leaks.

If your garage is tightly constructed, you'll need to supply fresh air in another way. Some people just open a window when the fan is on. But air-to-air heat exchangers are a high-end alternative. These electric units draw warm, dusty air from the garage and dump it outside. At the same time, they pull cool, fresh air from outside into the garage. When these air streams pass each other (confined to separate tubes), the outgoing air preheats the incoming air.

## Lighting

It may require work to pick a good heater and ventilator, but lighting for

**Concrete floors,** above, are durable, but they require much maintenance to keep them looking good.

**Fluorescent fixtures,** above, are inexpensive. Newer models offer truer color renderings than older types.

**Hanging pendant lights,** opposite, are a good way to provide task lighting for counters and worktables.

# SMARTtip

## Garage Safety

The following safety checklist is worth reviewing for those who plan to spend a lot of time in their garages. It was compiled by the Home Safety Council (homesafetycouncil.org), a nonprofit, industry-supported group created to help prevent injuries in the home.

1. Organize all items in designated, easy-to-reach places so that large piles don't accumulate.

2. Store shovels, rakes, lawn chairs, bikes, and other sharp and large objects on the wall to prevent trips and falls.

3. Clear floors and steps of clutter, grease, and spills.

4. Keep children's playthings in one area and within their reach to prevent kids from exploring potentially dangerous areas.

5. Light your garage brightly with maximum safe wattage as designated by light fixtures.

6. Protect light bulbs near work areas with substantial guards to reduce risk of breakage and fire.

7. Light stairs brightly, and install on both sides secure handrails or banisters that extend the entire length of the stairs.

8. Make sure poisonous products, such as pesticides, automotive fluids, lighter fluid, paint thinner, antifreeze, and turpentine, have child-resistant caps, are clearly labeled, and are stored either on a high shelf or in a locked cabinet.

9. Do not use barbecue grills and electric generators inside the garage, as they emit carbon monoxide (CO) and pose a fire hazard.

10. Install a smoke alarm and CO detector in the garage.

11. Never leave cars running inside a closed or open garage to prevent CO poisoning.

12. Store gasoline in small quantities only and in a proper, tightly sealed container labeled "gasoline."

13. Do not keep gasoline in a garage with an appliance that contains a pilot light.

14. Mount a fire extinguisher and stocked first-aid kit in the garage, and make sure every family member knows where they are and how to use them.

15. Store pool chemicals according to the manufacturers' directions to prevent combustion and potential poisoning exposures.

16. Do not overload outlets, and make sure the electrical ratings on extension cords have been checked to ensure they are carrying no more than their proper loads.

17. Lock electrical supply boxes to prevent children from opening them.

18. Clean the garage of dust, cobwebs, and trash, which can interfere with the electrical system.

19. Properly secure shelving units to the wall; make sure they are not overloaded; and store heavier items closest to the ground.

20. Keep a sturdy step stool within easy reach to aid in reaching items stored high off the ground.

the garage is much easier. Simply put, it's hard to beat overhead fluorescent lighting for general room illumination. These units provide good light, are easy to install, and are cheap to run. Higher-end models are often sold without bulbs. Of course buying the bulbs lets you choose the bulb wattage (typically from 20 to 40 watts) and color temperature to match your needs.

Task lighting can be accomplished the old fashioned way, with small shop lights installed just where you need them. Some wall storage systems also have light fixtures that mount in the panel slots.

Rear View

Kitchen

*Images provided by designer/architect.*

## Plan #141030

**Dimensions:** 38' W x 32' D
**Levels:** 2
**Square Footage:** 2,323
**Main Level Sq. Ft.:** 1,179
**Upper Level Sq. Ft.:** 1,144
**Bedrooms:** 4
**Bathrooms:** 2½
**Foundation:** Basement
**Materials List Available:** Yes
**Price Category:** E

This European-style home provides visual excitement, with its many rooflines and multiple gables. Its distinctive design creates a rich, solid appearance.

**Features:**

- Living Room: Your guests will appreciate the elegance and style that characterize this formal living room.

- Dining Room: A fitting complement to the living room, this formal dining room is well suited for special occasions.

- Kitchen: The well-designed kitchen, with ample cabinet and counter space, makes food preparation a pleasure.

- Master Suite: Enjoy the quiet luxury of this large master suite, sure to become your favorite retreat at the end of the day.

- Bonus Room: This impressive home features an optional bonus room above the garage.

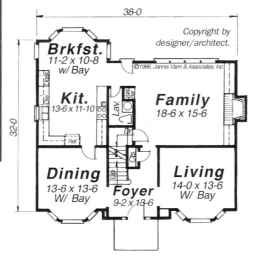

38-0

**Brkfst.**
11-2 x 10-8
w/ Bay

**Kit.**
13-6 x 11-10

*Copyright by designer/architect.*
©1986, Jannis Vann & Associates, Inc.

**Family**
18-6 x 15-6

**Dining**
13-6 x 13-6
W/ Bay

**Foyer**
9-2 x 13-6

**Living**
14-0 x 13-6
W/ Bay

**Main Level Floor Plan**

**Bdrm.4**
10-10 x 13-6

**Bth.2**

**M.Bath**

**Lnd.**
W/D

**Bdrm.3**
13-6 x 11-6

**M.Bdrm.**
12-4 x 18-4

**Bdrm.2**
10-10 x 13-6

**Upper Level Floor Plan**

Living Room

## Plan #131060

**Dimensions:** 60' W x 57' D
**Levels:** 1
**Square Footage:** 2,282
**Bedrooms:** 3
**Bathrooms:** 2½
**Foundation:** Crawl space, slab, or basement
**Materials List Available:** Yes
**Price Category:** F

Beautifully trimmed flat bay windows flank each side of a tall covered porch in this formally balanced country-style ranch.

### Features:

- **Great Room:** An 11-ft.-high stepped ceiling makes this large gathering area feel even larger. The French door beside the fireplace leads out to the future deck. The open snack counter from the adjacent kitchen connects the two areas.

- **Kitchen:** This peninsula kitchen is open to the vaulted breakfast room. The laundry room is close by. The 13-ft.-tall ceiling adds an open and airy feeling to the area.

- **Master Suite:** This master suite boasts a stepped ceiling and a bay window in the sleeping area. His and her walk-in closets are a welcome feature. The master bath features dual vanities and a whirlpool tub.

- **Secondary Bedrooms:** Two equally sized bedrooms are located near the master suite. Bedroom #2 boasts a walk-in closet.

- **Bonus Room:** An upper-level bonus room with vaulted ceiling can be finished to your liking.

*Images provided by designer/architect.*

**Rear Elevation**

*Copyright by designer/architect.*

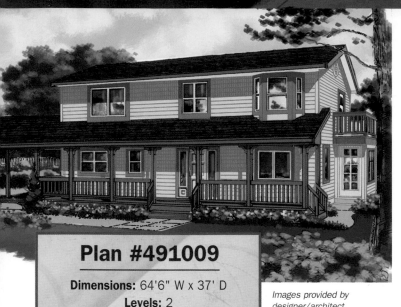

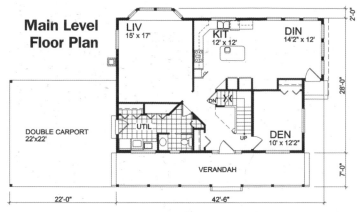

**Main Level Floor Plan**

LIV 15' x 17'
KIT 12' x 12'
DIN 14'2" x 12'
DOUBLE CARPORT 22'x22'
UTIL
DEN 10' x 12'2"
DN
UP
VERANDAH

22'-0"    42'-6"
2'-0"
28'-0"
7'-0"

*Images provided by designer/architect.*

**Upper Level Floor Plan**

BR 2 15' x 10'
MBR 17'6" x 14'4"
BALCONY
DN
OPEN
RAILING
BR 3 15' x 10'
LIN
SEAT

*Copyright by designer/architect.*

# Plan #491009

**Dimensions:** 64'6" W x 37' D

**Levels:** 2

**Square Footage:** 2,215

**Main Level Sq. Ft.:** 1,149

**Upper Level Sq. Ft.:** 1,066

**Bedrooms:** 3

**Bathrooms:** 2½

**Foundation:** Basement

**Material List Available:** Yes

**Price Category:** E

# Plan #511012

**Dimensions:** 50' W x 57'8" D

**Levels:** 1

**Square Footage:** 1,573

**Bedrooms:** 3

**Bathrooms:** 2

**Foundation:** Crawl space or slab

**Material List Available:** No

**Price Category:** C

*Images provided by designer/architect.*

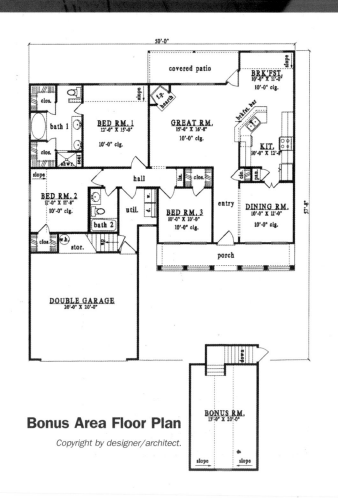

50'-0"

covered patio
BRK FST 10'-6" X 11'-6" 10'-0" clg.
bath 1
BED RM. 1 12'-0" X 15'-0" 10'-0" clg.
GREAT RM. 15'-4" X 16'-6" 10'-0" clg.
KIT. 10'-0" X 12'-8"
hall
BED RM. 2 11'-0" X 11'-8" 10'-0" clg.
util.
BED RM. 3 10'-0" X 10'-0" 10'-0" clg.
entry
DINING RM. 10'-0" X 11'-0" 10'-0" clg.
bath 2
stor.
porch
DOUBLE GARAGE 20'-0" X 20'-0"

57'-8"

**Bonus Area Floor Plan**

BONUS RM. 13'-0" X 20'-0"
slope    slope

*Copyright by designer/architect.*

Copyright by designer/architect.

## Plan #421008

**Dimensions:** 74'6" W x 43' D

**Levels:** 1

**Square Footage:** 1,954

**Bedrooms:** 3

**Bathrooms:** 2½

**Foundation:** Crawl space, slab, or basement

**Material List Available:** Yes

**Price Category:** D

*Images provided by designer/architect.*

**Optional Basement Level Floor Plan**

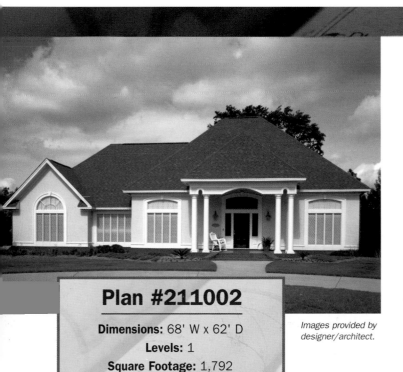

## Plan #211002

**Dimensions:** 68' W x 62' D

**Levels:** 1

**Square Footage:** 1,792

**Bedrooms:** 3

**Bathrooms:** 2

**Foundation:** Crawl space

**Materials List Available:** Yes

**Price Category:** C

*Images provided by designer/architect.*

Copyright by designer/architect.

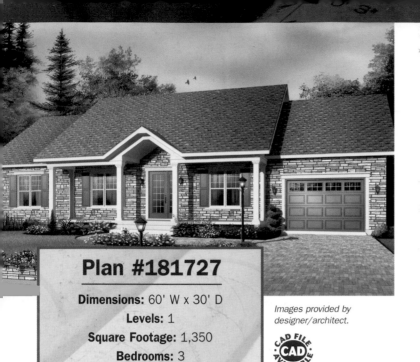

## Plan #181727

**Dimensions:** 60' W x 30' D

**Levels:** 1

**Square Footage:** 1,350

**Bedrooms:** 3

**Bathrooms:** 1

**Foundation:** Basement

**Material List Available:** Yes

**Price Category:** B

*Images provided by designer/architect.*

**CAD FILE AVAILABLE**

*Copyright by designer/architect.*

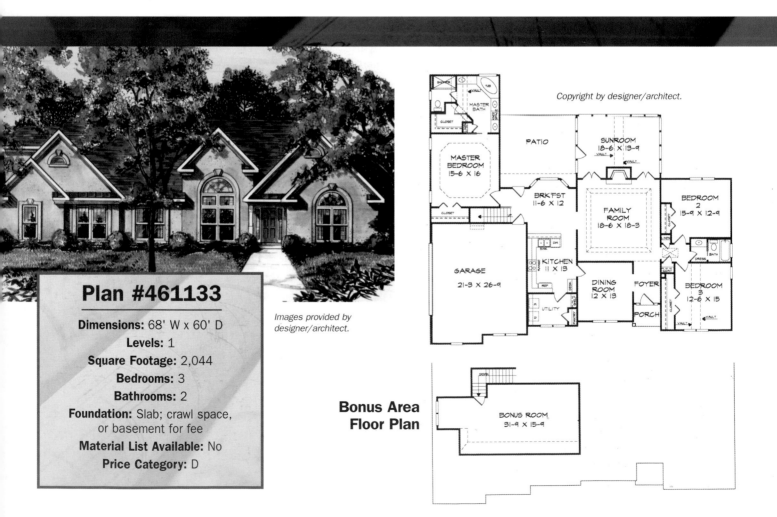

## Plan #461133

**Dimensions:** 68' W x 60' D

**Levels:** 1

**Square Footage:** 2,044

**Bedrooms:** 3

**Bathrooms:** 2

**Foundation:** Slab; crawl space, or basement for fee

**Material List Available:** No

**Price Category:** D

*Images provided by designer/architect.*

*Copyright by designer/architect.*

**Bonus Area Floor Plan**

## Plan #151007

**Dimensions:** 54'2" W x 56'2" D

**Levels:** 1

**Square Footage:** 1,787

**Bedrooms:** 3

**Bathrooms:** 2

**Foundation:** Crawl space, slab, basement, or walkout

**CompleteCost List Available:** Yes

**Price Category:** C

*Images provided by designer/architect.*

**CAD FILE AVAILABLE**

*Copyright by designer/architect.*

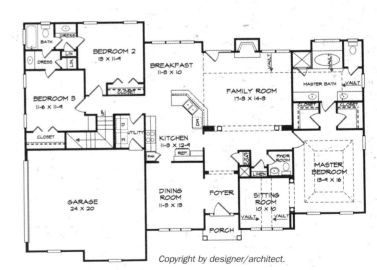

## Plan #461136

**Dimensions:** 67' W x 47' D

**Levels:** 1

**Square Footage:** 2,087

**Bedrooms:** 3

**Bathrooms:** 2½

**Foundation:** Crawl space, slab, or basement

**Material List Available:** No

**Price Category:** D

*Images provided by designer/architect.*

*Copyright by designer/architect.*

**Bonus Area Floor Plan**

*Images provided by designer/architect.*

# Plan #421001

**Dimensions:** 54' W x 41' D

**Levels:** 1

**Square Footage:** 1,433

**Bedrooms:** 3

**Bathrooms:** 2

**Foundation:** Crawl space, slab, or basement

**Material List Available:** Yes

**Price Category:** B

# Plan #161016

**Dimensions:** 59'4" W x 58'8" D

**Levels:** 2

**Square Footage:** 2,101

**Main Level Sq. Ft.:** 1,626

**Upper Level Sq. Ft.:** 475

**Bedrooms:** 3

**Bathrooms:** 2½

**Foundation:** Basement; crawl space option available for fee

**Materials List Available:** Yes

**Price Category:** D

*Images provided by designer/architect.*

*Note: Home in photo reflects a modified garage entrance.*

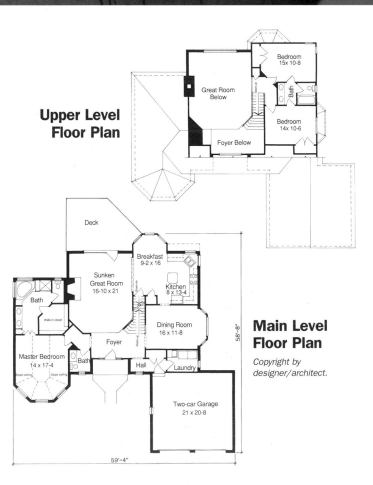

**Upper Level Floor Plan**

**Main Level Floor Plan**

*Copyright by designer/architect.*

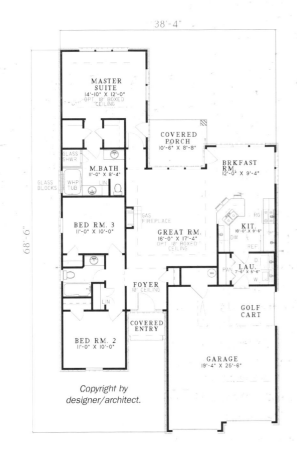

# Plan #151010

**Dimensions:** 38'4" W x 68'6" D

**Levels:** 1

**Square Footage:** 1,379

**Bedrooms:** 3

**Bathrooms:** 2

**Foundation:** Crawl space, slab

**CompleteCost List Available:** Yes

**Price Category:** B

*Images provided by designer/architect.*

*Copyright by designer/architect.*

---

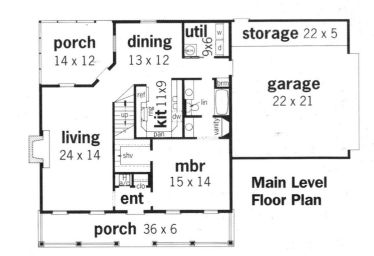

**Main Level Floor Plan**

**Upper Level Floor Plan**

# Plan #211069

**Dimensions:** 58' W x 42' D

**Levels:** 1½

**Square Footage:** 1,600

**Main Level Sq. Ft.:** 1,136

**Upper Level Sq. Ft.:** 464

**Bedrooms:** 3

**Bathrooms:** 2

**Foundation:** Crawl space

**Materials List Available:** Yes

**Price Category:** C

*Images provided by designer/architect.*

*Copyright by designer/architect.*

## Plan #131047

**Dimensions:** 69'10" W x 51'8" D
**Levels:** 1
**Square Footage:** 1,793
**Bedrooms:** 3
**Bathrooms:** 2
**Foundation:** Crawl space, slab, or basement
**Materials List Available:** Yes
**Price Category:** D

*Images provided by designer/architect.*

The country charm of this well-designed home is mixed with the convenience and luxury normally reserved for more contemporary plans.

**Features:**

- Great Room: The spaciousness of this great room is enhanced by the 11-ft. stepped ceiling. A fireplace makes it cozy on cool evenings or on chilly winter days, and two sets of French sliding glass doors open to the back porch.

- Kitchen: In addition to the convenient layout of this design, you'll also love its bright, airy position. It includes an old-fashioned pantry,

a sink under a window, and a sunny breakfast area that opens to the wraparound porch.

- Master Suite: You'll find 11-ft. ceilings in both the master bedroom and the bayed sitting area that the suite includes. In the bath, the circular spa tub is surrounded by a glass-block wall.

- Bonus Space: A permanent staircase leads to an unfinished bonus space on the upper level.

**Rear Elevation**

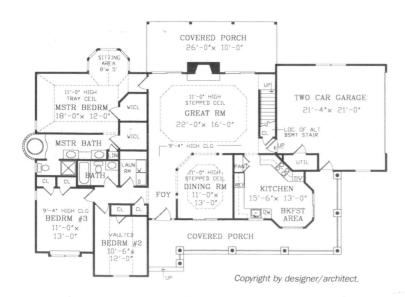

*Copyright by designer/architect.*

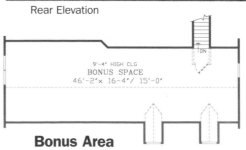

**Bonus Area**

## Plan #151002

**Dimensions:** 67' W x 66' D

**Levels:** 1

**Square Footage:** 2,444

**Bedrooms:** 3

**Bathrooms:** 2½

**Foundation:** Crawl space, slab, or basement

**CompleteCost List Available:** Yes

**Price Category:** E

*Images provided by designer/architect.*

This gracious, traditional home is designed for practicality and convenience.

**CAD FILE AVAILABLE**

### Features:

- **Ceiling Height:** 9 ft. except as noted below.

- **Great Room:** This room is ideal for entertaining, thanks to its lovely fireplace and French doors that open to the covered rear porch. Built-in cabinets give convenient storage space.

- **Family Room:** With access to the kitchen as well as the rear porch, this room will become your family's "headquarters."

- **Study:** Enjoy the quiet in this room with its 12-ft. ceiling and doorway to a private patio on the side of the house.

- **Dining Room:** Take advantage of the 8-in. wood columns and 12-ft. ceilings to create a formal dining area.

- **Kitchen:** An eat-in bar is a great place to snack, and the handy computer nook allows the kids to do their homework while you cook.

- **Breakfast Room:** Opening from the kitchen, this area gives added space for the family to gather any time.

- **Master Suite:** Featuring a 10-ft. boxed ceiling, the master bedroom also has a door way that opens onto the covered rear porch. The master bathroom has a step-up whirlpool tub, separate shower, and twin vanities with a makeup area.

*Copyright by designer/architect.*

## Plan #351001

**Dimensions:** 72'8" W x 51' D
**Levels:** 1
**Square Footage:** 1,855
**Bedrooms:** 3
**Bathrooms:** 2½
**Foundation:** Crawl space, slab, or basement
**Materials List Available:** Yes
**Price Category:** D

From the lovely arched windows on the front to the front and back covered porches, this home is as comfortable as it is beautiful.

### Features:

- **Great Room:** Come into this room with 12-ft. ceilings, and you're sure to admire the corner gas fireplace and three windows overlooking the porch.

- **Dining Room:** Set off from the open design, this room is designed to be used formally or not.

- **Kitchen:** You'll love the practical walk-in pantry, broom closet, and angled snack bar here.

- **Breakfast Room:** Brightly lit and leading to the covered porch, this room will be a favorite spot.

- **Bonus Room:** Develop a playroom or study in this area.

- **Master Suite:** The large bedroom is complemented by the private bath with garden tub, separate shower, double vanity, and spacious walk-in closet.

**CAD FILE AVAILABLE**

*Images provided by designer/architect.*

*Copyright by designer/architect.*

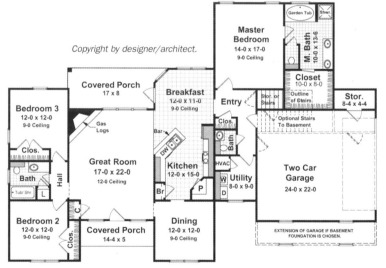

**Kitchen/Great Room**

## Bonus Area Floor Plan

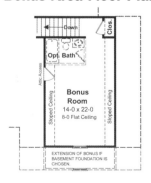

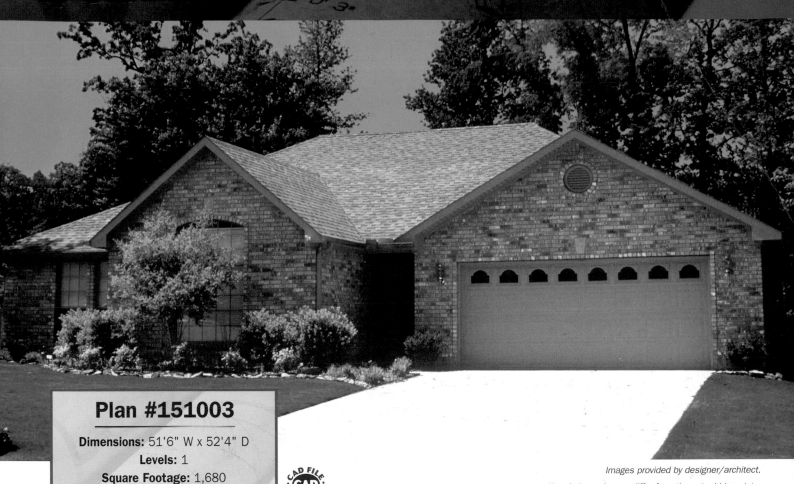

## Plan #151003

**Dimensions:** 51'6" W x 52'4" D

**Levels:** 1

**Square Footage:** 1,680

**Bedrooms:** 3

**Bathrooms:** 2

**Foundation:** Crawl space, slab, or basement

**CompleteCost List Available:** Yes

**Price Category:** C

A lovely front porch, bay windows, and dormers add sparkle to this country-style home.

**Features:**

- **Great Room:** Perfect for entertaining, this room features a tray ceiling, wet bar, and a quiet screened porch nearby.

- **Dining Room:** This bayed dining room facing the front porch is cozy yet roomy enough for family parties during the holidays.

- **Kitchen:** This eat-in kitchen also faces the front and is ideal for preparing meals for any occasion.

- **Master Suite:** The tray ceiling here gives an added feeling of space, while the distance from the other bedrooms allows for all the privacy you'll need.

*Images provided by designer/architect.*

*This home, as shown in the photograph, may differ from the actual blueprints. For more detailed information, please check the floor plans carefully.*

*Copyright by designer/architect.*

# Plan #341071

**Dimensions:** 72'7" W x 38'6" D

**Levels:** 1

**Square Footage:** 1,500

**Bedrooms:** 3

**Bathrooms:** 2

**Foundation:** Crawl space, slab, basement, or walkout

**Materials List Available:** Yes

**Price Category:** C

A contemporary ranch design with classic features and country charm, this home promises a relaxing environment that is sure to please.

**Features:**

- Vaulted Ceilings: The living room and dining room feature vaulted ceilings, giving these rooms the feeling of spaciousness.

- Master Suite: This private area is located toward the rear of the home to add to its seclusion. The walk-in closet has an abundance of space. The master bath boasts dual vanities and a garden tub.

- Secondary Bedrooms: Bedroom 2 makes the perfect child's room and is in close proximity to the second full bathroom. Bedroom 3 has built-in bookshelves and a light well for natural illumination.

- Garage: A front-loading two-car garage has easy access to the pantry in the kitchen, making grocery unloading simple. The washer and dryer are also close by.

Copyright by designer/architect.

## Plan #151004

**Dimensions:** 64'8" W x 62'1" D

**Levels:** 1

**Square Footage:** 2,107

**Bedrooms:** 4

**Bathrooms:** 2½

**Foundation:** Crawl space, slab, or basement

**CompleteCost List Available:** Yes

**Price Category:** D

*Images provided by designer/architect.*

*Copyright by designer/architect.*

You'll love the spacious feeling in this comfortable home designed for a family.

### Features:

- Foyer: A 10-ft. ceiling greets you in this home.

- Great Room: A 10-ft. ceiling complements this large room, with its fireplace, built-in cabinets, and easy access to the rear covered porch.

- Dining Room: The 9-ft. boxed ceiling in this large room helps to create a beautiful formal feeling.

- Kitchen: The island in this kitchen is open to the breakfast room for true convenience.

- Breakfast Room: Morning light will stream through the bay window here.

- Master Suite: A 9-ft. pan ceiling adds a distinctive note to this room with access to the rear porch. In the bath, you'll find a whirlpool tub, separate shower, double vanities, and two walk-in closets.

## Plan #161001

**Dimensions:** 67'2" W x 47' D

**Levels:** 1

**Square Footage:** 1,782

**Bedrooms:** 3

**Bathrooms:** 2

**Foundation:** Basement

**Materials List Available:** Yes

**Price Category:** C

An all-brick exterior displays the solid strength that characterizes this gracious home.

### Features:

- **Great Room:** A feeling of spaciousness permeates the gathering area created by the foyer, great room, and dining room. Multiple windows provide natural light that dances along a sloped ceiling, spilling onto decorative columns and a fireplace.

- **Breakfast Area:** A continuation of the sloped ceiling leads to the breakfast area where French doors open to a screened porch.

- **Kitchen:** An abundance of cabinets and counter space are the hallmarks of this large kitchen with its easy access to a spacious laundry room and storage area.

- **Master Suite:** A tray ceiling and spacious walk-in closet in the master bedroom, along with a whirlpool tub and double-bowl vanity in the bathroom, enable you to pamper yourself.

*Images provided by designer/architect.*

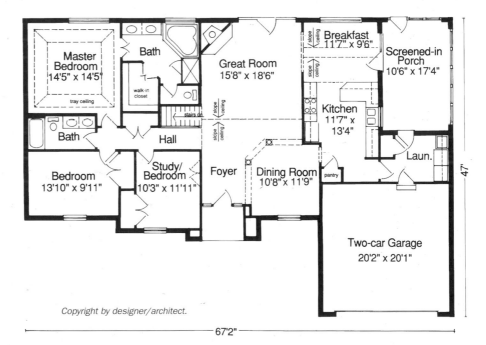

*Copyright by designer/architect.*

Rear Elevation

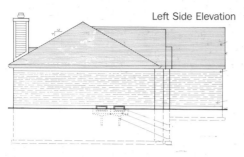

Left Side Elevation

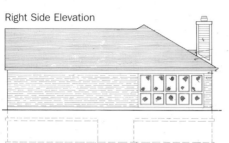

Right Side Elevation

Front View

Great Room / Foyer

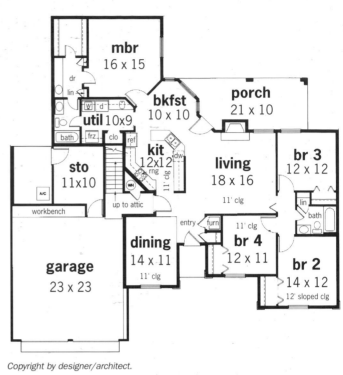

## Plan #211004

**Dimensions:** 64' W x 62' D

**Levels:** 1

**Square Footage:** 1,828

**Bedrooms:** 4

**Bathrooms:** 2

**Foundation:** Crawl space, slab, or basement

**Materials List Available:** Yes

**Price Category:** D

*Images provided by designer/architect.*

*Copyright by designer/architect.*

---

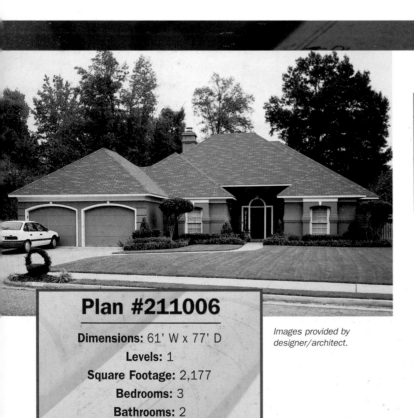

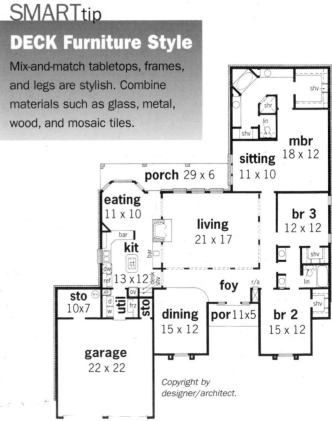

## SMARTtip

### DECK Furniture Style

Mix-and-match tabletops, frames, and legs are stylish. Combine materials such as glass, metal, wood, and mosaic tiles.

## Plan #211006

**Dimensions:** 61' W x 77' D

**Levels:** 1

**Square Footage:** 2,177

**Bedrooms:** 3

**Bathrooms:** 2

**Foundation:** Crawl space or slab

**Materials List Available:** Yes

**Price Category:** D

*Images provided by designer/architect.*

*Copyright by designer/architect.*

## Plan #211005

**Dimensions:** 68' W x 64' D
**Levels:** 1
**Square Footage:** 2,000
**Bedrooms:** 3
**Bathrooms:** 2
**Foundation:** Slab
**Materials List Available:** Yes
**Price Category:** D

A brick veneer exterior complements the columned porch to make this a striking home.

## SMARTtip

### Do-It-Yourself Ponds

To avoid disturbing utility lines, contact your utility companies before doing any digging. Locate a freestanding container pond on your deck near an existing (GFCI) outlet. For an in-ground pond, have an electrician run a buried line and install a GFCI outlet near the pond so you can plug in a pump or fountain.

**Features:**

- Ceiling Height: 9 ft. unless otherwise noted.
- Living Room: From the front porch, the foyer unfolds into this expansive living room. Family and friends will be drawn to the warmth of the living room's cozy fireplace.
- Formal Dining Room: This elegant room is designed for dinner parties of any size.
- Kitchen: Located between the formal dining room and the dinette, the kitchen can serve formal meals as easily as quick family repasts.
- Master Suite: There's plenty of room to unwind at the end of a long day in the huge master bedroom. Luxuriate in the private bath, with its spa tub, separate shower, dual sinks, and two walk-in closets.
- Home Office: The home office, accessible from the master bedroom, is the perfect quiet spot to work, study, or pay the bills.

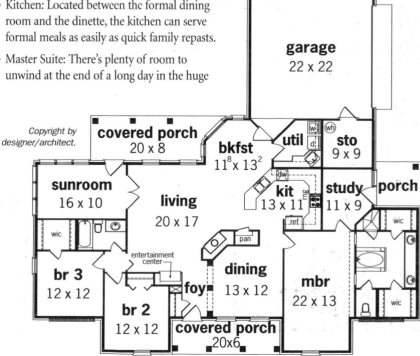

*Copyright by designer/architect.*

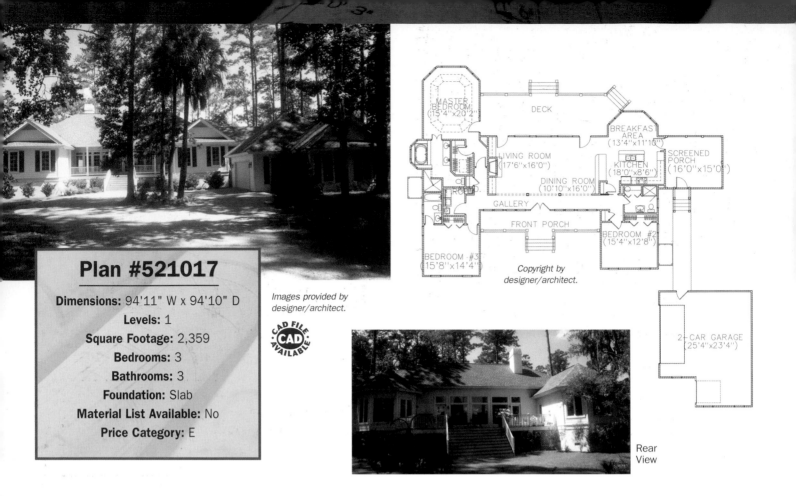

# Plan #521017

**Dimensions:** 94'11" W x 94'10" D

**Levels:** 1

**Square Footage:** 2,359

**Bedrooms:** 3

**Bathrooms:** 3

**Foundation:** Slab

**Material List Available:** No

**Price Category:** E

*Images provided by designer/architect.*

CAD FILE AVAILABLE

*Copyright by designer/architect.*

Rear View

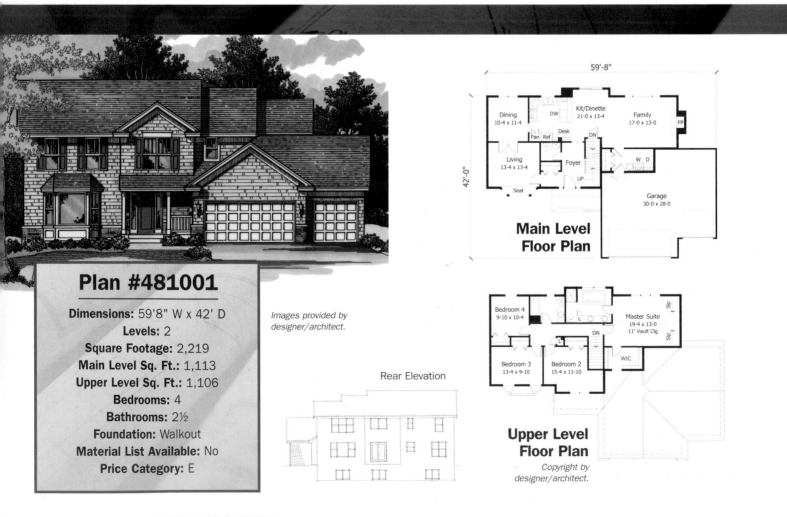

# Plan #481001

**Dimensions:** 59'8" W x 42' D

**Levels:** 2

**Square Footage:** 2,219

**Main Level Sq. Ft.:** 1,113

**Upper Level Sq. Ft.:** 1,106

**Bedrooms:** 4

**Bathrooms:** 2½

**Foundation:** Walkout

**Material List Available:** No

**Price Category:** E

*Images provided by designer/architect.*

**Main Level Floor Plan**

Rear Elevation

**Upper Level Floor Plan**

*Copyright by designer/architect.*

## Plan #311033

**Dimensions:** 70' W x 78'11" D
**Levels:** 1
**Square Footage:** 2,475
**Bedrooms:** 3
**Bathrooms:** 2½
**Foundation:** Crawl space, slab, or basement
**Material List Available:** No
**Price Category:** E

*Images provided by designer/architect.*

### Bonus Area Floor Plan

*Copyright by designer/architect.*

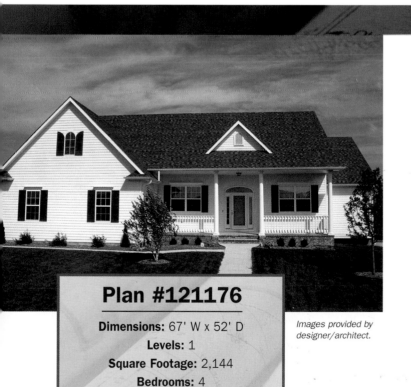

## Plan #121176

**Dimensions:** 67' W x 52' D
**Levels:** 1
**Square Footage:** 2,144
**Bedrooms:** 4
**Bathrooms:** 2
**Foundation:** Slab; basement for fee
**Material List Available:** Yes
**Price Category:** D

*Images provided by designer/architect.*

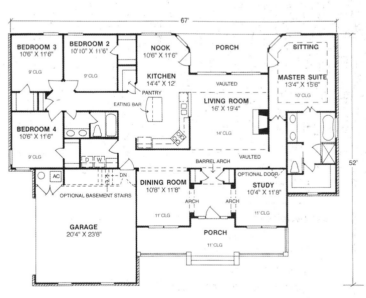

*Copyright by designer/architect.*

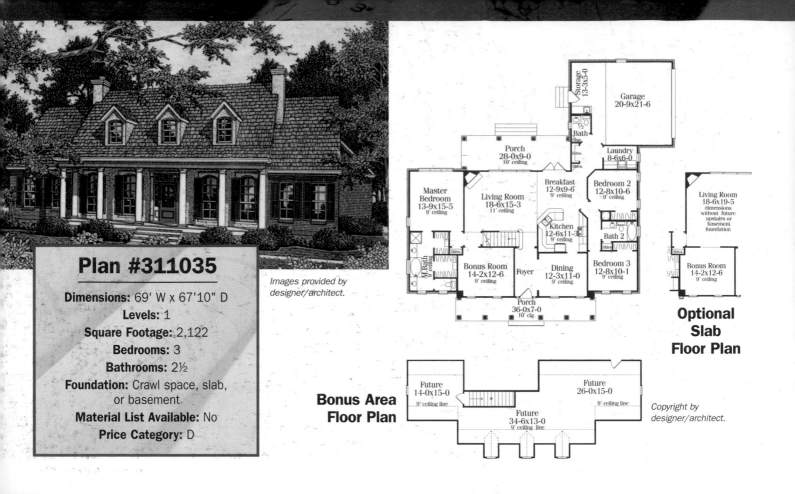

## Plan #311035

**Dimensions:** 69' W x 67'10" D

**Levels:** 1

**Square Footage:** 2,122

**Bedrooms:** 3

**Bathrooms:** 2½

**Foundation:** Crawl space, slab, or basement

**Material List Available:** No

**Price Category:** D

Images provided by designer/architect.

Storage 13-3x5-0

Garage 20-9x21-6

Porch 28-0x9-0 10' ceiling

Bath

Laundry 8-6x6-0

Master Bedroom 13-9x15-5 9' ceiling

Living Room 18-6x15-3 11' ceiling

Breakfast 12-9x9-6 9' ceiling

Bedroom 2 12-8x10-6 9' ceiling

Kitchen 12-6x11-3 9' ceiling

Bath 2

M. Bath

Bonus Room 14-2x12-6 9' ceiling

Foyer

Dining 12-3x11-0 9' ceiling

Bedroom 3 12-8x10-1 9' ceiling

Porch 36-0x7-0 10' clg.

**Optional Slab Floor Plan**

Living Room 18-6x19-5 dimensions without future upstairs or basement foundation

Bonus Room 14-2x12-6 9' ceiling

**Bonus Area Floor Plan**

Future 14-0x15-0 9' ceiling line

Future 26-0x15-0 9' ceiling line

Future 34-6x13-0 9' ceiling line

Copyright by designer/architect.

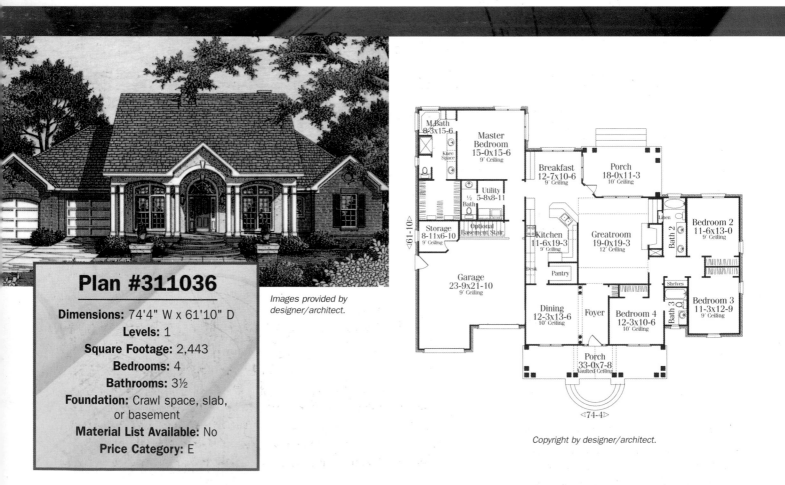

## Plan #311036

**Dimensions:** 74'4" W x 61'10" D

**Levels:** 1

**Square Footage:** 2,443

**Bedrooms:** 4

**Bathrooms:** 3½

**Foundation:** Crawl space, slab, or basement

**Material List Available:** No

**Price Category:** E

Images provided by designer/architect.

M. Bath 8-3x15-6

Master Bedroom 15-0x15-6 9' Ceiling

Knee Space

Breakfast 12-7x10-6 9' Ceiling

Porch 18-0x11-3 10' Ceiling

Utility 5-8x8-11

½ Bath

Bath 2

Bedroom 2 11-6x13-0 9' Ceiling

Storage 8-11x6-10 9' Ceiling

Optional Basement Stair

Kitchen 11-6x19-3 9' Ceiling

Greatroom 19-0x19-3 12' Ceiling

Linen

Garage 23-9x21-10 9' Ceiling

Pantry

Desk

Shelves

Bath 3

Bedroom 3 11-3x12-9 9' Ceiling

Dining 12-3x13-6 10' Ceiling

Foyer

Bedroom 4 12-3x10-6 10' Ceiling

Porch 33-0x7-8 Vaulted Ceiling

<61-10>

<74-4>

Copyright by designer/architect.

## Plan #101010

**Dimensions:** 70' W x 47' D

**Levels:** 1

**Square Footage:** 2,187

**Bedrooms:** 4

**Bathrooms:** 2½

**Foundation:** Crawl space, slab, or basement

**Materials List Available:** Yes

**Price Category:** D

CAD FILE AVAILABLE

*Images provided by designer/architect.*

This stately ranch features a brick-and-stucco exterior, layered trim, and copper roofing returns.

**Features:**

- Ceiling Height: 11 ft. unless otherwise noted.

- Special Ceilings: Vaulted and raised ceilings adorn the living room, family room, dining room, foyer, kitchen, breakfast room, and master suite.

- Kitchen: This roomy kitchen is brightened by an abundance of windows.

- Breakfast Room: Located off the kitchen, this breakfast room is the perfect spot for informal family meals.

- Master Suite: This truly exceptional master suite features a bath, and a spacious walk in closet.

- Morning Porch: Step out of the master bedroom, and greet the day on this lovely porch.

- Additional Bedrooms: The three additional bedrooms each measure approximately 11 ft. x 12 ft. Two of them have walk-in closets.

*Copyright by designer/architect.*

## SMARTtip

### Using Slipcovers in Your Dining Area

Change the look of your dining room by slipcovering chairs. Short-skirted slipcovers give a more informal appearance; fabrics in graphic patterns, such as checks or floral prints, complement this style of slipcover best. Long-skirted covers are elegant additions to a formal dining room, particularly in solid color or tone-on-tone fabrics. Ties, buttons, or trim can add personality.

## Plan #141042

**Dimensions:** 54'4" W x 30' D
**Levels:** 2
**Square Footage:** 1,855
**Main Level Sq. Ft.:** 874
**Upper Level Sq. Ft:** 981
**Bedrooms:** 3
**Bathrooms:** 2½
**Foundation:** Basement
**Materials List Available:** No
**Price Category:** D

This colonial-inspired home features all the amenities today's family could want.

*Images provided by designer/architect.*

**Features:**

• Family Room: This grand room dominates one side of the main level of the home, just off the entry. The fireplace will remove the chill on a cold night.

• Dining Room: Located near the entry, this formal eating area features a nook for your hutch. Being steps away from the kitchen makes entertaining easy in this area.

• Kitchen: This island kitchen is open to the breakfast area and in close proximity to the half bath. The garage is close by for ease in unloading groceries.

• Upper Level: Two bedrooms, a master suite, and a bonus room occupy this level. The master suite features a whirlpool tub, stall shower, and dual vanities.

Rear Elevation

## Main Level Floor Plan

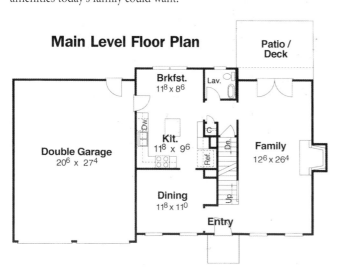

Patio / Deck

Brkfst.
11⁸ x 8⁶

Lav.

Double Garage
20⁶ x 27⁴

Kit.
11⁸ x 9⁶

Family
12⁶ x 26⁴

Dining
11⁸ x 11⁰

Entry

## Upper Level Floor Plan

Bdrm.3
11⁸ x 11⁰

Bath 2

M. Bath

W. D.

Lnd.

Bonus
15⁸ x 21¹⁰

Linen

Master Bdrm.
12⁶ x 17⁸

Bdrm.2
11⁰ x 11⁰

*Copyright by designer/architect.*

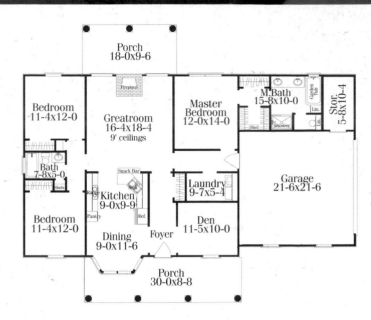

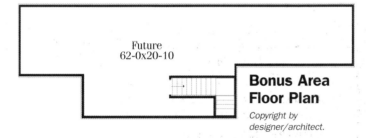

Porch
18-0x9-6

Bedroom
11-4x12-0

Greatroom
16-4x18-4
9' ceilings

Master
Bedroom
12-0x14-0

M.Bath
15-8x10-0

Stor.
5-8x10-4

Bath
7-8x5-0

Kitchen
9-0x9-9

Snack Bar

Laundry
9-7x5-4

Garage
21-6x21-6

Bedroom
11-4x12-0

Dining
9-0x11-6

Foyer

Den
11-5x10-0

Porch
30-0x8-8

*Images provided by designer/architect.*

## Plan #311037

**Dimensions:** 63' W x 53'2" D

**Levels:** 1

**Square Footage:** 1,644

**Bedrooms:** 3

**Bathrooms:** 2

**Foundation:** Crawl space, slab, or basement

**Material List Available:** No

**Price Category:** C

### Basement Stair Location

Laundry

To Optional Basement

To Optional Upstairs

Garage

Porch

Future
62-0x20-10

### Bonus Area Floor Plan

*Copyright by designer/architect.*

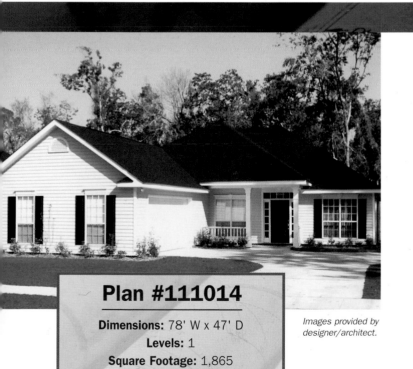

## Plan #111014

**Dimensions:** 78' W x 47' D

**Levels:** 1

**Square Footage:** 1,865

**Bedrooms:** 4

**Bathrooms:** 2

**Foundation:** Slab

**Materials List Available:** No

**Price Category:** D

*Images provided by designer/architect.*

Master
Bedroom
14'8"x 14'

Porch

Breakfast

Bedroom
11'x 10'

Living
19'4"x 15'6"

Bedroom
10'6"x 11'6"

Dining
10'6"x 11'6"

Bedroom
11'x 10'6"

Porch

Two Car
Garage
19'6"x 22'8"

*Copyright by designer/architect.*

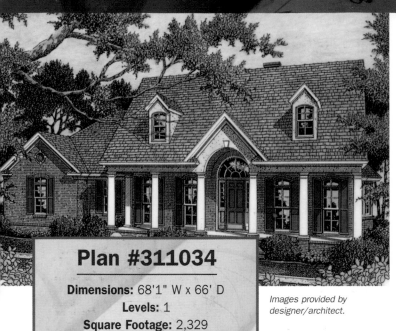

## Plan #311034

**Dimensions:** 68'1" W x 66' D

**Levels:** 1

**Square Footage:** 2,329

**Bedrooms:** 3

**Bathrooms:** 2½

**Foundation:** Crawl space, slab, or basement

**Material List Available:** No

**Price Category:** E

*Images provided by designer/architect.*

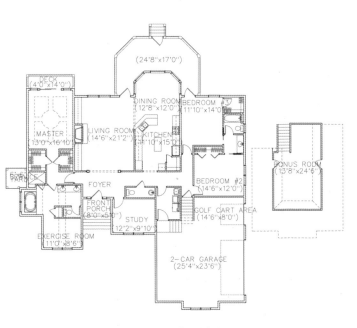

**Bonus Area Floor Plan**

*Copyright by designer/architect.*

## Plan #521016

**Dimensions:** 65'4" W x 79'2" D

**Levels:** 1

**Square Footage:** 2,389

**Bedrooms:** 3

**Bathrooms:** 2½

**Foundation:** Crawl space

**Material List Available:** No

**Price Category:** E

*Images provided by designer/architect.*

*Copyright by designer/architect.*

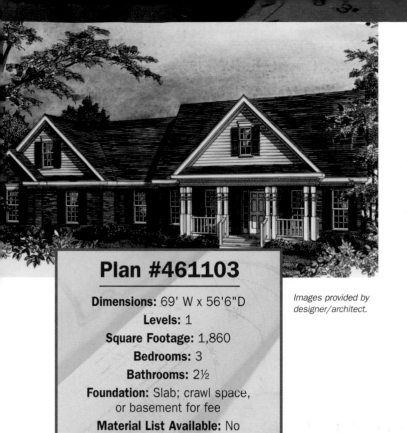

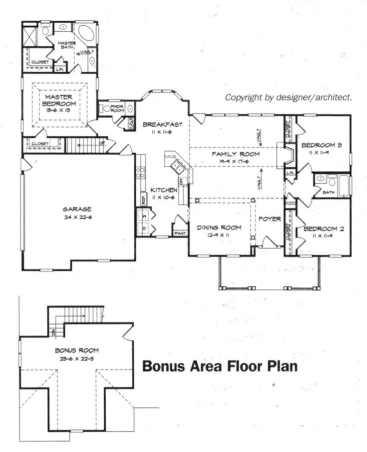

*Copyright by designer/architect.*

## Plan #461103

**Dimensions:** 69' W x 56'6"D

**Levels:** 1

**Square Footage:** 1,860

**Bedrooms:** 3

**Bathrooms:** 2½

**Foundation:** Slab; crawl space, or basement for fee

**Material List Available:** No

**Price Category:** D

*Images provided by designer/architect.*

**Bonus Area Floor Plan**

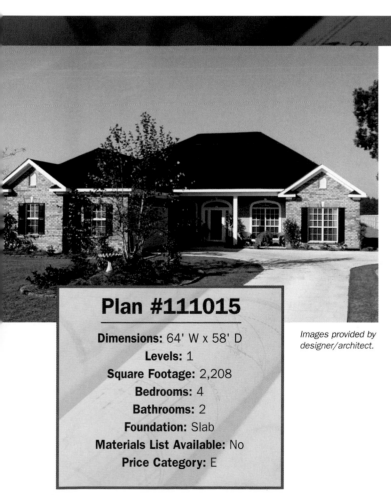

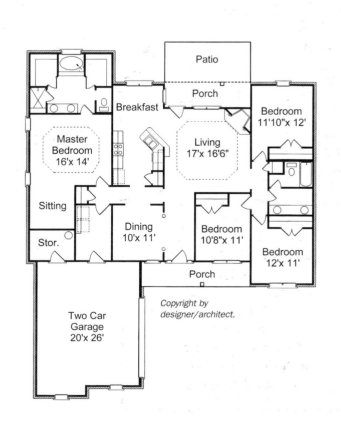

## Plan #111015

**Dimensions:** 64' W x 58' D

**Levels:** 1

**Square Footage:** 2,208

**Bedrooms:** 4

**Bathrooms:** 2

**Foundation:** Slab

**Materials List Available:** No

**Price Category:** E

*Images provided by designer/architect.*

*Copyright by designer/architect.*

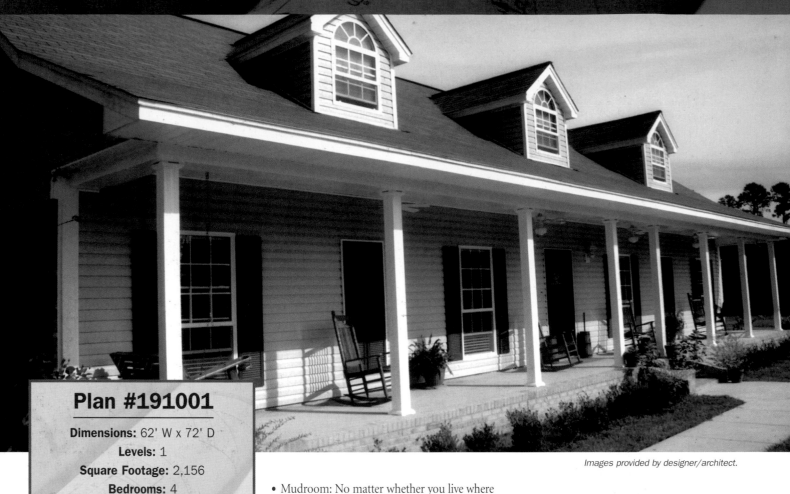

## Plan #191001

**Dimensions:** 62' W x 72' D

**Levels:** 1

**Square Footage:** 2,156

**Bedrooms:** 4

**Bathrooms:** 3

**Foundation:** Crawl space, slab, or basement

**Materials List Available:** No

**Price Category:** D

*Images provided by designer/architect.*

This lovely home has the best of old and new — a traditional appearance combined with fabulous comforts and conveniences.

### Features:

• **Great Room:** A tray ceiling gives stature to this expansive room, and its many windows let natural light stream into it.

• **Kitchen:** When you're standing at the sink in this gorgeous kitchen, you'll have a good view of the patio. But if you turn around, you'll see the island cooktop, wall oven, walk-in pantry, and snack bar, all of which make this kitchen such a pleasure.

• **Master Suite:** Somewhat isolated for privacy, this area is ideal for an evening or weekend retreat. Relax in the gracious bedroom or luxuriate in the spa-style bath, with its corner whirlpool tub, large shower, two sinks, and access to the walk-in closet, which measures a full 8 ft. x 10 ft.

• **Mudroom:** No matter whether you live where mud season is as reliable as spring thaws or where rain is a seasonal event, you'll love having a spot to confine the muddy mess.

Front View

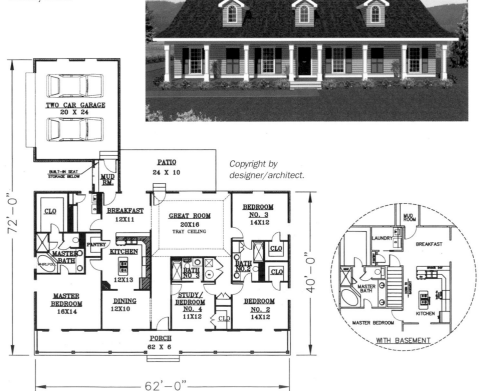

*Copyright by designer/architect.*

## Plan #151230

**Dimensions:** 59' W x 69' D

**Levels:** 1

**Square Footage:** 1,689

**Bedrooms:** 3

**Bathrooms:** 2

**Foundation:** Crawl space or slab

**CompleteCost List Available:** Yes

**Price Category:** C

This classic ranch home, with its lovely front porch, is waiting to entertain friends and family.

**CAD FILE AVAILABLE**

**Features:**

- **Living Room:** When you arrive home, this gathering area welcomes you with a vaulted ceiling and cozy fireplace. There is an abundance of wall space, allowing for many different ways to layout your furniture.

- **Kitchen:** This U-shape kitchen features plenty of counter space and cabinets and a window above the sink for a view of the backyard. Open to the dining room, which in turn is open to the living room, the area contributes to the home's open and spacious feeling.

- **Master Suite:** Located on the opposite side of the home from the secondary bedrooms, this retreat boasts privacy. The master bath features two large walk-in closets, a whirlpool tub, a stall shower, and a compartmentalized lavatory.

- **Secondary Bedrooms:** Two secondary bedrooms, each with a walk-in closet, share the second full bathroom, which is located in the hallway. Bedroom #2 boasts a built-in desk.

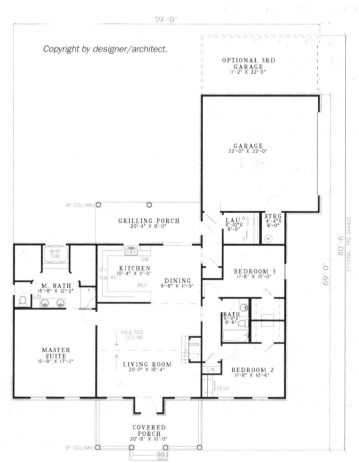

Copyright by designer/architect.

## Plan #171019

**Dimensions:** 68' W x 60' D

**Levels:** 1

**Square Footage:** 1,878

**Bedrooms:** 3

**Bathrooms:** 2

**Foundation:** Slab

**Materials List Available:** Yes

**Price Category:** D

*Images provided by designer/architect.*

Large columns on the front porch and brick accents give this home great curb appeal.

### Features:

- Living Room: This gathering area is perfect for friends and family to relax. The corner fireplace adds charm and warmth to the area. The wall of windows allows a view of the rear porch and backyard.

- Kitchen: This kitchen boasts an efficient cabinet layout and room for the family chef to prepare the meals. The large windows in the adjacent eating area will bring the natural light into the space. A convenient utility space located just off the kitchen features the washer and dryer.

- Master Suite: Located in a private wing of the home, this retreat boasts ample space for furnishings in the sleeping area. The master bath includes a walk-in closet, dual vanities, a whirlpool tub, and a compartmentalized lavatory.

- Garage: This side-loading two-car garage can hold two full-size cars and has an added storage room.

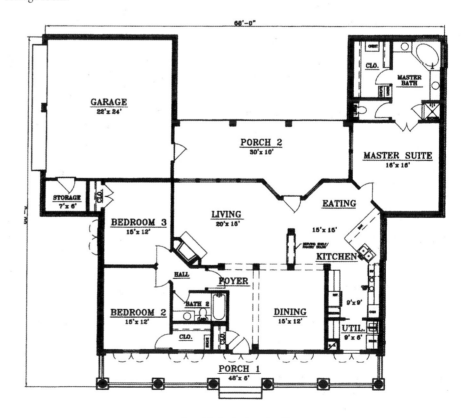

*Copyright by designer/architect.*

## Plan #111024

**Dimensions:** 46'10" W x 68'5" D
**Levels:** 2
**Square Footage:** 2,356
**Main Level Sq. Ft.:** 1,516
**Upper Level Sq. Ft.:** 840
**Bedrooms:** 4
**Bathrooms:** 2½
**Foundation:** Slab
**Materials List Available:** No
**Price Category:** E

A Southern-style home with a front porch and round-top windows, this is a great place to raise a family.

**Features:**

- **Living Room:** This gathering area features a ceiling that is two stories tall. The cozy fireplace will add warmth to a cool night.

- **Kitchen:** This U-shape kitchen with an abundance of cabinets and counter space would be a welcome addition to any home. The raised bar, which is open to the breakfast room, adds seating space to the area.

- **Master Suite:** Located on the main level for privacy, this oasis boasts a large walk-in closet. The master bath features his and her vanities, a stall shower, and a whirlpool tub.

- **Upper Level:** Three additional bedrooms and a full bathroom occupy this level. The balcony overlooks the living room.

*Images provided by designer/architect.*

**Main Level Floor Plan**

**Upper Level Floor Plan**
*Copyright by designer/architect.*

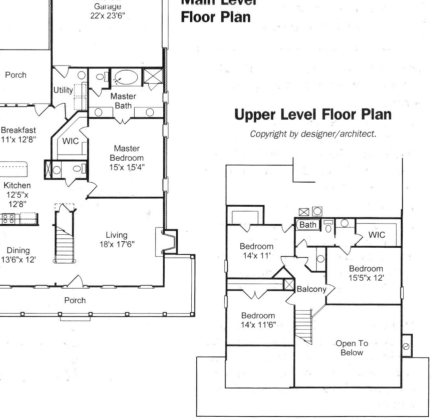

## Plan #181094

**Dimensions:** 50' W x 39' D
**Levels:** 2
**Square Footage:** 2,099
**Main Level Sq. Ft.:** 1,060
**Upper Level Sq. Ft.:** 1,039
**Bedrooms:** 4
**Bathrooms:** 2½
**Foundation:** Basement
**Materials List Available:** Yes
**Price Category:** D

*Images provided by designer/architect.*

The curved covered porch makes this is a great place to come home to.

**CAD FILE AVAILABLE**

**Features:**

- **Entry:** This air-lock entry area with closet will help keep energy costs down.

- **Family Room:** This gathering area features a fireplace and is open to the kitchen and the dining area.

- **Kitchen:** U-shaped and boasting an island and a walk-in pantry, this kitchen is open to the dining area.

- **Master Suite:** This large retreat features a fireplace and a walk-in closet. The master bath has dual vanities, a separate shower, and a large tub.

- **Bedrooms:** Located upstairs with the master suite are three additional bedrooms. They share a common bathroom, and each has a large closet.

Rear View

**Main Level Floor Plan**

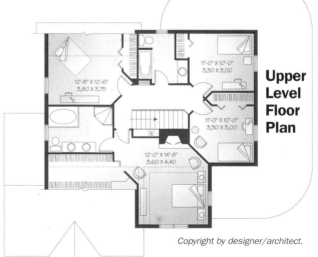

**Upper Level Floor Plan**

*Copyright by designer/architect.*

## Plan #181054

**Dimensions:** 54' W x 35'8" D

**Levels:** 2

**Square Footage:** 1,315

**Main Level Sq. Ft.:** 791

**Upper Level Sq. Ft:** 524

**Bedrooms:** 2

**Bathrooms:** 1½

**Foundation:** Basement

**Materials List Available:** Yes

**Price Category:** B

*Images provided by designer/architect.*

This is a charming home that would look great in any neighborhood.

### Features:

• Family Room: A bay window adds style and natural light to this family room. The fireplace, which it shares with the dining room, will add a warm and cozy feeling to this space.

• Home Office: Just off the entry is this efficient home office has a unique corner window seat. This space could also be used as a third bedroom.

• Kitchen: This L-shaped kitchen, with its built-in pantry, has room for a table for casual family meals. A full bathroom is just steps away and features a washer and dryer.

• Upper Level: The master bedroom and one secondary bedroom are located on this level. The single full bathroom is centrally located between the two bedrooms.

**CAD FILE — CAD — AVAILABLE**

**Main Level Floor Plan**

*Copyright by designer/architect.*

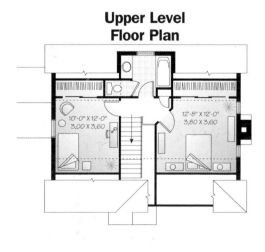

**Upper Level Floor Plan**

## Plan #211154

**Dimensions:** 40' W x 34' D

**Levels:** 1

**Square Footage:** 848

**Bedrooms:** 1

**Bathrooms:** 1

**Foundation:** Crawl space

**Materials List Available:** No

**Price Category:** A

This charming cottage is a perfect addition to your existing home for guests or live-in parents.

**Features:**

- **Porch:** This wraparound porch creates a warm and inviting entry, and it is a great place for spending a relaxing evening.

- **Dining and Living Room:** This combination space is surprisingly large for a compact home. The open design gives a feeling of spaciousness.

- **Kitchen:** Despite the compact design, this kitchen has plenty of cabinets and counter space. The two windows located in this space allow an abundance of natural light into this area.

- **Master Suite:** The only bedroom in this home features a tray ceiling. The full bathroom is just off the bedroom.

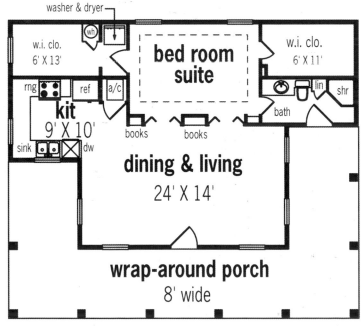

**Main Level Floor Plan**

Two Car Garage 21'2"x 21'1"

Patio

Porch

Storage

1/2 Ba.

Master Bedroom 15'x 15'

WIC

Living 19'4"x 17'1"

Breakfast 13'8"x 10'7"

Ma. Bath

Bath

WIC

Bedroom 12'x 11'7"

Dining 12'x 13'6"

Kitchen 10'8"x 12'3"

Utility

Porch

*Images provided by designer/architect.*

Open to Below

Bath

Balcony

**Upper Level Floor Plan**

Bedroom 12'x 11'7"

Bedroom 12'x 13'

*Copyright by designer/architect.*

## Plan #111026

**Dimensions:** 66' W x 65' D

**Levels:** 2

**Square Footage:** 2,406

**Main Level Sq. Ft.:** 1,796

**Upper Level Sq. Ft.:** 610

**Bedrooms:** 4

**Bathrooms:** 3½

**Foundation:** Crawlspace

**Materials List Available:** No

**Price Category:** E

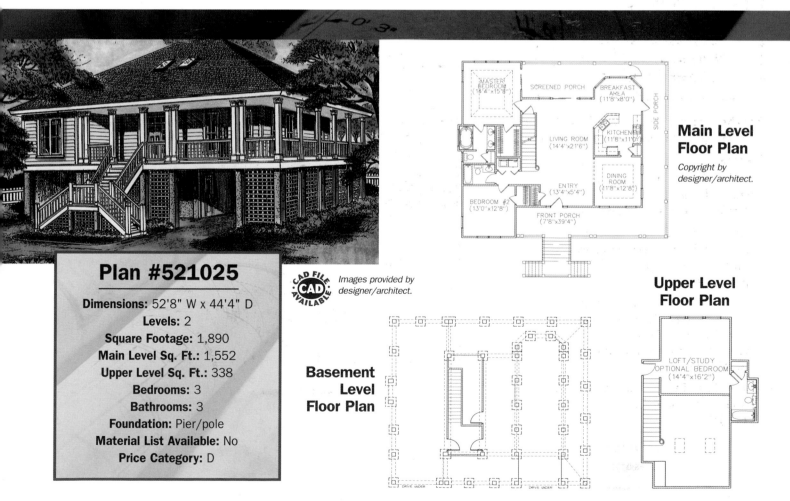

MASTER BEDROOM (16'4"x15'8")

SCREENED PORCH

BREAKFAST AREA (11'8"x8'0")

SIDE PORCH

LIVING ROOM (14'4"x 21'6")

KITCHEN (11'8"x11'0")

ENTRY (13'4"x5'4")

DINING ROOM (11'8"x12'8")

BEDROOM #2 (13'0"x12'8")

FRONT PORCH (7'8"x39'4")

**Main Level Floor Plan**

*Copyright by designer/architect.*

**CAD FILE AVAILABLE**

*Images provided by designer/architect.*

**Upper Level Floor Plan**

**Basement Level Floor Plan**

DRIVE UNDER

DRIVE UNDER

LOFT/STUDY OPTIONAL BEDROOM (14'4"x16'2")

## Plan #521025

**Dimensions:** 52'8" W x 44'4" D

**Levels:** 2

**Square Footage:** 1,890

**Main Level Sq. Ft.:** 1,552

**Upper Level Sq. Ft.:** 338

**Bedrooms:** 3

**Bathrooms:** 3

**Foundation:** Pier/pole

**Material List Available:** No

**Price Category:** D

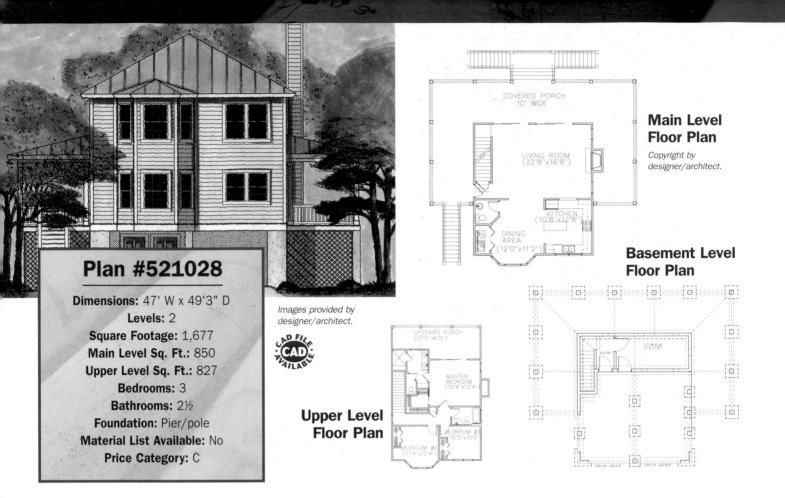

**Main Level Floor Plan**

*Copyright by designer/architect.*

COVERED PORCH 10' WIDE

LIVING ROOM (22'8"x16'8")

KITCHEN (10'8"x13'8")

DINING AREA (12'0"x11'2")

**Basement Level Floor Plan**

UPSTAIRS PORCH (27'0"x6'0")

MASTER BEDROOM (15'4"x13'8")

BEDROOM #3 (10'0"x10'0")

BEDROOM #2 (11'4"x12'4")

**Upper Level Floor Plan**

ENTRY

STORAGE (17'2"x18')

DRIVE UNDER | DRIVE UNDER

*Images provided by designer/architect.*

**CAD FILE AVAILABLE**

## Plan #521028

**Dimensions:** 47' W x 49'3" D

**Levels:** 2

**Square Footage:** 1,677

**Main Level Sq. Ft.:** 850

**Upper Level Sq. Ft.:** 827

**Bedrooms:** 3

**Bathrooms:** 2½

**Foundation:** Pier/pole

**Material List Available:** No

**Price Category:** C

---

## Plan #421003

**Dimensions:** 59' W x 61' D

**Levels:** 1

**Square Footage:** 1,698

**Bedrooms:** 3

**Bathrooms:** 2½

**Foundation:** Crawl space, slab, or basement

**Materials List Available:** Yes

**Price Category:** C

*Images provided by designer/architect.*

**CAD FILE AVAILABLE**

GARAGE 21'-0"x22'-0" (CARPORT OR NO GARAGE OPTIONAL)

16' OVERHEAD DOOR

WORK BENCH/STORAGE

PATIO 20'-0"x12'-0"

WALK-IN CLOSET

MSTR BATH

PWDR

HALL

PANTRY

KITCHEN 13'-0"x10'-0"

DINING 11'-0"x10'-0"

FRIG

COLUMNS

DESK

BEDROOM #3 13'-0"x11'-10"

LINEN

BATH

OPTIONAL PRIVACY DOOR (POCKET)

SITTING AREA

RIDGE OF VAULT

MASTER BEDROOM 15'-5"x16'-0" (VAULTED CLG)

FP

BUILT-IN

GREAT ROOM 24'-0"x20'-0" (10' CLG)

OPTIONAL ROOM DIVIDER

COAT

DESK

BEDROOM #2 13'-0"x11'-10"

COVERED PORCH 25'-0"x8'-0" (10' CLG)

*Copyright by designer/architect.*

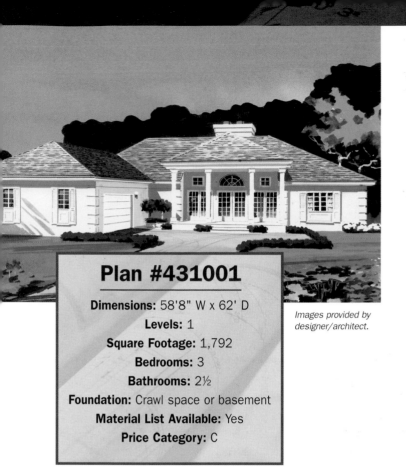

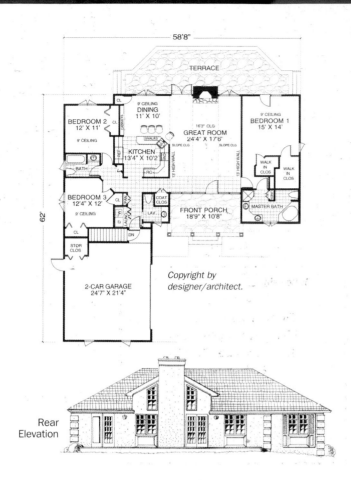

## Plan #431001

**Dimensions:** 58'8" W x 62' D

**Levels:** 1

**Square Footage:** 1,792

**Bedrooms:** 3

**Bathrooms:** 2½

**Foundation:** Crawl space or basement

**Material List Available:** Yes

**Price Category:** C

*Images provided by designer/architect.*

*Copyright by designer/architect.*

Rear Elevation

## Plan #111023

**Dimensions:** 46'11" W x 73'5" D

**Levels:** 2

**Square Footage:** 2,356

**Main Level Sq. Ft.:** 1,516

**Upper Level Sq. Ft.:** 840

**Bedrooms:** 4

**Bathrooms:** 2½

**Foundation:** Slab

**Materials List Available:** No

**Price Category:** E

*Images provided by designer/architect.*

**Main Level Floor Plan**

**Upper Level Floor Plan**

*Copyright by designer/architect.*

## Plan #221034

**Dimensions:** 63'8" W x 56'4" D
**Levels:** 2
**Square Footage:** 2,415
**Main Level Sq. Ft.:** 1,691
**Upper Level Sq. Ft.:** 724
**Bedrooms:** 4
**Bathrooms:** 2½
**Foundation:** Basement
**Materials List Available:** No
**Price Category:** C

This spacious two-story brick home features tons of amenities that you would normally expect in a much larger home.

*Images provided by designer/architect.*

**Features:**

- Kitchen: The breakfast bar in this kitchen overlooks both the nook and the great room, creating the illusion of additional space.

- Great Room: The two-story ceiling in this room is made comfortable by a wall that features a fireplace and built-ins.

- Master Suite: This suite features a spacious bath and large walk-in closet, while the bedroom itself has a stepped ceiling.

- Upper Level: Upstairs you'll love the balcony, which overlooks the great room from above, and you'll be pleasantly surprised to find three additional bedrooms and a full bathroom.

Rear Elevation

**Main Level Floor Plan**

**Upper Level Floor Plan**

*Copyright by designer/architect.*

# Plan #461009

**Dimensions:** 67'6" W x 43'6" D

**Levels:** 1

**Square Footage:** 1,758

**Bedrooms:** 3

**Bathrooms:** 2½

**Foundation:** Slab or basement; crawl space available for fee

**Material List Available:** No

**Price Category:** C

*Images provided by designer/architect.*

*Copyright by designer/architect.*

GARAGE 21-3 X 19-3

PORCH

UTILITY

CLOSET

MASTER BATH

KITCHEN 11 X 9-9

BREAKFAST 10 X 11

MASTER BEDROOM 13-3 X 13-9

DINING ROOM 10-3 X 12-6

PANTRY

STORAGE

BEDROOM 3 11 X 13

CLOSET

DRESS

CLOSET

FAMILY ROOM 13-9 X 17-3

FOYER

BEDROOM 2 11 X 10-9

BATH

DRESS

PORCH

---

# Plan #161115

**Dimensions:** 79'8" W x 44'2" D

**Levels:** 1

**Square Footage:** 2,253

**Bedrooms:** 4

**Bathrooms:** 3

**Foundation:** Walkout basement

**Material List Available:** Yes

**Price Category:** E

*Images provided by designer/architect.*

CAD FILE AVAILABLE

Deck

WALK IN CLOSET

Master Bedroom 15' x 14'6"

Breakfast 12'9" x 11' Incl. Bay

Guest Suite 14'8" x 10'8"

Bath

WALK IN CLOSET

Great Room 16'6" x 21'2"

Dressing

CLOSET

Kitchen 12'6" x

Laun.

Garage 12' x 21'

Bedroom 12' x 11'1"

Bath

Foyer

Dining Room 10'10" x 12'2"

Garage 19'8" x 21'

Bedroom 12'3" x 11'1"

CLOSET

Porch

*Copyright by designer/architect.*

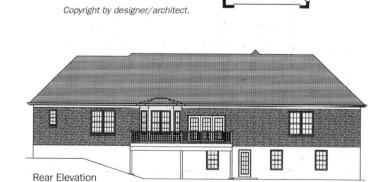

Rear Elevation

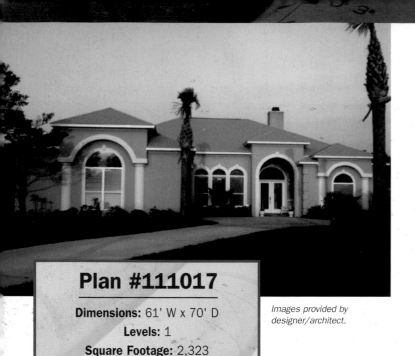

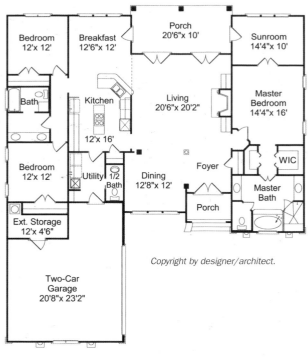

Images provided by
designer/architect.

Copyright by designer/architect.

## Plan #111017

**Dimensions:** 61' W x 70' D

**Levels:** 1

**Square Footage:** 2,323

**Bedrooms:** 3

**Bathrooms:** 2½

**Foundation:** Monolithic slab

**Materials List Available:** No

**Price Category:** E

## Plan #191016

**Dimensions:** 113' W x 56' D

**Levels:** 1

**Square Footage:** 2,421

**Bedrooms:** 3

**Bathrooms:** 2

**Foundation:** Crawl space or slab

**Material List Available:** No

**Price Category:** E

Images provided by
designer/architect.

Copyright by
designer/architect.

## Plan #271074

**Dimensions:** 68' W x 86' D
**Levels:** 1
**Square Footage:** 2,400
**Bedrooms:** 4
**Bathrooms:** 3
**Foundation:** Crawl space or slab
**Materials List Available:** No
**Price Category:** E

Perfect for families with aging relatives or boomerang children, this home includes a completely separate suite at the rear.

**Features:**

- **Living Room:** A corner fireplace casts a friendly glow over this gathering space.
- **Kitchen:** This efficient space offers a serving bar that extends toward the eating nook and the formal dining room.

- **Master Suite:** A cathedral ceiling presides over this deluxe suite, which boasts a whirlpool tub, dual-sink vanity, and walk-in closet.
- **In-law Suite:** This separate wing has its own vaulted living room, plus a kitchen, a dining room, and a bedroom suite.

**CAD FILE AVAILABLE**

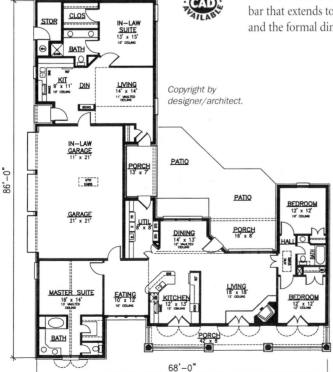

Copyright by designer/architect.

## SMARTtip

### Adding Professional Flair to Window Treatments

You can give your window treatment designs a professional look by using decorator tricks to customize readymades or dress your own home-sewn designs. These could include contrast linings, tassels, cording, ribbons, or couture trimmings such as buttons, coins, or bows applied to edges. Another trick is to sew a fine wire into the hem of curtains or valances to create a pliable edge that you can shape yourself. Small weights that you can sew into the hem of drapery panels or jabots will make them hang better. For more inspiration look at fashion magazines and visit showrooms.

## Plan #521066

**Dimensions:** 66'4" W x 53'8" D
**Levels:** 2
**Square Footage:** 2,245
**Main Level Sq. Ft.:** 1,390
**Lower Level Sq. Ft:** 855
**Bedrooms:** 3
**Bathrooms:** 2½
**Foundation:** Crawl space
**Materials List Available:** No
**Price Category:** E

The two level front porches gives classic styling to this wonderful home.

*Images provided by designer/architect.*

CAD FILE AVAILABLE

**Features:**

• **Living Room:** Just off the entry is this wonderful gathering area. The fireplace adds warmth in the winter while the front and rear windows can bring in the summer breeze.

• **Kitchen:** This efficiently designed kitchen features an oversize built-in pantry. The raised bar, which is open to the dining area, adds the much-needed additional dining space.

• **Master Suite:** This main-level master suite gives the privacy needed for a relaxing retreat.

The large sleeping area and spacious walk-in closet make the area special. The master bath boasts a large tub with a separate shower and dual vanities.

• **Upper Level:** Go up the stairway, and you will find two spacious bedrooms, each with a walk-in closet. In close proximity is the common bathroom that the two bedrooms share. The computer area will be the perfect place for the kids to do their homework.

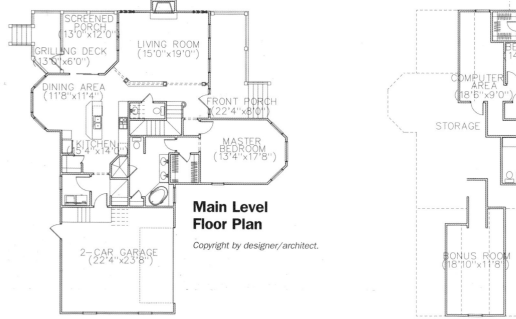

**Main Level Floor Plan**

*Copyright by designer/architect.*

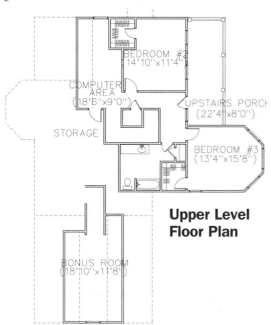

**Upper Level Floor Plan**

## Plan #441002

**Dimensions:** 70' W x 51' D

**Levels:** 1

**Square Footage:** 1,873

**Bedrooms:** 3

**Bathrooms:** 2

**Foundation:** Crawl space

**Materials List Available:** No

**Price Category:** D

Shutters flank tall windows to adorn the front of this charming home. A high roofline gives presence to the façade and allows vaulted ceilings in all the right places inside.

**Features:**

- **Great Room:** The entry hall overlooks this room, where a fireplace warms gatherings on chilly evenings and built-in shelves, to the right of the fireplace, add space that might be used as an entertainment center. A large three-panel window wall allows for a rear-yard view.

- **Dining Room:** This area is connected directly to the great room and features double doors to a covered porch.

- **Kitchen:** This open work area contains ample counter space with an island cooktop and large pantry.

- **Bedrooms:** The bedrooms are split, with the master suite in the back and additional bedrooms at the front.

*Images provided by designer/architect.*

- **Master Suite:** This suite boasts a 9-ft.-high ceiling and is graced by a luxurious bathroom and a walk-in closet.

*Copyright by designer/architect.*

Rear Elevation

## Plan #101004

**Dimensions:** 55'8" W x 56'6" D

**Levels:** 1

**Square Footage:** 1,787

**Bedrooms:** 3

**Bathrooms:** 2

**Foundation:** Crawl space, slab, or basement

**Materials List Available:** Yes

**Price Category:** C

*Images provided by designer/architect.*

This carefully designed ranch provides the feel and features of a much larger home.

**Features:**

- Ceiling Height: 9 ft. unless otherwise noted.

- Foyer: Guests will step up onto the inviting front porch and into this foyer, with its impressive 11-ft. ceiling.

- Dining Room: Open to the entry and to its left is this elegant dining room, perfect for entertaining or informal family gatherings.

- Family Room: This family gathering place features an 11-ft. ceiling to enhance its sense of spaciousness.

- Kitchen: This intelligently designed kitchen has an open plan. A breakfast bar and a serving bar are features that add to its convenience.

- Master Suite: This suite is loaded with amenities, including a double-step tray ceiling, direct access to the screened porch, a sitting room, deluxe bath, and his and her walk-in closets.

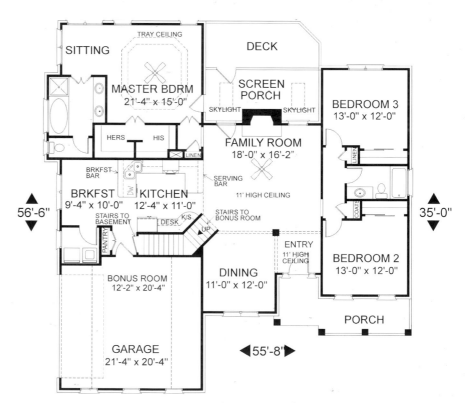

*Copyright by designer/architect.*

Kitchen

Family Room

Dining Room

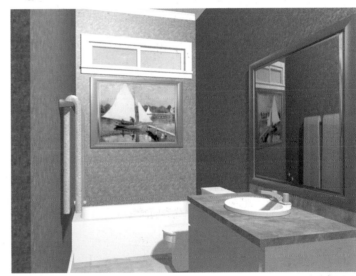

Master Bath

Bedroom

Master Bedroom

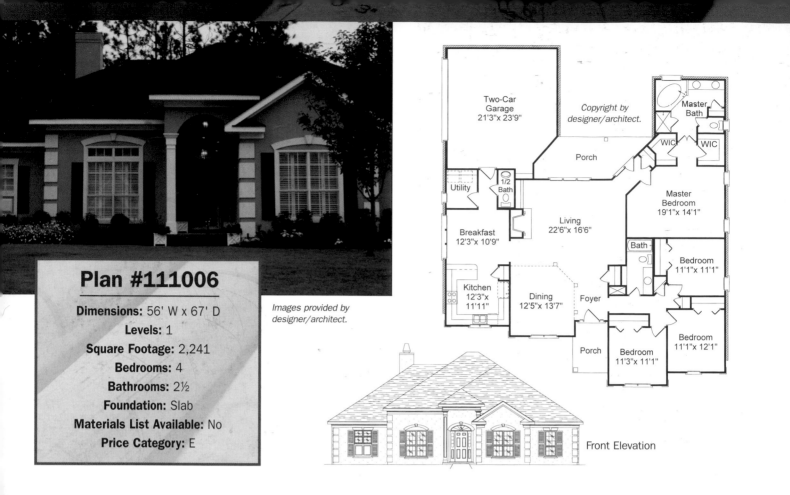

# Plan #111006

**Dimensions:** 56' W x 67' D

**Levels:** 1

**Square Footage:** 2,241

**Bedrooms:** 4

**Bathrooms:** 2½

**Foundation:** Slab

**Materials List Available:** No

**Price Category:** E

*Images provided by designer/architect.*

Two-Car Garage 21'3"x 23'9"

*Copyright by designer/architect.*

Porch

Master Bath

WIC

WIC

Utility

1/2 Bath

Master Bedroom 19'1"x 14'1"

Breakfast 12'3"x 10'9"

Living 22'6"x 16'6"

Bath

Bedroom 11'1"x 11'1"

Kitchen 12'3"x 11'11"

Dining 12'5"x 13'7"

Foyer

Porch

Bedroom 11'3"x 11'1"

Bedroom 11'1"x 12'1"

Front Elevation

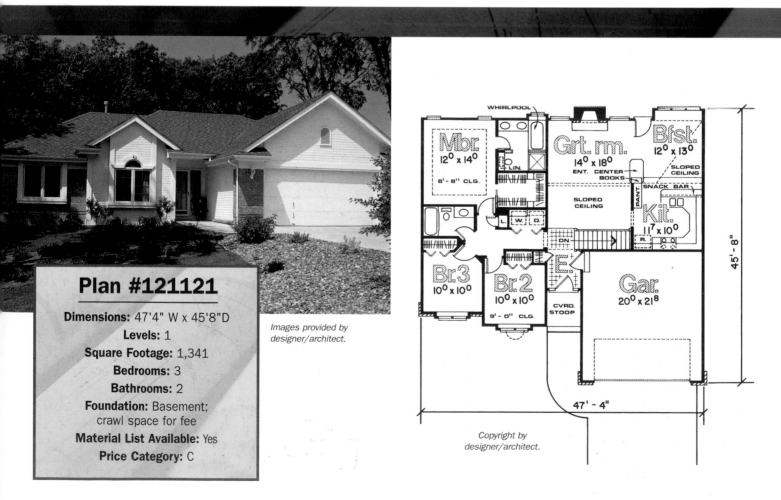

# Plan #121121

**Dimensions:** 47'4" W x 45'8"D

**Levels:** 1

**Square Footage:** 1,341

**Bedrooms:** 3

**Bathrooms:** 2

**Foundation:** Basement; crawl space for fee

**Material List Available:** Yes

**Price Category:** C

*Images provided by designer/architect.*

WHIRLPOOL

Mbr. 12⁰ x 14⁰
8'- 8"11 CLG.

Grt. rm. 14⁰ x 18⁰
ENT. CENTER BOOKS
SLOPED CEILING
SLOPED CEILING

Bfst. 12⁰ x 13⁰
SLOPED CEILING

LIN.

PANT.

SNACK BAR

Kit.
11'7 x 10⁰

Br.3 10⁰ x 10⁰

Br.2 10⁰ x 10⁰
9'- 0" CLG.

CVRD. STOOP

Gar. 20⁰ x 21⁸

45'- 8"

47'- 4"

*Copyright by designer/architect.*

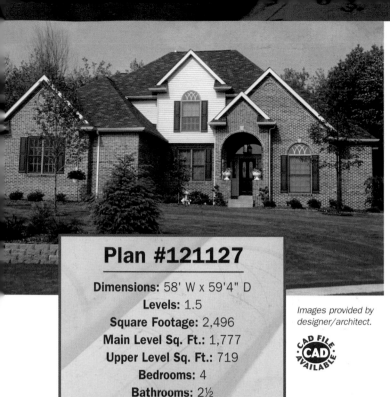

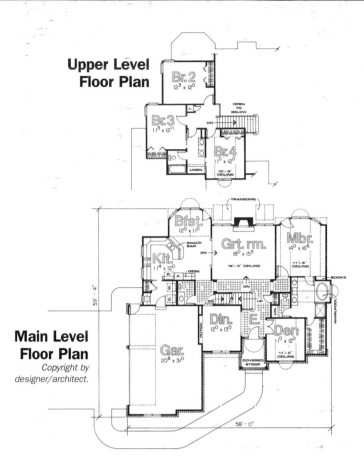

## Upper Level Floor Plan

Br. 2
12³ x 12⁰

Br. 3
11³ x 12'¹

Br. 4
11⁰ x 11⁰
10'-0" CEILING

OPEN TO BELOW

LINEN

## Main Level Floor Plan

*Copyright by designer/architect.*

Bfst.
12⁰ x 11⁰

Grt. rm.
18⁰ x 15⁵
18'-0" CEILING

Mbr.
14⁰ x 16⁶
11'-6" CEILING

Kit.
11⁴ x 12⁰

SNACK BAR

Gar.
20⁸ x 31⁰

Din.
12⁰ x 13⁰

Den
11⁰ x 11⁰
11'-0" CEILING

COVERED STOOP

58'-0"

59'-4"

# Plan #121127

**Dimensions:** 58' W x 59'4" D

**Levels:** 1.5

**Square Footage:** 2,496

**Main Level Sq. Ft.:** 1,777

**Upper Level Sq. Ft.:** 719

**Bedrooms:** 4

**Bathrooms:** 2½

**Foundation:** Basement; crawl space for fee

**Material List Available:** Yes

**Price Category:** E

*Images provided by designer/architect.*

CAD FILE AVAILABLE — **CAD**

---

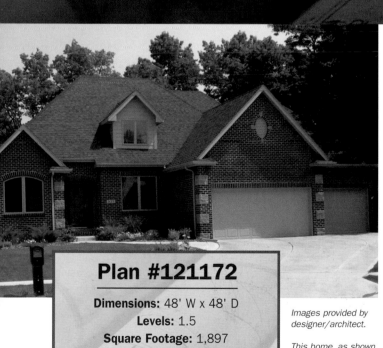

# Plan #121172

**Dimensions:** 48' W x 48' D

**Levels:** 1.5

**Square Footage:** 1,897

**Main Level Sq. Ft.:** 1,448

**Upper Level Sq. Ft.:** 449

**Bedrooms:** 3

**Bathrooms:** 2½

**Foundation:** Slab; basement for fee

**Material List Available:** Yes

**Price Category:** D

*Images provided by designer/architect.*

*This home, as shown in the photograph, may differ from the actual blueprints. For more detailed information, please check the floor plans carefully.*

## Main Level Floor Plan

48'

NOOK
10'4" X 10'2"
9' CLG.

FAMILY ROOM
15'8" X 18'
VAULTED CEILING
18' CLG.

MASTER BEDROOM
14'4" X 14'6"
9' CLG.

EATING BAR

KITCHEN
10'4" X 11'6"

MASTER BATH

DESK

REF.

BUTLER'S PANTRY

OPTIONAL BASEMENT STAIRS

UP

DINING ROOM
10'4" X 11'6"
12' CLG.

10' CLG.

LIVING ROOM
10'8" X 11'6"
9' CLG.

GARAGE
19'4" X 21'6"

48'

## Upper Level Floor Plan

*Copyright by designer/architect.*

BEDROOM 2
11'8" X 10'8"

OPEN TO BELOW

BEDROOM 3
10'6" X 11'10"

DN

ATTIC

## Plan #441045

**Dimensions:** 52' W x 33'6" D
**Levels:** 2
**Square Footage:** 2,206
**Main Level Sq. Ft.:** 1,294
**Upper Level Sq. Ft:** 912
**Bedrooms:** 4
**Bathrooms:** 3
**Foundation:** Slab or walkout
**Materials List Available:** No
**Price Category:** E

A sloped lot is no challenge for this comely design–it easily accommodates a site that slopes to the side or to the front.

**CAD FILE AVAILABLE — CAD**

**Features:**

- **Great Room:** A perfect place for friends and family to gather, this great room welcomes you to the home. The cozy gas fireplace will add charm to the atmosphere.

- **Kitchen:** An abundance of cabinets and counter space fill this gourmet island kitchen. The raised bar is open to the dining room and the great room.

- **Master Suite:** This master suite has a scissor-vaulted ceiling and a large sleeping area. The master bath features a spa tub, walk-in closet, and separate shower.

- **Secondary Bedrooms:** Two bedrooms are located upstairs with the master suite and share a common full bathroom. The third is on the main level and boasts a 9-ft.-high cciling, as do all rooms on this level.

**Upper Level Floor Plan**

**Rear Elevation**

**Main Level Floor Plan**

**Basement Level Floor Plan**

*Copyright by designer/architect.*

## Plan #271021

**Dimensions:** 39' W x 58' D
**Levels:** 2
**Square Footage:** 1,551
**Main Level Sq. Ft.:** 1,099
**Upper Level Sq. Ft.:** 452
**Bedrooms:** 3
**Bathrooms:** 2½
**Foundation:** Basement
**Materials List Available:** Yes
**Price Category:** C

*Images provided by designer/architect.*

The exterior of this cozy country-style home boasts a charming combination of woodwork and stone that lends an air of England to the facade.

**Features:**

• Living Room: An arched entryway leads into the living room, with its vaulted ceiling, tall windows, and fireplace.

• Dining Room: This space also features a vaulted ceiling, plus a view of the patio.

• Master Suite: Find a vaulted ceiling here, too, as well as a walk-in closet, and private bath.

Living Room

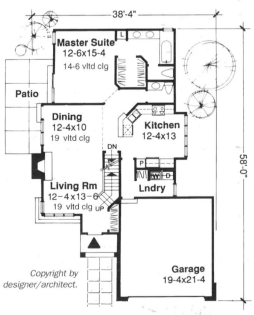

*Copyright by designer/architect.*

**Main Level Floor Plan**

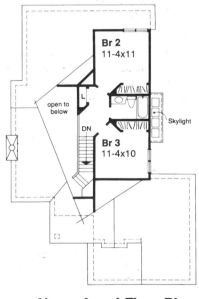

**Upper Level Floor Plan**

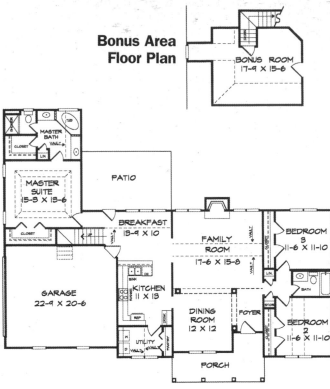

**Bonus Area Floor Plan**

BONUS ROOM 17-9 X 15-6

*Images provided by designer/architect.*

# Plan #461033

**Dimensions:** 67'6" W x 50'9"D

**Levels:** 1

**Square Footage:** 1,802

**Bedrooms:** 3

**Bathrooms:** 2

**Foundation:** Slab; crawl space, or basement for fee

**Material List Available:** No

**Price Category:** D

*Copyright by designer/architect.*

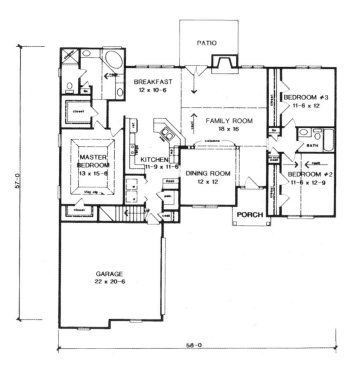

*Images provided by designer/architect.*

# Plan #461035

**Dimensions:** 58' W x 57' D

**Levels:** 1

**Square Footage:** 1,831

**Bedrooms:** 3

**Bathrooms:** 2

**Foundation:** Crawl space or slab; basement for fee

**Material List Available:** No

**Price Category:** D

*Copyright by designer/architect.*

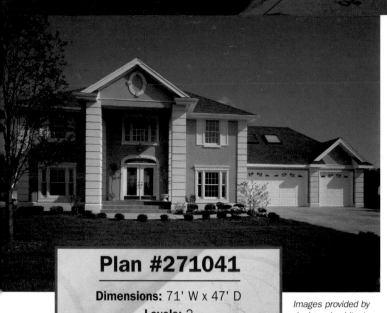

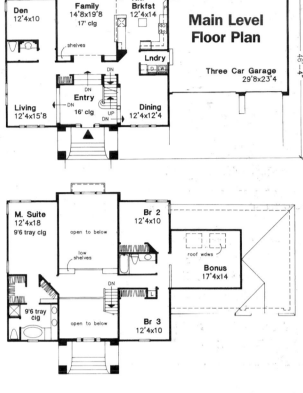

**Main Level Floor Plan**

Three Car Garage 29'8x23'4

Deck

Family 14'8x19'8 17' clg

Kit/ Brkfst 12'4x14

Den 12'4x10

Lndry

Living 12'4x15'8

Entry 16' clg

Dining 12'4x12'4

71'-0"

46'-4"

*Images provided by designer/architect.*

**Upper Level Floor Plan**

M. Suite 12'4x18 9'6 tray clg

open to below

low shelves

Br 2 12'4x10

roof wdws

Bonus 17'4x14

9'6 tray clg

open to below

Br 3 12'4x10

*Copyright by designer/architect.*

## Plan #271041

**Dimensions:** 71' W x 47' D

**Levels:** 2

**Square Footage:** 2,416

**Main Level Sq. Ft.:** 1,416

**Upper Level Sq. Ft.:** 1,000

**Bedrooms:** 4

**Bathrooms:** 2½

**Foundation:** Basement

**Materials List Available:** No

**Price Category:** E

63'-8"

DW

Kit/ Dinette 22-0 x 14-4 9' Clg

Great Rm 17-0 x 14-4 9' Clg

Built-In

Ref

FP

DN    UP

Built-In

Dining Rm 12-4 x 12-4 9' Clg

Foyer 6-8 x 12-4 9' Clg

Study 11-4 x 12-4 9' Clg

Garage 32-0 x 24-4

Porch 31-8 x 8-0

48'-0"

**Main Level Floor Plan**

*Images provided by designer/architect.*

**Upper Level Floor Plan**

WIC

Master Bath

Master Suite 13-4 x 13-4

DN

Desk

Bedroom 2 11-4 x 10-10

Bedroom 3 11-4 x 10-10

*Copyright by designer/architect.*

## Plan #481003

**Dimensions:** 63'8" W x 48' D

**Levels:** 2

**Square Footage:** 2,278

**Main Level Sq. Ft.:** 1,231

**Upper Level Sq. Ft.:** 1,047

**Bedrooms:** 3

**Bathrooms:** 2½

**Foundation:** Walkout

**Material List Available:** No

**Price Category:** E

## Plan #481007

**Dimensions:** 40' W x 55' D

**Levels:** 2

**Square Footage:** 2,176

**Main Level Sq. Ft.:** 1,154

**Upper Level Sq. Ft.:** 1,022

**Bedrooms:** 3

**Bathrooms:** 2½

**Foundation:** Walkout

**Material List Available:** No

**Price Category:** D

*Images provided by designer/architect.*

### Main Level Floor Plan

*Copyright by designer/architect.*

### Upper Level Floor Plan

Rear Elevation

## Plan #511013

**Dimensions:** 50' W x 58' D

**Levels:** 1

**Square Footage:** 1,931

**Bedrooms:** 4

**Bathrooms:** 2

**Foundation:** Crawl space or slab

**Material List Available:** No

**Price Category:** D

*Images provided by designer/architect.*

CAD FILE AVAILABLE

*Copyright by designer/architect.*

## Plan #441001

**Dimensions:** 44' W x 68' D

**Levels:** 1

**Square Footage:** 1,850

**Bedrooms:** 3

**Bathrooms:** 2

**Foundation:** Crawl space

**Materials List Available:** No

**Price Category:** D

*Images provided by designer/architect.*

With all the tantalizing elements of a cottage and the comfortable space of a family-sized home, this Arts and Crafts-style one-story design is the best of both worlds. Exterior accents such as stone wainscot, cedar shingles under the gable ends, and mission-style windows just add to the effect.

**CAD FILE AVAILABLE — CAD**

**Features:**

- **Great Room:** A warm hearth lights this room—right next to a built-in media center.

- **Dining Room:** This area features a sliding glass door to the rear patio for a breath of fresh air.

- **Den:** This quiet area has a window seat and a vaulted ceiling, giving the feeling of openness and letting your mind wander.

- **Kitchen:** This open corner kitchen features a 42-in. snack bar and a giant walk-in pantry.

- **Master Suite:** This suite boasts a tray ceiling and a large walk-in closet.

*Copyright by designer/architect.*

Rear Elevation

## Plan #271040

**Dimensions:** 44' W x 66'8" D

**Levels:** 2

**Square Footage:** 2,272

**Main Level Sq. Ft.:** 1,750

**Upper Level Sq. Ft.:** 522

**Bedrooms:** 3

**Bathrooms:** 2½

**Foundation:** Basement

**Materials List Available:** Yes

**Price Category:** E

*Images provided by designer/architect.*

Suitable for a narrow lot, this stylish home may have two, three, or four bedrooms, depending on the needs of your family.

### Features:

- **Family Room:** This spacious family room features a handsome fireplace and a ceiling that vaults to 17 ft. Sliding glass doors provide access to an inviting deck.

- **Kitchen:** This efficiently designed kitchen offers an angled serving counter and a pantry. The breakfast room and family room are open to this kitchen.

- **Master Suite:** A 10-ft.-high tray ceiling and private deck access highlights this master suite. His and her walk-in closets will provide for all of your storage needs.

- Upper Level: You'll find the second bedroom upstairs, along with a nice loft that overlooks the family room and could serve as a third bedroom. The unfinished bonus room may be completed later as a fourth bedroom, playroom, or home office.

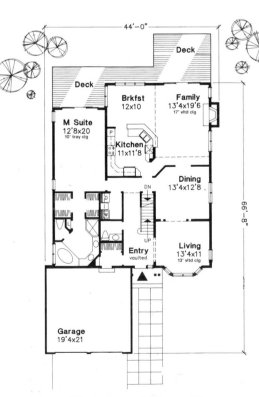

**Main Level Floor Plan**

### Upper Level Floor Plan

*Copyright by designer/architect.*

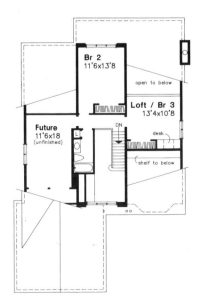

## Plan #181617

**Dimensions:** 33' W x 35' D
**Levels:** 2
**Square Footage:** 1,745
**Main Level Sq. Ft.:** 805
**Upper Level Sq. Ft.:** 940
**Bedrooms:** 3
**Bathrooms:** 2½
**Foundation:** Basement
**Materials List Available:** Yes
**Price Category:** C

Unique architectural details and classic beauty will make this home the envy of the neighborhood.

**CAD FILE AVAILABLE**

*Images provided by designer/architect.*

## Features:

- **Entry:** A covered entry and large foyer welcome guests in from the elements.

- **Living Room:** A triplet of windows lets the sunlight into this room, creating a warm atmosphere for lazy afternoons with the family or friendly gatherings.

- **Dining Room:** This formal dining room, just off the kitchen, creates simple meal transitions and a place for entertaining. A door to the backyard gives you a reason to buy patio furniture: drinks and dinner outside on warm summer afternoons.

- **Kitchen:** This spacious eat-in kitchen has plenty of workspace and storage to keep the family cook happy, including an extra

pantry. It opens into the laundry room for easy cleanup.

- **Second Floor:** For a restful atmosphere, the bedrooms are separated from the hum of daily life. The master suite includes a spacious bedroom, walk-in closet and full master bath, with his and her sinks, a stall shower, and a large tub. The secondary bedrooms are virtually identical to prevent squabbles between siblings, and they share access to the second full bathroom.

### Main Level Floor Plan

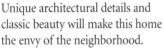

14'-8" X 10'-0"
4,40 X 3,00

10'-0" X 13'-0"
3,00 X 3,90

12'-0" X 16'-0"
3,60 X 4,80

11'-8" X 20'-4"
3,50 X 6,10

*Copyright by designer/architect.*

Rear Elevation

### Upper Level Floor Plan

12'-0" X 12'-0"
3,60 X 3,60

12'-0" X 15'-4"
3,60 X 4,60

12'-0" X 12'-0"
3,60 X 3,60

Images provided by designer/architect.

## Plan #291005

**Dimensions:** 16' W x 28' D

**Levels:** 2

**Square Footage:** 896

**Main Level Sq. Ft.:** 448

**Upper Level Sq. Ft.:** 448

**Bedrooms:** 2

**Bathrooms:** 1½

**Foundation:** Crawl space

**Materials List Available:** No

**Price Category:** A

You'll be as charmed by the interior of this small home as you are by the wood-shingled roof, scroll-saw rake detailing, and board-and-batten siding on the exterior.

**Features:**

- **Porch:** Relax on this porch, which is the ideal spot for a couple of rockers or a swing.

- **Entryway:** Double doors reveal an open floor plan that makes everyone feel welcome.

- **Living Room:** Create a cozy nook by the windows here.

- **Kitchen:** Designed for convenience, this kitchen has ample counter space as well as enough storage to suit your needs. The stairway to the upper floor and the half-bath divide the kitchen from the living and dining areas.

- **Upper Level:** 9-ft. ceilings give a spacious feeling to the two bedrooms and full bathroom that you'll find on this floor.

**Main Level Floor Plan**

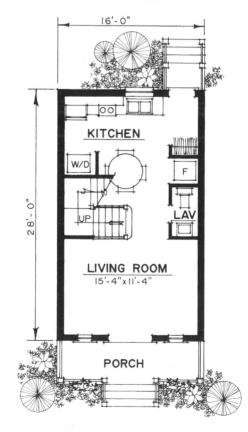

**Upper Level Floor Plan**

Copyright by designer/architect.

# Plan #271069

**Dimensions:** 63'5" W x 51'8" D

**Levels:** 2

**Square Footage:** 2,376

**Main Level Sq. Ft.:** 1,248

**Upper Level Sq. Ft.:** 1,128

**Bedrooms:** 4

**Bathrooms:** 2½

**Foundation:** Crawl space, basement

**Materials List Available:** No

**Price Category:** E

*Images provided by designer/architect.*

This home's Federal-style facade has a simple elegance that is still popular among today's homeowners.

**Features:**

• Living Room: This formal space is perfect for serious conversation or thoughtful reflection. Optional double doors would open directly into the family room beyond.

• Dining Room: You won't find a more elegant room than this for hosting holiday feasts.

• Kitchen: This room has everything the cook could hope for—a central island, a handy pantry, and a menu desk. Sliding glass doors in the dinette let you step outside for some fresh air with your cup of coffee.

• Family Room: Here's the spot to spend a cold winter evening. Have hot chocolate in front of a crackling fire!

• Master Suite: With an optional vaulted ceiling, the sleeping chamber is bright and spacious. The private bath showcases a splashy whirlpool tub.

## Main Level Floor Plan

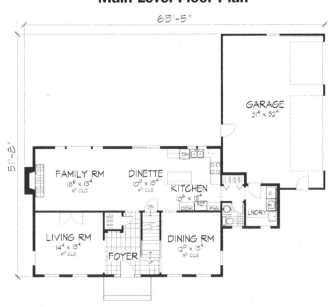

## Upper Level Floor Plan

*Copyright by designer/architect.*

## Plan #281016

**Dimensions:** 46' W x 44' D

**Levels:** 2

**Square Footage:** 1,945

**Main Level Sq. Ft.:** 1,211

**Upper Level Sq. Ft.:** 734

**Bedrooms:** 3

**Bathrooms:** 3

**Foundation:** Combination basement/slab

**Materials List Available:** Yes

**Price Category:** D

*Images provided by designer/architect.*

The fabulous window shapes on this Tudor-style home give just a hint of the beautiful interior design.

**Features:**

- **Living Room:** A vaulted ceiling in this raised room adds to its spectacular good looks.

- **Dining Room:** Between the lovely bay window and the convenient door to the covered sundeck, this room is an entertainer's delight.

- **Family Room:** A sunken floor, cozy fireplace, and door to the patio make this room special.

- **Study:** Just off the family room, this quiet spot can be a true retreat away from the crowd.

- **Kitchen:** The family cooks will be delighted by the ample counter and storage space here.

- **Master Suite:** A large walk-in closet, huge picture window, and private bath add luxurious touches to this second-floor retreat.

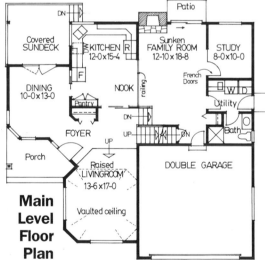

**Main Level Floor Plan**

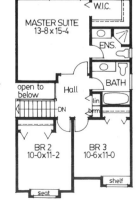

**Upper Level Floor Plan**

*Copyright by designer/architect.*

Rear Elevation

Left Side Elevation

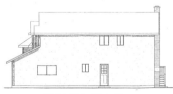

Right Side Elevation

## Plan #151816

**Dimensions:** 52'6" W x 55'6" D

**Levels:** 1.5

**Square Footage:** 1,723

**Bedrooms:** 3

**Bathrooms:** 2

**Foundation:** Crawl space or slab

**CompleteCost List Available:** Yes

**Price Category:** C

*Images provided by designer/architect.*

**CAD FILE AVAILABLE**

**Bonus Area Floor Plan**

*Copyright by designer/architect.*

## Plan #271082

**Dimensions:** 71' W x 62' D

**Levels:** 1

**Square Footage:** 2,074

**Bedrooms:** 4

**Bathrooms:** 2

**Foundation:** Crawl space or slab

**Materials List Available:** No

**Price Category:** D

*Images provided by designer/architect.*

**CAD FILE AVAILABLE**

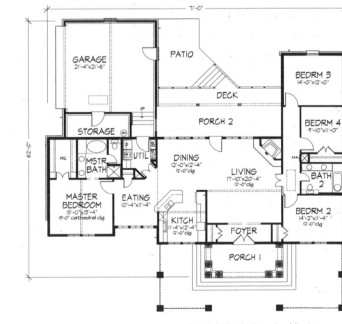

*Copyright by designer/architect.*

## Plan #461142

**Dimensions:** 48'6" W x 32' D

**Levels:** 1

**Square Footage:** 1,499

**Bedrooms:** 3

**Bathrooms:** 2

**Foundation:** Slab or basement

**Material List Available:** No

**Price Category:** B

*Images provided by designer/architect.*

### Bonus Area Floor Plan

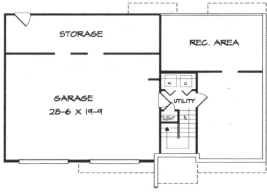

*Copyright by designer/architect.*

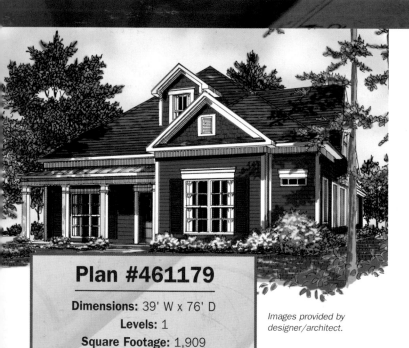

## Plan #461179

**Dimensions:** 39' W x 76' D

**Levels:** 1

**Square Footage:** 1,909

**Bedrooms:** 3

**Bathrooms:** 2½

**Foundation:** Slab; crawl space, or basement for fee

**Material List Available:** No

**Price Category:** D

*Images provided by designer/architect.*

### Bonus Area Floor Plan

*Copyright by designer/architect.*

## Plan #441007

**Dimensions:** 70' W x 64' D
**Levels:** 1
**Square Footage:** 2,197
**Bedrooms:** 4
**Bathrooms:** 2½
**Foundation:** Crawl space
**Materials List Available:** No
**Price Category:** D

*Images provided by designer/architect.*

Welcome to this roomy ranch, embellished with a brick facade, intriguing roof peaks, and decorative quoins on all the front corners.

**CAD FILE AVAILABLE**

**Features:**

- **Great Room:** There's a direct sightline from the front door through the trio of windows in this room. The rooms are defined by columns and changes in ceiling height rather than by walls, so light bounces from dining room to breakfast nook to kitchen.

- **Kitchen:** The primary workstation in this kitchen is a peninsula, which faces the fireplace. The peninsula is equipped with a sink, dishwasher, downdraft cooktop, and snack counter.

- **Den/Home Office:** Conveniently located off the foyer, this room would work well as a home office.

- **Master Suite:** The double doors provide an air of seclusion for this suite. The vaulted bedroom features sliding patio doors to the backyard and an arch-top window. The adjoining bath is equipped with a whirlpool tub, shower, double vanity, and walk-in closet.

- **Secondary Bedrooms:** The two additional bedrooms, each with direct access to the shared bathroom, occupy the left wing of the ranch.

Rear Elevation

*Copyright by designer/architect.*

## Plan #441003

**Dimensions:** 50' W x 48' D

**Levels:** 1

**Square Footage:** 1,580

**Bedrooms:** 3

**Bathrooms:** 2½

**Foundation:** Crawl space; slab or basement available for fee

**Materials List Available:** No

**Price Category:** C

*Images provided by designer/architect.*

Craftsman styling with modern floor planning—that's the advantage of this cozy design. Covered porches at front and back enhance both the look and the livability of the plan.

**Features:**

- Great Room: This vaulted entertaining area boasts a corner fireplace and a built-in media center. The area is open to the kitchen and the dining area.

- Kitchen: This large, open island kitchen will please the chef in the family. The raised bar is open to the dining area and the great room.

- Master Suite: Look for luxurious amenities such as double sinks and a separate tub and shower in the master bath. The master bedroom has a vaulted ceiling and a walk-in closet with built-in shelves.

- Bedrooms: Two secondary bedrooms are located away from the master suite. Each has a large closet and access to a common bathroom.

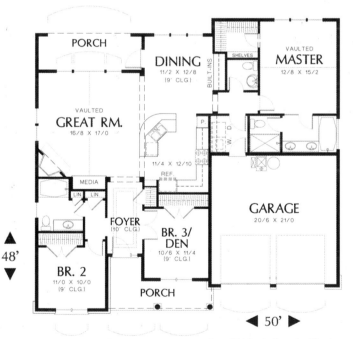

*Copyright by designer/architect.*

Rear Elevation

## Plan #441004

**Dimensions:** 55' W x 48' D

**Levels:** 1

**Square Footage:** 1,728

**Bedrooms:** 2

**Bathrooms:** 2

**Foundation:** Crawl space; slab or basement available for fee

**Materials List Available:** No

**Price Category:** C

*Images provided by designer/architect.*

Empty nesters and first-time homeowners will adore the comfort within this charming home. Rooms benefit from the many windows, which welcome light into the home.

### Features:

- **Great Room:** This vaulted room is equipped with a media center and fireplace. Windows span across the back of the room and the adjoining dining room, extending the perceived area and offering access to the covered patio.

- **Kitchen:** Taking advantage of corner space, this kitchen provides ample cabinets and countertops to store goods and prepare meals. Every chef will appreciate the extra space afforded by the pantry.

- **Master Suite:** This luxurious escape has a large sleeping area with views of the back-yard. The master bath features a spa tub, dual vanities, and a walk-in closet.

- **Garage:** This front-loading two-car garage has a shop area located in the rear.

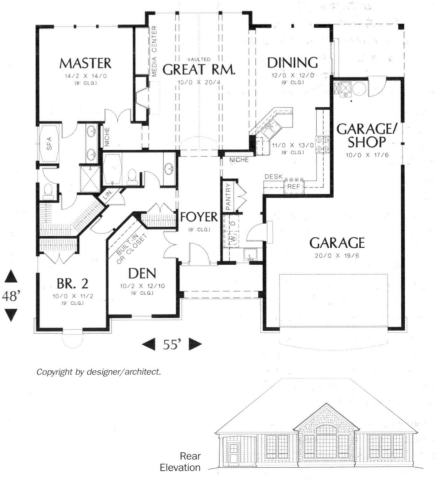

*Copyright by designer/architect.*

Rear Elevation

## Plan #221076

**Dimensions:** 56' W x 43' D

**Levels:** 2

**Square Footage:** 2,401

**Main Level Sq. Ft.:** 1,311

**Upper Level Sq. Ft:** 1,090

**Bedrooms:** 4

**Bathrooms:** 3

**Foundation:** Basement

**Materials List Available:** No

**Price Category:** E

This European-inspired two-story home makes full use of all the square footage available.

**CAD FILE CAD AVAILABLE**

*Images provided by designer/architect.*

**Features:**

• Entry: The columns on the front porch frame the front door. As you step into the home, this two-story entry area gives a spacious feel to the floor plan.

• Great Room: Complete with a cozy fireplace and a built-in cabinet, this great room will be the perfect place to entertain. Open to the kitchen and breakfast nook, this area provides an open feeling.

• Kitchen: This kitchen features a breakfast bar that overlooks the great room. Easy access to the dinning room makes formal meals a breeze.

• Master Suite: The stepped ceiling sets off this retreat and adds a feeling of elegance. The master bath boasts an oversize shower and walk-in closet.

Rear Elevation

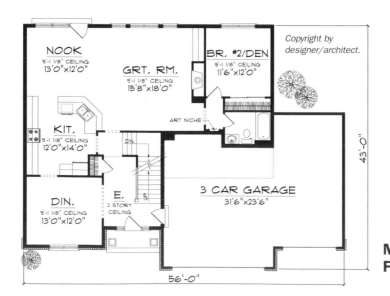

*Copyright by designer/architect.*

**Main Level Floor Plan**

**Upper Level Floor Plan**

## Plan #271043

**Dimensions:** 57'8" W x 36'4" D

**Levels:** 2

**Square Footage:** 2,396

**Main Level Sq. Ft.:** 1,238

**Upper Level Sq. Ft.:** 1,158

**Bedrooms:** 4

**Bathrooms:** 2½

**Foundation:** Basement

**Materials List Available:** Yes

**Price Category:** E

This grand home receives guests well, with brilliant windows, classic columns, and gorgeous gables.

**Features:**

• Living Room: Stately columns introduce this equally elegant room, which comes complete with a handsome fireplace flanked by shelves. A vaulted ceiling soars above it all.

• Dining Room: Opposite, the dining room is defined by its own columns. A butler's pantry joins it to the kitchen.

• Kitchen: This island-equipped kitchen and the breakfast area merge for easy casual dining. You'll find a built-in desk, two pantry closets, and laundry facilities here, too.

• Family Room: Corner windows brighten this fun space, which opens to a backyard deck through a lovely French door.

• Master Suite: The upper-floor master bedroom flaunts a vaulted ceiling and a private bath with dual vanities, a garden tub and a separate shower.

**CAD FILE AVAILABLE**

**Main Level Floor Plan**

### Upper Level Floor Plan

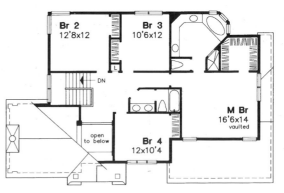

*Copyright by designer/architect.*

## Plan #441005

**Dimensions:** 50' W x 59' D
**Levels:** 1
**Square Footage:** 1,800
**Bedrooms:** 3
**Bathrooms:** 2
**Foundation:** Crawl space
**Materials List Available:** No
**Price Category:** D

*Images provided by designer/architect.*

This home looks as if it's a quaint little abode—with its board-and-batten siding, cedar shingle detailing, and column-covered porch—but even a quick peek inside will prove that there is much more to this plan than meets the eye.

**Features:**

• **Foyer:** This entry area rises to a 9-ft.-high ceiling. On one side is a washer-dryer alcove with a closet across the way; on the other is another large storage area. Just down the hallway is a third closet.

• **Kitchen:** This kitchen features a center island, built-in desk/work center, and pantry. This area and the dining area also boast 9-ft.-high ceilings and are open to a vaulted great room with corner fireplace.

• **Dining Room:** Sliding doors in this area lead to a covered side porch, so you can enjoy outside dining.

• **Master Suite:** This suite has a vaulted ceiling. The master bath is wonderfully appointed with a separate shower, spa tub, and dual sinks.

• **Bedrooms:** Three bedrooms (or two plus an office) are found on the right side of the plan.

Rear Elevation

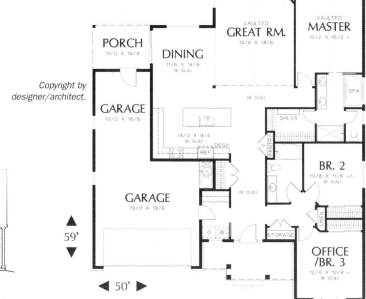

*Copyright by designer/architect.*

## Plan #221077

**Dimensions:** 57'8" W x 44' D
**Levels:** 2
**Square Footage:** 2,440
**Main Level Sq. Ft.:** 1,206
**Upper Level Sq. Ft:** 1,234
**Bedrooms:** 4
**Bathrooms:** 2½
**Foundation:** Basement
**Materials List Available:** No
**Price Category:** E

From the shutters on the windows to the columns on the porch, you'll love how the European details of this two-story home attract attention.

**CAD FILE AVAILABLE**

*Images provided by designer/architect.*

### Features:

- **Great Room:** The open floor plan and two-story ceiling make this gathering area spacious and practical. The rear wall of windows brings natural light into this room.

- **Kitchen:** This island kitchen features a raised bar and is open to the breakfast nook and great room. The attached computer nook and large walk-in pantry are just what you have been looking for.

- **Master Suite:** This oasis has a stepped ceiling in the sleeping area. The master bath boasts

a large walk-in closet, dual vanities, and a whirlpool tub.

- **Upper Level:** In addition to the master suite, there are three additional secondary bedrooms, each with ample closet space. The laundry room is also located on this level to save trips up and down the stairs.

**Rear Elevation**

## Main Level Floor Plan

## Upper Level Floor Plan

*Copyright by designer/architect.*

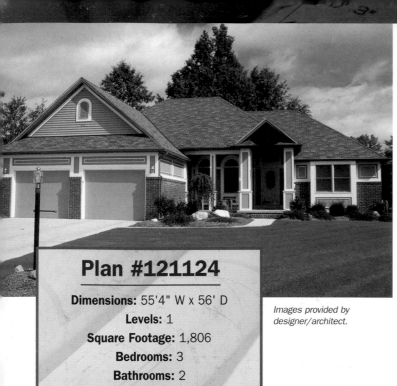

## Plan #121124

**Dimensions:** 55'4" W x 56' D

**Levels:** 1

**Square Footage:** 1,806

**Bedrooms:** 3

**Bathrooms:** 2

**Foundation:** Basement; crawl space for fee

**Material List Available:** Yes

**Price Category:** D

*Images provided by designer/architect.*

*Copyright by designer/architect.*

---

## Plan #121125

**Dimensions:** 54' W x 58'8" D

**Levels:** 1

**Square Footage:** 1,978

**Bedrooms:** 3

**Bathrooms:** 2½

**Foundation:** Basement; crawl space for fee

**Material List Available:** Yes

**Price Category:** D

*Images provided by designer/architect.*

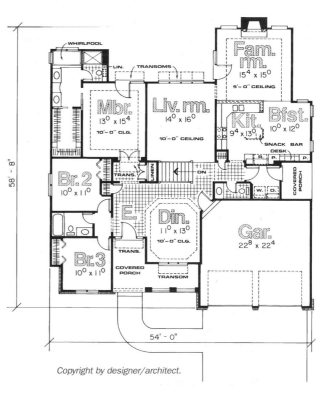

*Copyright by designer/architect.*

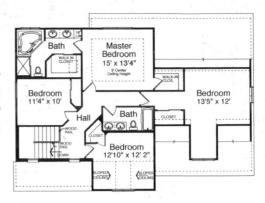

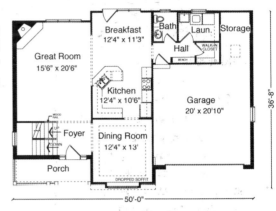

# Plan #161114

**Dimensions:** 50' W x 36'8" D

**Levels:** 2

**Square Footage:** 2,246

**Main Level Sq. Ft.:** 1,072

**Upper Level Sq. Ft.:** 1,174

**Bedrooms:** 4

**Bathrooms:** 2½

**Foundation:** Basement

**Material List Available:** Yes

**Price Category:** E

*Images provided by designer/architect.*

**CAD FILE AVAILABLE**

Rear Elevation

**Upper Level Floor Plan**

Bath · Master Bedroom 15' x 13'4" · 9' Center Ceiling Height · WALK IN CLOSET · WALK-IN CLOS. · Bedroom 11'4" x 10' · Bedroom 13'5" x 12' · Hall · Bath · CLOSET · WOOD RAIL · CLOSET · WOOD RAIL · DOWN · Bedroom 12'10" x 12' 2" · SLOPED CEILING · SLOPED CEILING

**Main Level Floor Plan**

Breakfast 12'4" x 11'3" · Bath · Laun. · Storage · Great Room 15'6" x 20'6" · Hall · WALK-IN CLOSET · BENCH · Kitchen 12'4" x 10'6" · Garage 20' x 20'10" · WOOD RAIL · UP · DOWN · Foyer · Dining Room 12'4" x 13' · Porch · DROPPED SOFFIT

36'-8"

50'-0"

*Copyright by designer/architect.*

---

# Plan #161119

**Dimensions:** 44'9" W x 67'10" D

**Levels:** 2

**Square Footage:** 2,334

**Main Level Sq. Ft.:** 1,858

**Upper Level Sq. Ft.:** 476

**Bedrooms:** 4

**Bathrooms:** 3

**Foundation:** Basement

**Material List Available:** Yes

**Price Category:** E

*Images provided by designer/architect.*

**CAD FILE AVAILABLE**

Rear Elevation

**Main Level Floor Plan**

Screened Porch 16'2" x 12'5" · Great Room 20'2" x 19'9" · Master Bedroom 16'2" x 13' · Dining Area 10'5" x 16'6" · WALK-IN CLOSET · Bath · Kitchen 11'10" x 14' · PANTRY · Laun. · Foyer · Bath · Garage · Porch · Guest Room/Library 12'4" x 14'1"

**Upper Level Floor Plan**

Bedroom 13'10" x 11' · Hall · Bath · Bedroom 12'4" x 11' · Foyer Below

*Copyright by designer/architect.*

## Plan #351086

**Dimensions:** 82'6" W x 65' D

**Levels:** 1

**Square Footage:** 2,201

**Bedrooms:** 3

**Bathrooms:** 2½

**Foundation:** Crawl space or slab

**Material List Available:** Yes

**Price Category:** E

This stunning European country home is designed with the contemporary family in mind.

**CAD FILE AVAILABLE**

### Features:

- **Porches:** Beautiful brick arches welcome guests into your covered front porch, indicating the warmth and hospitality within the home. A screened back porch, accessible from the dining area, is ideal for enjoying meals in the fresh air.

- **Great Room:** Three entrances from the covered porch, elegant archways into the kitchen and dining area, raised ceilings, a fireplace, and built-in cabinets combine to make this an ideal space for entertaining.

- **Kitchen:** The efficient L-shaped design of this work area includes an island with a vegetable sink and raised bar. The kitchen is open to the dining area and great room to provide a feeling of openness and informality.

- **Master Suite:** This suite features vaulted ceilings and a walk-in closet. But the compartmentalized master bath, with its second walk-in closet, his and her sinks and linen cabinets, standing shower, vanity, and jetted tub, really makes the suite special.

- **Secondary Bedrooms:** The secondary bedrooms have a wing of their own, and both include computer desks, large closets, and shared access to a bathtub through their individual half-baths.

- **Garages:** Two separate garages house up to three cars, or use the one-car bay for storage or hobby needs.

Rear Elevation

## Plan #181710

**Dimensions:** 32'4" W x 40'4" D
**Levels:** 2
**Square Footage:** 1,767
**Main Level Sq. Ft.:** 857
**Upper Level Sq. Ft.:** 910
**Bedrooms:** 3
**Bathrooms:** 2½
**Foundation:** Basement
**Materials List Available:** Yes
**Price Category:** C

*Images provided by designer/architect.*

This stone home will give any neighborhood an elegant look.

### Features:

- **Family Room:** This two-story space will welcome friends and family into your home. The convenient coat closet is waiting to take their coats.

- **Kitchen:** This island kitchen, with an abundance of cabinets and counter space, is a welcome addition. The adjacent dining room has access to the rear porch.

- **Master Suite:** Just off the balcony looking down into the family room is this nice-size master suite. The master bath boasts a compartmentalized lavatory and a stall shower.

- **Secondary Bedrooms:** Two equal-size bedrooms and a common bathroom round out the upper level. One bedroom boasts a walk-in closet.

**Main Level Floor Plan**

*Copyright by designer/architect.*

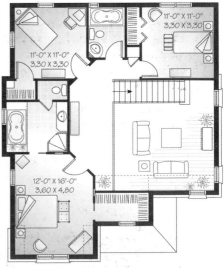

**Upper Level Floor Plan**

## Plan #181615

**Dimensions:** 36' W x 40' D

**Levels:** 2

**Square Footage:** 1,613

**Main Level Sq. Ft.:** 845

**Upper Level Sq. Ft.:** 768

**Bedrooms:** 3

**Bathrooms:** 1½

**Foundation:** Basement

**Materials List Available:** Yes

**Price Category:** C

This classic beauty with European styling will enchant you with its stone facade, columned entry, two-story bay windows, and a design that meets all your needs with style.

**Features:**

- Entry: A covered entry and large foyer welcome guests in from the elements.

- Family Room: The glow of natural light from the bay windows and the fireplace envelops this room. Whether you are relaxing with your family or entertaining guests, this room is ideal for coming together.

- Dining Room: This formal dining room is close to the kitchen for simple serving transitions and opens onto the covered back patio for meals indoors and out.

- Kitchen: From culinary expert to family cook, everyone will find in this room the workspace and storage they need to create beautiful meals. A sunlit breakfast area shares the space and opens onto the back covered patio for a variety of meal options.

- Second Floor: For a restful atmosphere, the bedrooms are separated from the hum of daily life. The spacious master bedroom finds light from the bay windows and has an adjacent walk-in closet. All three bedrooms share access to the single full bathroom with dual sinks, a large tub, and a stall shower.

### Main Level Floor Plan

### Upper Level Floor Plan

Rear Elevation

## Plan #361481

**Dimensions:** 78' W x 46' D

**Levels:** 2

**Square Footage:** 2,471

**Main Level Sq. Ft.:** 1,903

**Upper Level Sq. Ft.:** 568

**Bedrooms:** 4

**Bathrooms:** 3

**Foundation:** Crawl space

**Materials List Available:** No

**Price Category:** E

**CAD FILE AVAILABLE**

This home, with stone accents, has a European flair.

**Features:**

- **Entry:** As you enter this home from the covered porch, this vaulted entry welcomes you home. The convenient coat closet is close by.
- **Great Room:** This two-story gathering area is flooded with natural light from the back wall of windows. The fireplace, flanked by built-ins, adds a cozy feel to the room.
- **Master Suite:** This main level oasis features a large sleeping area with access to the rear patio. The master bathroom boasts a large walk-in closet, dual vanities, and a compartmentalized lavatory.
- **Upper Level:** The stairs take you from the great room to this second level of the home with a view down into entry. Two large bedrooms share a common bathroom. The bonus room can be finished as a playroom or the fourth bedroom.

### Main Level Floor Plan

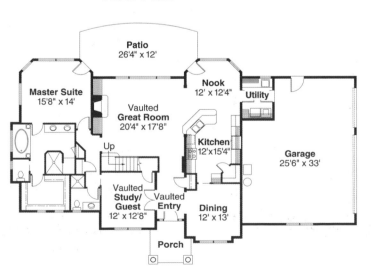

### Upper Level Floor Plan

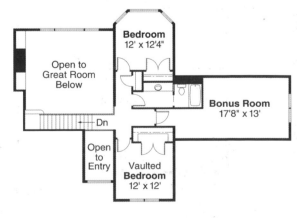

# Plan #281018

**Dimensions:** 50' W x 52'6" D
**Levels:** 1
**Square Footage:** 1,565
**Bedrooms:** 3
**Bathrooms:** 2
**Foundation:** Basement
**Materials List Available:** Yes
**Price Category:** C

*Images provided by designer/architect.*

You'll love the arched window that announces the grace of this home to the rest of the world.

**Features:**

- Living Room: Scissor trusses on the ceiling and a superb window design make this room elegant.

- Dining Room: Open to the living room, this dining room features an expansive window area and contains a convenient, inset china closet.

- Family Room: A gas fireplace in the corner and a doorway to the patio make this room the heart of the house.

- Breakfast Room: The bay window here makes it a lovely spot at any time of day.

- Kitchen: A raised snack bar shared with both the family and breakfast rooms adds a nice touch to this well-planned, attractive kitchen.

- Master Suite: A bay window, walk-in closet, and private bath add up to luxurious comfort in this suite.

Rear Elevation

Left Side Elevation

Right Side Elevation

*Copyright by designer/architect.*

## Plan #371104

**Dimensions:** 57' W x 52'6" D

**Levels:** 1

**Square Footage:** 1,795

**Bedrooms:** 3

**Bathrooms:** 2

**Foundation:** Crawl space or slab

**Materials List Available:** No

**Price Category:** C

This classic looking home will look great in any neighborhood.

**Features:**

- Dining Room: Just off the foyer is this formal eating area, in conveniently close proximity to the kitchen. The 10-ft.-high ceiling gives the space a dramatic feeling.

- Living Room: This large gathering area features large windows with a view to the backyard. The built-in bookcase and cozy fireplace add charm to the area.

- Kitchen: This U-shape peninsula kitchen features a raised bar and is open into the breakfast nook. The corner sink's two windows will bring an abundance of light into the area.

- Master Suite: Located in the rear of the home for privacy, the ceiling in the sleeping area soars up to 10 ft. The oversize master bathroom boasts his and her vanities, two large walk-in closets, and a compartmentalized lavatory.

## Plan #151350

**Dimensions:** 47' W x 50' D

**Levels:** 1.5

**Square Footage:** 1,684

**Main Level Sq. Ft.:** 1,155

**Upper Level Sq. Ft.:** 529

**Bedrooms:** 3

**Bathrooms:** 2½

**Foundation:** Crawl space or slab; basement or walkout for fee

**CompleteCost List Available:** Yes

**Price Category:** C

*Images provided by designer/architect.*

This charming European-style home is both practical and beautiful, the perfect place to raise a family and welcome friends.

**CAD FILE AVAILABLE**

### Features:

- **Great Room:** Imagine coming home from a hard day working or chauffeuring the kids, and this is the first room you find. A comfy couch and a warm fire welcome you home and help you unwind. Your guests will feel the same way.

- **Kitchen:** The heart of any home, this kitchen forms a hub between a formal dining room, a breakfast nook, and an outdoor grilling porch for easy transitions. It's also adjacent to the master suite, making breakfast in bed tempting. With plenty of workspace and storage,

this kitchen also features an island with a raised breakfast bar.

- **Master Suite:** Luxury meets your lifestyle with this romantic master suite. A spacious bedroom leads into a full master bath with separated his and her sinks, a standing shower, and a whirlpool tub. A walk-in closet through the bathroom simplifies your morning.

- **Second Floor:** With two bedrooms, a full bath, and a bonus area for you to design, the second floor makes a great children's suite. Use the bonus space for entertainment, study, or both.

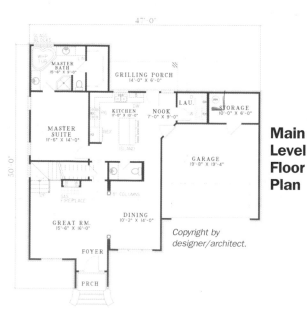

**Main Level Floor Plan**

*Copyright by designer/architect.*

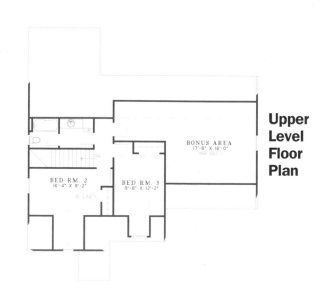

**Upper Level Floor Plan**

## Plan #181643

**Dimensions:** 42' W x 34' D

**Levels:** 2

**Square Footage:** 1,929

**Main Level Sq. Ft.:** 938

**Upper Level Sq. Ft.:** 991

**Bedrooms:** 4

**Bathrooms:** 2½

**Foundation:** Basement

**Materials List Available:** Yes

**Price Category:** D

This formidable home has a European grace and a unique style both indoors and out.

**Features:**

- **Great Room:** With sunlight streaming from a wall stacked with windows and a fireplace shared with the dining room, this room will be the most inviting area in the home. Imagine transitioning by firelight from a formal dinner to drinks and conversation in the quiet space.

- **Kitchen:** This uniquely design kitchen has a breakfast bar that is both attached to and separate from the space. An informal area for the family, a living room is also adjacent.

- **Master Bedroom:** A large space with a walk-in closet and room for a reading area this master bedroom will be your retreat. Just a few steps away is the full bathroom, with both a large tub and a standing shower.

- **Secondary Bedrooms:** All three bedrooms are approximately the same size, which prevents family squabbles. One shares the full bath room with the master bedroom, while the other two share direct access to a full bath room of their own. The hallway is large enough to have a small sitting area in the sunlight of the dual windows.

## Main Level Floor Plan

## Upper Level Floor Plan

*Copyright by designer/architect.*

Rear Elevation

## Plan #151275

**Dimensions:** 58'4" W x 68'6" D

**Levels:** 1

**Square Footage:** 2,180

**Bedrooms:** 3

**Bathrooms:** 2½

**Foundation:** Crawl space or slab

**CompleteCost List Available:** Yes

**Price Category:** D

*Images provided by designer/architect.*

*Copyright by designer/architect.*

## Plan #131003

**Dimensions:** 60' W x 39'10" D

**Levels:** 1

**Square Footage:** 1,466

**Bedrooms:** 3

**Bathrooms:** 2

**Foundation:** Crawl space, slab, or basement

**Materials List Available:** Yes

**Price Category:** C

*Images provided by designer/architect.*

*Copyright by designer/architect.*

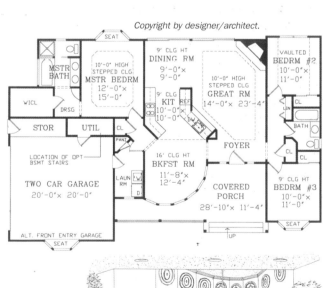

Breakfast Room

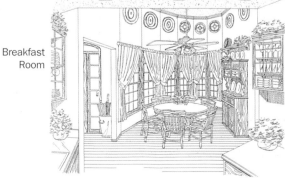

## Plan #441008

**Dimensions:** 60' W x 50' D

**Levels:** 1

**Square Footage:** 2,001

**Bedrooms:** 3

**Bathrooms:** 2

**Foundation:** Crawl space; slab or basement available for fee

**Materials List Available:** No

**Price Category:** D

*Images provided by designer/architect.*

A fine design for a country setting, this one-story plan offers a quaint covered porch at the entry, cedar shingles in the gables, and stonework at the foundation line.

**Features:**

- Entry: The pretty package on the outside is prelude to the fine floor plan on the inside. It begins at this entry foyer, which opens on the right to a den with a 9-ft.-high ceiling and space for a desk or closet.

- Great Room: This entertaining area is vaulted and contains a fireplace and optional media center. The rear windows allow a view onto the rear deck.

- Kitchen: Open to the dining room and great room to form one large space, this kitchen boasts a raised bar and a built-in desk.

- Master Suite: The vaulted ceiling in this master suite adds an elegant touch. The master bath features a dual vanities and a spa tub.

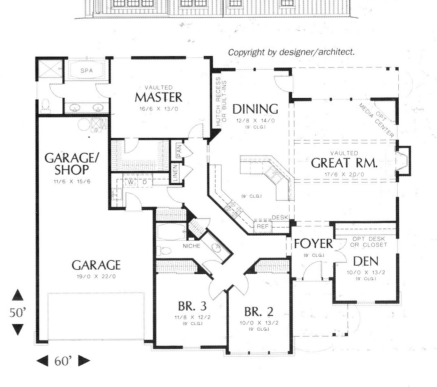

*Copyright by designer/architect.*

## Plan #141005

**Dimensions:** 38' W x 66' D

**Levels:** 1

**Square Footage:** 1,532

**Bedrooms:** 3

**Bathrooms:** 2

**Foundation:** Slab, basement

**Materials List Available:** Yes

**Price Category:** C

*Images provided by designer/architect.*

Board and batten combine with shake siding to give this cottage an appealing Tudor style.

**Features:**

• Ceiling Height: 8 ft. unless otherwise noted.

• Entry: This front entry is highlighted by a dormer that opens to the cathedral ceiling of the spacious open great room.

• Open Floor Plan: The living room, dining areas, and kitchen all flow together to create the feeling of a much larger home.

• Kitchen: This kitchen is defined by a curved bar, which can house a bench seat to service a small cafe-style table.

• Master Suite: This private suite is separated from the rest of the bedrooms. It features a volume ceiling and separate sitting area.

• Basement Option: The house is designed primarily for a slab on a narrow lot but can also be built over a basement.

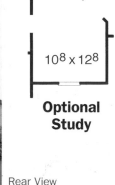

**Optional Study** $10^8 \times 12^8$

Rear View

Living Room

Kitchen

Living Room

Master Bath

Master Bedroom

Master Bedroom

## Plan #441018

**Dimensions:** 36' W x 44' D
**Levels:** 2
**Square Footage:** 1,500
**Main Level Sq. Ft.:** 716
**Upper Level Sq. Ft.:** 784
**Bedrooms:** 3
**Bathrooms:** 2½
**Foundation:** Crawl space
**Materials List Available:** No
**Price Category:** C

*Images provided by designer/architect.*

A trio of gables and a porch entry create a charming exterior for this home. With a compact footprint especially suited for smaller lots, it offers all the amenities important to today's sophisticated homebuyer.

**Features:**

• Great Room: From the entry, view this spacious two-story room, which features a fireplace and a wall of windows overlooking the porch.

• Dining Room: A French door to the porch is located in this room, along with a planning desk and a large pantry.

• Kitchen: Family will gravitate to this corner kitchen. It offers plenty of cabinet space and countertops including a center island, complete with a breakfast bar to add more space and convenience.

• Master Suite: Located upstairs, this vaulted suite features a walk-in closet and private bathroom.

### Main Level Floor Plan

*Copyright by designer/architect.*

### Upper Level Floor Plan

# Plan #441019

**Dimensions:** 38' W x 35' D
**Levels:** 3
**Square Footage:** 2,044
**Main Level Sq. Ft.:** 1,106
**Upper Level Sq. Ft.:** 872
**Lower Level Sq. Ft.:** 66
**Bedrooms:** 3
**Bathrooms:** 2½
**Foundation:** Slab
**Materials List Available:** No
**Price Category:** D

Images provided by designer/architect.

**Main Level Floor Plan**

**Garage Level Floor Plan**

**Upper Level Floor Plan**

Copyright by designer/architect.

**Rear Elevation**

Designed for a sloping lot, this tri-level home intrigues the eye and lifts the spirits.

**Features:**

- **Open Plan:** Sunlight filters into the grand two-story foyer and living room from tall windows.

- **Living Room:** From the loft overlooking this room you can view flames dancing in the fireplace, which is shared by the family room.

- **Dining Room:** From the windows or optional French doors in this space you can behold the outdoor vista.

- **Kitchen:** This spacious kitchen houses an island with a downdraft cooktop. Serve food informally in front of the breakfast-nook windows or at the island.

- **Master Suite:** This master bedroom is embellished with a vaulted ceiling and elegant front-facing windows; the attached master bath has a separate tub and shower and a private toilet enclosure.

## Plan #441050

**Dimensions:** 50' W x 52'6" D
**Levels:** 2
**Square Footage:** 2,296
**Main Level Sq. Ft.:** 1,464
**Upper Level Sq. Ft.:** 832
**Bedrooms:** 3
**Bathrooms:** 2½
**Foundation:** Crawl space;
slab or basement for fee
**Materials List Available:** No
**Price Category:** E

• Second Floor: Two bedrooms have the upstairs to themselves, a full bathroom with dual sinks just footsteps away. A large bonus space waits for you to mold it to your needs. Create another bedroom, if needed, or an extra entertainment or study space for your family.

Attention to architectural detail gives this Craftsman style home a unique contemporary appeal.

### Features:

• **Garage:** A three-car garage provides plenty of space for the multi-tasking family and all of their hobbies. If two vehicles are enough, use the third bay for workspace or storage.

• **Kitchen:** This efficient L-shaped kitchen includes a working island with raised bar. The room opens into a sunlit, formal dining room and the fireplace-warmed great room, both vaulted.

• **Patio:** Through a door in the dining room is a covered patio, perfect for enjoying the breeze and the view while you eat out on warm summer days.

• **Master Suite:** A vaulted master bedroom opens into a compartmentalized full bath, with his and her sinks, a spa tub and large stall shower.

**Main Level Floor Plan**

*Copyright by designer/architect.*

**Upper Level Floor Plan**

**Rear Elevation**

# Let Us Help You
## Plan Your
# Dream Home

**W**hether you've always dreamed of building your own home or you can't find the right house from among the dozens you've toured, our collection of two-story plans can help you achieve the home of your dreams. You could have an architect create a one-of-a-kind home for you, but the design services alone could end up costing up to 15 percent of the cost of construction—a hefty premium for any building project. Isn't it a better idea to select from among the hundreds of unique designs shown in our collection for a fraction of the cost?

## What does Creative Homeowner Offer?

In this book, Creative Homeowner provides hundreds of home plans from the country's best architects and designers. Our designs are among the most popular available. Whether your taste runs from traditional to contemporary, Victorian to early American, you are sure to find the best house design for you and your family. Our plans packages include detailed drawings to help you or your builder construct your dream house. **(See page 294.)**

## Can I Make Changes to the Plans?

Creative Homeowner offers three ways to help you achieve a truly unique home design. Our customizing service allows for extensive changes to our designs. **(See page 295.)** We also provide reverse images of our plans, or we can give you and your builder the tools for making minor changes on your own. **(See page 298.)**

## Can You Help Me Stay on Budget?

Building a house is a large financial investment. To help you stay within your budget, Creative Homeowner can provide you with general construction costs based on your zip code. **(See page 298.)** Also, many of our plans come with the option of buying detailed materials lists to help you price out construction costs.

## How Can I Get Started with the Building Process?

We've teamed up with the leading estimating company to provide one of the most accurate, complete, and reliable building material take-offs in the industry. **(See page 296.)** If you plan on doing all or part of the work yourself, or want to keep tabs on your builder, we offer best-selling building and design books at attractive prices. See our Web site at www.creativehomeowner.com.

# Our Plans Packages Offer:

All of our home plans are the result of many hours of work by leading architects and professional designers. Most of our home plans include each of the following.

## Frontal Sheet

This artist's rendering of the front of the house gives you an idea of how the house will look once it is completed and the property landscaped.

## Detailed Floor Plans

These plans show the size and layout of the rooms. They also provide the locations of doors, windows, fireplaces, closets, stairs, and electrical outlets and switches.

## Foundation Plan

A foundation plan gives the dimensions of basements, walk-out basements, crawl spaces, pier foundations, and slab construction. Each house design lists the type of foundation included. If the plan you choose does not have the foundation type you require, our customer service department can help you customize the plan to meet your needs.

## Roof Plan

In addition to providing the pitch of the roof, these plans also show the locations of dormers, skylights, and other elements.

## Exterior Elevations

These drawings show the front, rear, and sides of the house as if you were looking at it head on. Elevations also provide information about architectural features and finish materials.

## Interior Elevations and Details

Interior elevations show specific details of such elements as fireplaces, kitchen and bathroom cabinets, built-ins, and other unique features of the design.

## Cross Sections

These show the structure as if it were sliced to reveal construction requirements, such as insulation, flooring, and roofing details.

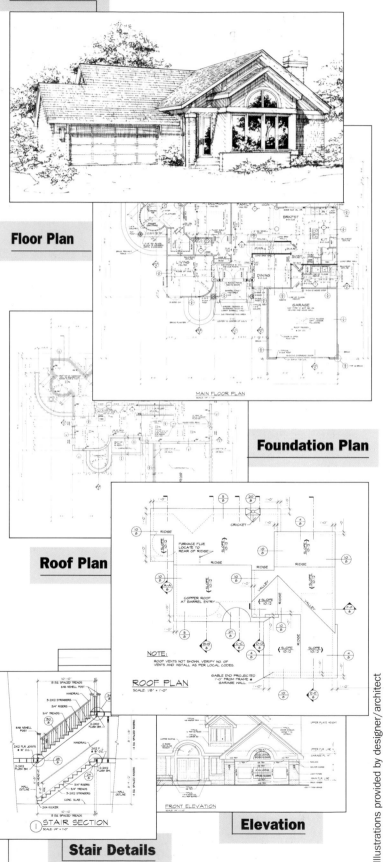

**Frontal Sheet**

**Floor Plan**

**Foundation Plan**

**Roof Plan**

**Elevation**

**Stair Details**

**Cross Sections**

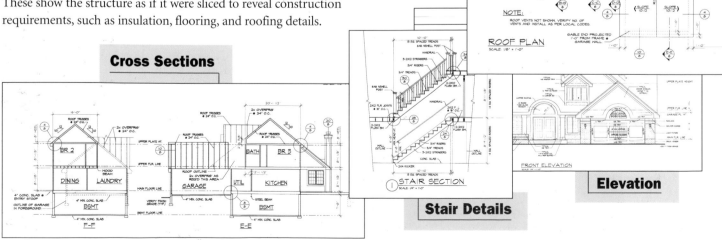

Illustrations provided by designer/architect

# Customize Your Plans in 4 Easy Steps

**1** **Select the home plan** that most closely meets your needs. Purchase of a reproducible master is necessary in order to make changes to a plan.

**2** **Call 1-800-523-6789 to place your order.** Tell our sales representative you are interested in customizing your plan. To receive your customization cost estimate, we will send you a checklist (via fax or email) for you to complete indicating the changes you would like to make to your plan. There is a $50 nonrefundable consultation fee for this service. If you decide to continue with the custom changes, the $50 fee is credited to the total amount charged.

**3** **Fax the completed checklist** to 1-201-760-2431 or email it to us at customize@creativehomeowner.com. Within three business days of receipt of your checklist, a detailed cost estimate will be provided to you.

**4** **Once you approve the estimate,** a 75% retainer fee is collected and customization work begins. Preliminary drawings typically take 10 to 15 business days. After approval, we will collect the balance of your customization order cost before shipping the completed plans. You will receive five sets of blueprints or a reproducible master, plus a customized materials list if desired.

## Modification Pricing Guide

| Categories | Average Cost For Modification |
|---|---|
| Add or remove living space | Quote required |
| Bathroom layout redesign | Starting at $120 |
| Kitchen layout redesign | Starting at $120 |
| Garage: add or remove | Starting at $400 |
| Garage: front entry to side load or vice versa | Starting at $300 |
| Foundation changes | Starting at $220 |
| Exterior building materials change | Starting at $200 |
| Exterior openings: add, move, or remove | $65 per opening |
| Roof line changes | Starting at $360 |
| Ceiling height adjustments | Starting at $280 |
| Fireplace: add or remove | Starting at $90 |
| Screened porch: add | Starting at $280 |
| Wall framing change from 2x4 to 2x6 | Starting at $200 |
| Bearing and/or exterior walls changes | Quote required |
| Non-bearing wall or room changes | $65 per room |
| Metric conversion of home plan | Starting at $400 |
| Adjust plan for handicapped accessibility | Quote required |
| Adapt plans for local building code requirements | Quote required |
| Engineering stamping only | Quote required |
| Any other engineering services | Quote required |
| Interactive illustrations (choices of exterior materials) | Quote required |

**Note:** *Any home plan can be customized to accommodate your desired changes. The average prices above are provided only as examples of the most commonly requested changes, and are subject to change without notice. Prices for changes will vary according to the number of modifications requested, plan size, style, and method of design used by the original designer. To obtain a detailed cost estimate, please contact us.*

**Before Customization**

**After**

# Turn your dream home into reality with

# UltimateEstimate

When purchasing a home plan with Creative Homeowner, we recommend you order one of the most complete materials lists in the industry.

## 1 | What comes with an Ultimate Estimate?

### Quote

- Basis of the entire estimate.

- Detailed list of all the framing materials needed to build your project, listed from the bottom up, in the order that each one will actually be used.

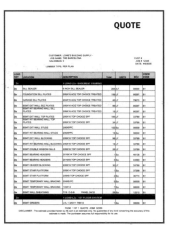

### Comments

- Details pertinent information beyond the cost of materials.

- Includes any notes from our estimator.

### Express List

- A version of the Quote with space for SKU numbers listed for purchasing the items at your local lumberyard.

- Your local lumberyard can then price out the materials list.

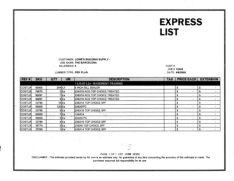

### Construction-Ready Framing Diagrams

- Your "map" to exact roof and floor framing.

### Millwork Report

- A complete count of the windows, doors, molding, and trim.

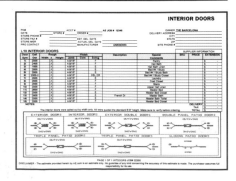

### Man-Hour Report

- Calculates labor on a line-by-line basis for all items quoted and presented in man-hours.

order direct: 1-800-523-6789

##  **2** Why an Ultimate Estimate?

**Accurate.** Professional estimators break down each individual item from the blueprints using advanced software, techniques, and equipment.

**Timely.** You will be able to start your home-building project quickly—knowing the exact framing materials you need to order from your local lumberyard.

**Detailed.** Work with your local lumberyard associate to complete your quote with the remaining products needed for your new home.

## **3** So how much does it cost?

Pricing is determined by the total square feet of the home plan—including living area, garages, decks, porches, finished basements, and finished attics.

| Square Feet Range | UE Tier* | Price |
|---|---|---|
| Up to 2,000 total square feet | XA | $249.00 |
| 2,001 to 5,000 total square feet | XB | $339.00 |
| 5,001 to 10,000 total square feet | XC | $499.00 |

\* Please see the Plan Index to determine your plan's Material Take-off Tier (MT Tier).

Call our toll-free number (800-523-6789), or visit ultimateplans.com to order your Material Take-off.

##  **4** What else do I need to know?

Call our toll-free number (800-523-6789), or visit
**ultimateplans.com** to order your Ultimate Estimate.

# Turn your dream home into reality.

# Decide What Type of Plan Package You Need

## How many Plans Should You Order?

**Standard 8-Set Package.** We've found that our 8-set package is the best value for someone who is ready to start building. Once the process begins, a number of people will require their own set of blueprints. The 8-set package provides plans for you, your builder, the subcontractors, mortgage lender, and the building department.

**Minimum 5-Set Package.** If you are in the bidding process, you may want to order only five sets for the bidding round and reorder additional sets as needed.

**1-Set Study Package.** The 1-set package allows you to review your home plan in detail. The plan will be marked as a study print, and it is illegal to build a house from a study print alone. It is a violation of copyright law to reproduce a blueprint without permission.

## Buying Additional Sets

If you require additional copies of blueprints for your home construction, you can order additional sets within 60 days of the original order date at a reduced price. The cost is $45.00 for each additional set. For more information, contact customer service.

## Reproducible Masters

If you plan to make minor changes to one of our home plans, you can purchase reproducible masters. Printed on vellum paper, an erasable paper that you can reproduce in a copying machine, reproducible masters allow an architect, designer, or builder to alter our plans to give you a customized home design. This package also allows you to print as many copies of the modified plans as you need for construction.

## CAD Files

CAD files are the complete set of home plans in an electronic file format. Choose this option if there are multiple changes you wish made to the home plans and you have a local design professional able to make the changes. Not available for all plans. Please contact our order department or visit our website to check the availability of CAD files for your plan.

## Mirror-Reverse Sets/Right-Reading Reverse

Plans can be printed in mirror-reverse—we can "flip" plans to create a mirror image of the design. This is useful when the house would fit your site or personal preferences if all the rooms were on the opposite side than shown. As the image is reversed, the lettering and dimensions will also be reversed, meaning they will read backwards. Therefore, when ordering mirror-reverse drawings, you must order at least one set of right-reading plans. A $50.00 fee per plan order will be charged for mirror-reverse (regardless of the number of mirror-reverse sets ordered). Some plans are available in right-reading reverse, this feature will show the plan in reverse, but the writing on the plan will be readable. A $150.00 fee per plan order will be charged for right-reading reverse (regardless of the number of right-reading reverse sets ordered). Please contact our order department or visit our website to check the availibility of this feature for your chosen plan.

## EZ Quote: Home Cost Estimator

EZ Quote is our response to one of the most frequently asked questions we hear from customers: "How much will the house cost me to build?" EZ Quote: Home Cost Estimator will enable you to obtain a calculated building cost to construct your home, based on labor rates and building material costs within your zip code area. This summary is useful for those who want to get an idea of the total construction costs before purchasing sets of home plans. It will also provide a level of comfort when you begin soliciting bids. The cost is $29.95 for the first EZ Quote and $14.95 for each additional one. Available only in the U.S. and Canada.

## Materials List

Available for most of our plans, the Materials List provides you an invaluable resource in planning and estimating the cost of your home. Each Materials List outlines the quantity, dimensions, and type of materials needed to build your home (with the exception of mechanical systems). You will get faster, more-accurate bids from your contractors and building suppliers. A Materials List may only be ordered with the purchase of at least five sets of home plans.

## CompleteCost Estimator

CompleteCost Estimator is a valuable tool for use in planning and constructing your new home. It provides more detail than a materials list and will act as a checklist for all items you will need to select or coordinate during your building process. CompleteCost Estimator is only available for certain plans (please see Plan Index) and may only be ordered with the purchase of at least five sets of home plans. The cost is $125.00 for CompleteCost Estimator.

---

**Order Toll Free by Phone**
**1-800-523-6789**
**By Fax: 201-760-2431**

Regular office hours are
8:30AM–7:30PM ET, Mon–Fri
Orders received 3PM ET, will be processed and
shipped within two business days.

**Order Online**
**www.ultimateplans.com**

**Mail Your Order**
Creative Homeowner
Attn: Home Plans
24 Park Way
Upper Saddle River, NJ 07458

**Canadian Customers**
**Order Toll Free 1-800-393-1883**

**Mail Your Order (Canada)**
Creative Homeowner Canada
Attn: Home Plans
113-437 Martin St., Ste. 215
Penticton, BC V2A 5L1

# Before You Order

## Our Exchange Policy

Blueprints are nonrefundable. However, should you find that the plan you have purchased does not fit your needs, you may exchange that plan for another plan in our collection within 60 days from the date of your original order. The entire content of your original order must be returned before an exchange will be processed. You will be charged a processing fee of 20% of the amount of the original order, the cost difference between the new plan set and the original plan set (if applicable), and all related shipping costs for the new plans. Contact our order department for more information. Please note: reproducible masters may only be exchanged if the package is unopened and CAD files cannot be exchanged and are nonrefundable.

## Building Codes and Requirements

At the time of creation, our plans meet the building code requirements published by the Building Officials and Code Administrators International, the Southern Building Code Congress International, the International Conference of Building Officials, or the Council of American Building Officials. Because building codes vary from area to area, some drawing modifications and/or the assistance of a professional designer or architect may be necessary to comply with your local codes or to accommodate specific building site conditions. We strongly advise you to consult with your local building official for information regarding codes governing your area.

## Blueprint Price Schedule

| Price Code | 1 Set | 5 Sets | 8 Sets | Reproducible Masters | CAD | Materials List |
|---|---|---|---|---|---|---|
| A | $300 | $345 | $395 | $530 | $950 | $85 |
| B | $375 | $435 | $480 | $600 | $1,100 | $85 |
| C | $435 | $500 | $550 | $650 | $1,200 | $85 |
| D | $490 | $560 | $610 | $710 | $1,300 | $95 |
| E | $550 | $620 | $660 | $770 | $1,400 | $95 |
| F | $610 | $680 | $720 | $830 | $1,500 | $95 |
| G | $670 | $740 | $780 | $890 | $1,600 | $95 |
| H | $760 | $830 | $870 | $980 | $1,700 | $95 |
| I | $860 | $930 | $970 | $1,080 | $1,800 | $105 |
| J | $960 | $1,030 | $1,070 | $1,190 | $1,900 | $105 |
| K | $1,070 | $1,150 | $1,190 | $1,320 | $2,030 | $105 |
| L | $1,180 | $1,270 | $1,310 | $1,460 | $2,170 | $105 |

Note: All prices subject to change

## Ultimate Estimate Tier (UE Tier)

| MT Tier* | Price |
|---|---|
| XA | $249 |
| XB | $339 |
| XC | $499 |

\* Please see the Plan Index to determine your plan's Ultimate Estimate Tier (UE Tier).

## Shipping & Handling

| | 1-4 Sets | 5-7 Sets | 8+ Sets or Reproducibles | CAD |
|---|---|---|---|---|
| **US Regular** (7–10 business days) | $18 | $20 | $25 | $25 |
| **US Priority** (3–5 business days) | $25 | $30 | $35 | $35 |
| **US Express** (1–2 business days) | $40 | $45 | $50 | $50 |
| **Canada Express** (1–2 business days) | $60 | $70 | $80 | $80 |
| **Worldwide Express** (3–5 business days) | $80 | $80 | $80 | $80 |

---

# Order Form   Please send me the following:

**Plan Number:** _____ **Price Code:** _____ (See Plan Index.)

Indicate Foundation Type: (Select ONE. See plan page for availability.)

❏ Slab   ❏ Crawl space   ❏ Basement   ❏ Walk-out basement

❏ Optional Foundation for Fee _____ $_____
*(Please enter foundation here)*

*Please call all our order department or visit our website for optional foundation fee*

| **Basic Blueprint Package** | **Cost** |
|---|---|
| ❏ Reproducible Masters | $_____ |
| ❏ 8-Set Plan Package | $_____ |
| ❏ 5-Set Plan Package | $_____ |
| ❏ 1-Set Study Package | $_____ |
| ❏ Additional plan sets: __ sets at $45.00 per set | $_____ |
| ❏ Print in mirror-reverse: $50.00 per order *Please call all our order department or visit our website for availibility* | $_____ |
| ❏ Print in right-reading reverse: $150.00 per order *Please call all our order department or visit our website for availibility* | $_____ |

**Important Extras**

❏ Materials List   $_____

❏ CompleteCost Materials Report at $125.00   $_____
Zip Code of Home/Building Site _____

❏ EZ Quote for Plan #_____ at $29.95   $_____

❏ Additional EZ Quotes for Plan #s_____ at $14.95 each   $_____

❏ Ultimate Estimate (See Price Tier above.)   $_____

**Shipping** (see chart above)   $_____

**SUBTOTAL**   $_____

**Sales Tax** (NJ residents only, add 6%)   $_____

**TOTAL**   $_____

Order Toll Free: 1-800-523-6789   By Fax: 201-760-2431
Creative Homeowner
24 Park Way
Upper Saddle River, NJ 07458

Name _____
*(Please print or type)*

Street _____
*(Please do not use a P.O. Box)*

City _____ State _____

Country _____ Zip _____

Daytime telephone ( ____ )_____

Fax ( ____ )_____
*(Required for reproducible orders)*

E-Mail _____

**Payment**   ❏ Check/money order   *Make checks payable to Creative Homeowner*

❏ VISA   ❏ MasterCard   ❏ American Express   ❏ Discover

Credit card number _____

Expiration date (mm/yy) _____

Signature _____

*Please check the appropriate box:*
❏ Licensed builder/contractor   ❏ Homeowner   ❏ Renter

SOURCE CODE **CA250**   www.ultimateplans.com

# Copyright Notice

All home plans sold through this publication are protected by copyright. Reproduction of these home plans, either in whole or in part, including any form and/or preparation of derivative works thereof, for any reason without prior written permission is strictly prohibited. The purchase of a set of home plans in no way transfers any copyright or other ownership interest in it to the buyer except for a limited license to use that set of home plans for the construction of one, and only one, dwelling unit. The purchase of additional sets of the home plans at a reduced price from the original set or as a part of a multiple-set package does not convey to the buyer a license to construct more than one dwelling.

Similarly, the purchase of reproducible home plans (sepias, mylars) carries the same copyright protection as mentioned above. It is generally allowed to make up to a maximum of 10 copies for the construction of a single dwelling only. To use any plans more than once, and to avoid any copyright license infringement, it is necessary to contact the plan designer to receive a release and license for any extended use. Whereas a purchaser of reproducible plans is granted a license to make copies, it should be noted that because blueprints are copyrighted, making photocopies from them is illegal.

Copyright and licensing of home plans for construction exist to protect all parties. Copyright respects and supports the intellectual property of the original architect or designer. Copyright law has been reinforced over the past few years. Willful infringement could cause settlements for statutory damages to $150,000.00 plus attorney fees, damages, and loss of profits.

# Index *For pricing, see page 299.*

| Plan # | Price Code | Page | Total Finished Area Square Feet | Materials List Available | Complete Cost | UE Tier |
|---|---|---|---|---|---|---|
| 101004 | C | 252 | 1,787 | Y | N | XA |
| 101004 | C | 253 | 1,787 | Y | N | XA |
| 101005 | D | 14 | 1,992 | Y | N | XA |
| 101005 | D | 15 | 1,992 | Y | N | XA |
| 101008 | D | 25 | 2,088 | Y | N | XB |
| 101010 | D | 231 | 2,187 | Y | N | XB |
| 101011 | D | 24 | 2,184 | Y | N | XB |
| 101012 | E | 35 | 2,288 | N | N | XB |
| 101015 | C | 155 | 1,647 | N | N | XA |
| 111006 | E | 254 | 2,241 | N | N | XB |
| 111010 | D | 139 | 1,804 | N | N | XA |
| 111013 | C | 178 | 1,606 | N | N | XA |
| 111014 | D | 233 | 1,865 | N | N | XA |
| 111015 | E | 235 | 2,208 | N | N | XB |
| 111017 | E | 248 | 2,323 | N | N | XB |
| 111021 | E | 177 | 2,221 | N | N | XB |
| 111022 | E | 74 | 2,331 | N | N | XB |
| 111023 | E | 245 | 2,356 | N | N | XB |
| 111024 | E | 239 | 2356 | N | N | XB |
| 111026 | E | 243 | 2,406 | N | N | XB |
| 111040 | C | 166 | 1,650 | N | N | XA |
| 111041 | C | 148 | 1,743 | N | N | XA |
| 111042 | C | 146 | 1,779 | N | N | XA |
| 111044 | D | 134 | 1,819 | N | N | XA |
| 111045 | D | 16 | 1,880 | N | N | XA |
| 111046 | C | 113 | 1,768 | N | N | XA |
| 111047 | D | 142 | 1,863 | N | N | XA |
| 111049 | E | 180 | 2,205 | N | N | XB |
| 111049 | E | 181 | 2,205 | N | N | XB |
| 121001 | D | 10 | 1,911 | Y | N | XA |
| 121003 | E | 184 | 2,498 | Y | N | XB |
| 121004 | C | 182 | 1,666 | Y | N | XA |
| 121006 | C | 72 | 1,762 | Y | N | XA |
| 121008 | C | 188 | 1,651 | Y | N | XA |
| 121014 | D | 101 | 1,869 | Y | N | XA |
| 121021 | E | 102 | 2,270 | Y | N | XB |
| 121035 | B | 89 | 1,463 | Y | N | XA |
| 121037 | E | 129 | 2,292 | Y | N | XB |
| 121045 | C | 90 | 1,575 | Y | N | XA |
| 121050 | D | 191 | 1,996 | Y | N | XA |
| 121051 | D | 194 | 1,808 | Y | N | XA |
| 121064 | D | 13 | 1,846 | Y | N | XA |
| 121066 | D | 67 | 2,078 | Y | N | XB |
| 121074 | E | 200 | 2,486 | Y | N | XB |
| 121080 | E | 55 | 2,384 | Y | N | XB |
| 121085 | D | 52 | 1,948 | Y | N | XA |
| 121086 | D | 65 | 1,998 | Y | N | XA |
| 121088 | E | 18 | 2,340 | Y | N | XB |
| 121092 | D | 199 | 1,887 | Y | N | XA |
| 121105 | B | 23 | 1,125 | Y | N | XA |
| 121106 | D | 63 | 2,133 | Y | N | XB |
| 121107 | C | 53 | 1,604 | Y | N | XA |
| 121109 | C | 37 | 1,735 | Y | N | XA |
| 121112 | C | 77 | 1,650 | Y | N | XA |
| 121115 | D | 26 | 1,993 | Y | N | XA |
| 121116 | E | 28 | 2,276 | Y | N | XB |
| 121117 | D | 50 | 2,172 | Y | N | XB |
| 121118 | C | 57 | 1,636 | Y | N | XA |
| 121119 | D | 61 | 1,850 | Y | N | XA |
| 121121 | C | 254 | 1,341 | Y | N | XA |
| 121123 | E | 91 | 2,277 | Y | N | XB |
| 121124 | D | 276 | 1,806 | Y | N | XA |
| 121125 | D | 276 | 1,978 | Y | N | XA |
| 121127 | E | 255 | 2,496 | Y | N | XB |
| 121137 | B | 143 | 1,392 | Y | N | XA |
| 121144 | B | 145 | 1,195 | Y | N | XA |
| 121147 | D | 73 | 2,051 | Y | N | XB |
| 121148 | D | 66 | 2,076 | N | N | XB |
| 121153 | D | 74 | 1,984 | Y | N | XA |
| 121160 | D | 166 | 2,188 | Y | N | XB |
| 121165 | C | 105 | 1,678 | Y | N | XA |
| 121172 | D | 255 | 1,807 | Y | N | XA |
| 121176 | D | 229 | 2,144 | Y | N | XB |
| 121190 | E | 96 | 2,252 | Y | N | XB |
| 121212 | E | 99 | 2,219 | Y | N | XB |
| 121215 | B | 27 | 1,271 | Y | N | XA |
| 121216 | B | 34 | 1,205 | Y | N | XA |
| 121217 | B | 33 | 1,212 | Y | N | XA |
| 131001 | D | 110 | 1,615 | Y | N | XA |
| 131002 | C | 94 | 1,709 | Y | N | XA |
| 131003 | C | 286 | 1,466 | Y | N | XA |
| 131005 | C | 19 | 1,595 | Y | N | XA |
| 131007 | D | 58 | 1,595 | Y | N | XA |
| 131007 | D | 59 | 1,595 | Y | N | XA |
| 131008 | B | 162 | 1,299 | Y | N | XA |
| 131022 | E | 12 | 2,092 | Y | N | XB |
| 131032 | F | 31 | 2,455 | Y | N | XB |
| 131037 | C | 157 | 1,416 | Y | N | XA |
| 131047 | D | 218 | 1,793 | Y | N | XA |
| 131051 | F | 36 | 2,431 | Y | N | XB |
| 131056 | C | 167 | 1,396 | Y | N | XA |
| 131057 | D | 20 | 1,843 | Y | N | XA |
| 131058 | D | 149 | 1,648 | Y | N | XA |
| 131060 | F | 211 | 2,282 | Y | N | XB |
| 131063 | E | 185 | 1,996 | Y | N | XA |
| 131064 | D | 186 | 1,783 | Y | N | XA |
| 141005 | C | 288 | 1,532 | Y | N | XA |
| 141005 | C | 289 | 1,532 | Y | N | XA |
| 141012 | D | 88 | 1,870 | Y | N | XA |
| 141016 | E | 114 | 2,416 | Y | N | XB |
| 141023 | C | 134 | 1,715 | Y | N | XA |
| 141025 | C | 30 | 1,721 | Y | N | XA |
| 141026 | D | 112 | 1,993 | Y | N | XA |
| 141028 | E | 34 | 2,215 | Y | N | XB |
| 141030 | E | 210 | 2,323 | Y | N | XB |
| 141031 | E | 39 | 2,367 | N | N | XB |
| 141032 | E | 51 | 2,476 | Y | N | XB |
| 141037 | C | 131 | 1,735 | N | N | XA |
| 141038 | C | 104 | 1,668 | Y | N | XA |
| 141041 | D | 141 | 1,821 | N | N | XA |

# Index